Interactive Composition

Interactive Composition

Strategies Using Ableton Live and
Max for Live

V. J. Manzo and Will Kuhn

OXFORD
UNIVERSITY PRESS

Oxford University Press is a department of the University of Oxford.
It furthers the University's objective of excellence in research, scholarship,
and education by publishing worldwide.

Oxford   New York
Auckland   Cape Town   Dar es Salaam   Hong Kong   Karachi
Kuala Lumpur   Madrid   Melbourne   Mexico City   Nairobi
New Delhi   Shanghai   Taipei   Toronto

With offices in
Argentina   Austria   Brazil   Chile   Czech Republic   France   Greece
Guatemala   Hungary   Italy   Japan   Poland   Portugal   Singapore
South Korea   Switzerland   Thailand   Turkey   Ukraine   Vietnam

Oxford is a registered trade mark of Oxford University Press in the UK and
certain other countries.

Published in the United States of America by
Oxford University Press
198 Madison Avenue, New York, NY 10016

Library of Congress Cataloging-in-Publication Data
Manzo, V. J., author. Interactive composition : strategies using Ableton Live and
Max for Live / V. J. Manzo and Will Kuhn.
    pages cm
Includes bibliographical references and index.
ISBN 978-0-19-997381-1 (alk. paper) — ISBN 978-0-19-997382-8 (alk. paper)
1. Ableton Live.   2. Max for Live.   3. Digital audio editors.   4. Software
synthesizers.   5. Composition Music)—Computer programs.   I. Kuhn, Will,
author.   II. Title.
ML74.4.A23M35   2015
781.3453—dc23   2014020346

Contents

Foreword • xi

Preface • xiii

Acknowledgments • xxi

About the Companion Website • xxv

1 Basics • 1

This chapter looks at the ways that interactive composition can be facilitated using Ableton Live, a powerful digital audio workstation. It also serves as an overview of the tools and functions available within Live and how they can be used to allow composition and performance. Even if you are already familiar with Live, you may find it useful to follow along as we discuss concepts related to interactive music-making using this tool.

• Companion Site and Files • 1
• Basic Setup • 2
• Working in Live • 6
• On Your Own • 23

2 Session View • 26

Here we examine Live's *Session View*, a unique way of working with audio and MIDI offering real-time accessibility for composition and performance. We also discuss the basics of audio recording within Live and how to apply audio effects to the signal source.

• Session View • 26
• Adding Effects • 37
• Key and MIDI Mapping • 39
• Record to *Arrangement* View • 41
• On Your Own • 42

3 Introduction to Max for Live • 44

We look at using Max for Live, the add-on for Live that allows users to incorporate the powerful graphical programming language Max/MSP/Jitter into their Live sessions. The chapter also discusses the advantages of using Max for Live, which include creating custom MIDI effects, instruments, and audio effects for use in Live.

• Why Would I Want to Start Programming? • 45
• Writing a MIDI Program • 45
• On Your Own • 56

4 Ambient • 57

The focus of this chapter is learning how to build scales and chords and play them back in a variety of ways. You will also learn how to write a program that allows users to play diatonic chords in a specified key using just the number keys on your computer keyboard.

• Getting Started • 57
• Other Instruments • 60
• Form • 62
• On Your Own • 74

5 Pop and Rock Music • 75

There are many ways that popular music ensembles can enhance their performances through interactive methods. These techniques include triggering the playback of drum machine patterns or studio-created sounds that can't be produced live, creating karaoke-style backing tracks, and using an array of effects to enhance live instruments and vocals. We begin with raw, unprocessed, recorded files from a studio session and show how to add effects to create a produced mix. Then we examine ways to implement these production techniques in a live setting. Much of the chapter discusses the various, sometimes confusing ways of working with multiple audio outputs and the overall signal path of our session.

• Enhancing the Recording with Effects • 75
• Automation • 79
• Making It Performable in a Live Situation • 81
• Using the *Return* Tracks as Monitor Mixes • 86
• Multiple Sessions in One Session • 90
• Live for Practicing • 94
• On Your Own • 95
• Monkey FX Guide • 96

6 Electroacoustic Music • 100

This chapter discusses approaches to electroacoustic composition in which a performer is playing music that has been noted while simultaneously interacting with computer processes. We have already discussed a number of ways to generate pitches algorithmically using Max for Live as well as how to use various effect devices inside of Live, so our focus here will address making the compositional process easier for composers and the performance process easier for performers.

- Preparing the Canvas • 101
- Preparing the Form • 104
- Preparing Computer-Generated Sounds • 108
- Preparing the Session for Performance • 111
- Composition Examples • 114
- On Your Own • 119

7 Modern Hip-Hop and Trap Music • 120

In this chapter's example, we recreate a modern trap-style instrumental, with a bit of a buildup and plenty of the common tropes found in these producers' works. We will use the method of composing using a clip-centric workflow, similar to producers in the early days of the genre.

- Drum Patterns • 122
- Sub Kicks and Bass Lines • 123
- Buildup Patterns • 125
- Chord Sequences • 126
- Stabs • 127
- Lasers • 128
- Chipmunk Vocals and Shouts • 129
- Composition Examples • 131
- On Your Own • 132

8 House Music • 133

Here we construct the essential elements of house music including the typical drum, pad, and bass sounds associated with the genre. We also explore some of the regional differences in house music subgenres.

- Kick Drum and Essential Elements • 134
- Electro Bass Synth • 135
- Setting Up Mix Groups and Sidechain Ducking • 138
- Form and Arrangement • 140
- On Your Own • 141

9 Breakbeat/Drum and Bass • 142

This chapter explores various methods of sampling drum beats as whole-pattern loops and as slices of sound in a drum rack. We also demonstrate how to make the characteristic Reese bass sound and construct a drum and bass song using original samples.

- Creating a Sampled Loop • 143
- Reese Bass • 148
- Sub Bass and Advanced Reese • 150
- Sampled Sirens and Other Instruments • 151
- Buildup Scene • 153
- Mixing • 155
- Form Considerations • 157
- On Your Own • 158

10 Chiptune • 159

The focus of this chapter is building a Max for Live instrument capable of making characteristic chip-synth sounds reminiscent of video games from the 80s and 90s.

- Designing a Custom Chip Instrument • 161
- Using the Custom Chip Sounds • 170
- Auto-Chords and MIDI Reuse • 171
- Sampled Chip Sounds • 173
- 8-Bit Drums • 173
- Form and Structure • 175
- On Your Own • 176

11 Granular Synthesis • 177

In this chapter we will create a song reminiscent of artists who use granular synthesis extensively. We will also create an entire song from one voice sample.

- Basic Sampling • 178
- Wavetable Synthesis with Simpler • 181
- Granular Synthesis with Granulator II • 182
- Drums from a Voice • 185
- Mixing • 187
- On Your Own • 188

12 Dubstep • 189

Here we will create a dance track with many of the instruments and form elements of early 2010's U.K. dubstep, with a bit of flair from U.S. dubstep as well. We will incorporate advanced FM synthesis techniques for sound generation and explore unique ways to stitch together a complex bass sequence.

- Drum Patterns • 191
- Bass Instruments and Resampling • 192
- Treble Leads • 198
- Risers • 199
- Initial Mixing • 201
- On Your Own • 203

13 Remixing and Loop Sampling • 205

The focus in the chapter is to learn the techniques behind remixing, mashups, and sampling isolated loops from preexisting songs. The examples created can be made from music in your collection. The first two examples show how to combine and match the tempo and key of two preexisting songs, and the final example is a song made of smaller bits and pieces from several existing songs.

- Simple Remixing • 206
- Mashups • 207
- Sampling Loops from Preexisting Songs • 209
- Remixing an Acapella • 214
- On Your Own • 217

14 Mastering • 219

Mastering one's music is mandatory, whether the music is by yourself or another. Maybe you have heard a track from a bedroom producer that sounds much softer or weaker than a professional track played from a CD. This chapter will address some very simple ways to master a track sound and make it fit in well sonically with professional tracks.

- Generic Mixing Technique • 220
- The Master Track • 221
- The Limiter • 221
- The Mastering Chain • 223
- Compression on the Master Track • 224
- Equalizing on the Master Track • 225
- Multiband Dynamics • 226
- The Loudness War • 227
- Exporting • 227
- On Your Own • 229

Contents

15 Analysis of Projects • 230

Here we will look at some larger-scale projects in Live. Many of the projects involve some heavy-duty Max programming. We will describe the portions of the Max for Live patches that take advantage of using Live and allow it to function in novel ways.

- Live Rig • 230
- Pedalman Pro • 237
- Wrap-Up • 239
- On Your Own • 239

Bibliography • 241

Index • 245

Foreword

When I began my career as a musician and composer, entry into the world of fine art music was limited to a very small percentage of the population. To hear music, you would listen to the radio once a week or attend a concert. To create or perform music required the privilege of musical education and the inclination to work at it from an early age, a very daunting experience unavailable to the vast majority of people. Shortly after my entrance into that world a little over 50 years ago, the transistor was developed; promising a future of cheap electronic devices, and Bank of America delivered the first credit card with a large base of merchants. These two advancements sparked awareness that electronics would become very economical and, if you didn't have the money to buy the object, you could purchase the item with NO money up front. We were about to witness a significant change in the world of music; the creation, delivery, and enjoyment of music would soon be available to everyone. Most saw it, and still do, as a means of producing music easily and inexpensively. Others saw it as an opportunity to find new resources and tools, bypassing traditional methods and discovering new ways to be musically creative and expressive. Ultimately, you might say and believe that you can do anything you want with a piano. But, can you? Yes, if anything means to never make a crescendo on a single note, or never slide through pitches, and so on. The black and white keyboard defines the limits of your creative needs and expression. It was the time and dawning of Marshall McLuhan's "the medium is the message"! What I imagined was an electronic music easel that would have a neutral message. To this end, Ramon Sender and I commissioned Donald Buchla to create such an instrument—the birth of the Buchla Synthesizer, by some, the first analog synthesizer.

I was attracted to Ableton Live several years ago because of its simple and unassuming metaphor of being a single mixer module that could be used, multiplied, and configured at the user's will. Then, Ableton added Max, which uses the patching paradigm that we used in those early years to allow for a nonprescribed musical control flow. I have been using Ableton Live and Max along with the Buchla Synthesizer and it was very easy for me to see the potential of this union. But I suspected that it was not so easy for people to see these possibilities without some information about the power of the application union. This book does exactly that. By chapter 3 of *Interactive Composition* the reader is being introduced not only on how to use Max as an extra set of plug-ins but also on how to personalize everything from the modulation of a sound to the creation of individual ways in which the music will flow. In Manzo and Kuhn's words, "the powerful graphical programming language of Max/MSP/Jitter" is implemented in Ableton Live, giving composers newfound tools for creativity. The authors' simple and direct approach to teaching how to use these powerful tools within a single environment will empower anyone to experiment with their own musical creativity and expressiveness.

Morton Subotnik
August 2014

Preface

This book strives to empower readers with the skills and insight to compose and perform music in a variety of popular styles using technology. The focus is on the implementation of compositional and production concepts, and each chapter culminates with a newly composed piece created by the reader using these concepts. The book is divided into two units, the first of which addresses the tools involved in the creation of interactive composition. This is where the reader will learn the basics of using the available technology. The second unit presents chapters describing particular musical styles and the ways that one can compose and perform within each style using the software. Ideally, as the reader progresses through the book, they will learn to use the software to facilitate their compositional objectives.

A particular feature of this book is that it discusses the historical context of several electronic music styles used by DJs, electronic musicians, and other artists and then describes, using software, some of the technical processes used in the composition and performance of these styles. Each chapter presents attainable activities that require the reader to compose music according to a specific style and then use the technological tools to properly engineer and produce that style.

The intended audience for this book is individuals interested in creating music through a hands-on approach that centers on composing and performing with technological tools used in studios and clubs today. It will also be an ideal resource for secondary and higher education instructors interested in teaching courses on popular composition in a structured, yet creatively free, context. The book will primarily use *Ableton Live*, one of the most versatile software tools in the industry. We will also explain the production and engineering techniques for various styles that use *Ableton Live* and *Max for Live* as the technological tools. Each chapter will provide historic background on the popular music style being explored and discuss the pedagogical implications for classroom learning. The chapters then culminate in helping the reader to create an original composition in a given style and discuss the techniques used to perform the piece in an idiomatic fashion.

Why Implement Technology in Composition at All?

These days, you can't walk into a convenience store without seeing seven or eight computers being actively used to facilitate specific intended outcomes—why should music performance venues be any different? From stages, to galleries, to installations, to you name it: incorporating technology can truly help facilitate our creative musical objectives.

Electronic musical instruments, then, can be thought of as controllers for some musical elements. A variable is something that changes. A control is something that changes a variable. In music, there are many variables, such as pitch, dynamics, and timbre, that change as a result of the instrument's control device, also known as a *control interface*.

The control interface for a violin is typically a bow. Without buttons, knobs, or sensors, the bow is capable of controlling numerous variables within a single, simple interface. For example, if you angle the bow differently as it hits the strings, the timbre will change; apply more pressure and the dynamics will change.

The Buchla 200e, for example, is a modular synthesizer capable of controlling numerous musical variables. In fact, the Buchla is capable of creating more diverse timbres than the violin. However, controlling musical variables on the Buchla, with the control interface of knobs, buttons, and patch cables, involves more gestures than the violinist and bow.

For the intent of performance, some control interfaces are more accessible than others for real-time use. With a computer, you can arguably achieve any sound imaginable if you tweak the right numbers and press the right buttons. A well-designed control interface, however, allows a performer to readily control musical variables in a less cumbersome way than clicking on menu items from pull-down lists and checking boxes.

Throughout history, people have created new musical instruments that generally reflect the technological resources available at the time. Early primitive instruments had few moving parts, if any. The Industrial Revolution made way for the modern piano to evolve using steel and iron. In the Information Age, it stands to reason that newly created instruments may largely involve computers and electronics.

The paradigm of traditional musical instrument design, up until recently, has been focused primarily on the principles of acoustics. Design concepts that might inhibit string vibration or airflow, thus compromising timbral qualities and dynamic range in undesirable ways, are concerns for makers of traditional acoustic instruments. With electronic instruments, however, the mapping of musical variables to controls can be similar to traditional instruments or completely unrelated. In this way, instrument designers can pursue concepts that allow for novel idiomatic writing and performance without the acoustical concerns of sound reproduction. Considerations like body type, physical ability, accessibility, and so on may now become determinant factors regarding musical instrument use and design. New instrument creation can be designed to fit specific activities or people. These possibilities simply did not exist only a few short years ago, yet they are now available through advances in technology.

One obvious implementation of technology in compositions and performance can be seen in the work of DJs, interactive artists, and more. Walk onto a college campus that holds music technology concerts and prepare yourself for repurposed video game controllers, newly designed Theremins, musical gloves, more newly designed Theremins, Tesla coils, traditional instruments outfitted with technology, color-tracking systems, and still more newly designed Theremins. Yet, once the new instruments are made, how do we use those instruments to make interesting music? After all, with music technology, it's really easy to make really bad music.

You don't have to throw out your traditional instrument in order to implement technology. In fact, you don't even have to change your style to take advantage of the ways that technology can help facilitate musicianship in traditional popular or art music contexts. In the recording studio, many music groups overdub more parts onto their recording than they can possibly play in a live situation in order to produce a certain sound. So how do you pull it off live? Some groups do this by playing in sync with a sequencer that "performs" those additional tracks. Bands striving for that "orchestral rock" sound on their studio recordings may not find it feasible to tour with a full string orchestra. However, they may be able to more reasonably afford touring with a keyboardist who performs live with a software-based sample library sound.

In many cases, the objectives of the performers are the most important to consider. As much as the overall objectives of performing musicians may very well include "get rich and famous," "enjoy life," and "move people with my music," there are other questions about performance they must account for. Is an objective of performance to demonstrate the virtuosity of the performers? How do you want to feature that virtuosity: in novel ideas employed within the compositions you write, or in the way you perform them, or both? Perhaps the performers are more interested in creating an enjoyable experience for the audience through crowd interaction, an energetic stage show, and playing familiar but less-complicated songs than on showcasing their skills as virtuosic live performers. Choosing to demonstrate your technical ability in a live context could, and probably would, diminish the group's ability to simultaneously dance around a dimly lit stage. A religious ensemble may prefer to focus their performance on leading a congregation into worship more so than on executing the music without mistakes. These are philosophical issues that musicians need to answer honestly for themselves.

Once these issues are addressed and reconciled, there are a number of technical ways to facilitate creative objectives. For example, imagine the room volume inside a venue where the objective of the band is to get people dancing and partying, as compared to a venue where the objective of the band is to showcase the articulation and clarity of their overall balance. If playing at a moderate volume is a priority for the ensemble, then actions to facilitate that objective are implemented. It may mean that the guitarist considers using amp-simulation software instead of playing through a full-stack amplifier, and perhaps the drummer considers using an electronic drum kit instead of an acoustic one. These technologies certainly have pros and cons, and it is up to the ensemble to discuss them and consider the potential benefits with regard to the overall objective.

In a live performance, some may consider a vocalist who uses a pitch-correction processor to be a form of deception, while others may view it as simply another effect that enhances the final sound—no different from adding EQ, reverb, and compression. After all, pitch, just like tone and dynamics, is but one variable a singer controls, and we certainly have no qualms about using processors to correct tone and dynamics. Is it any more deceptive to use pitch-correction on a grad-school audition recording than it is to use EQ and reverb? In a recording studio, is using a pitch-correction processor different from asking a singer to rerecord the same phrase over and over again until they sing it better? Eventually, the singer is bound to sing that phrase in tune once (in the same way that monkeys left alone with a typewriter will eventually randomly type the works of Shakespeare!). Perhaps you are asked to engineer a recording for your elderly neighbor who wants to sing some songs for a CD she intends to give as a gift. If necessary, would you use pitch-correction and other effects to help her efforts or insist that she practice harder and come back to the studio when her singing is more polished? The production and compositional process of recording can be thought of as creating an experience for the listener, or creating the illusion that the listener has been transported and is now listening somewhere else. The engineering and tracking process of a recording is sometimes less magical.

However you feel about the above scenarios, technology can be used to help facilitate your creative goals. Consider the audience you are trying to reach and the type of experience that will reach them; then create that experience using music, software, or whatever else you need. What moves your peers is probably different than what moves your parents, young children, your teachers, and so on. As you proceed in this book, be creative and think of ways that technology can be used to help you do what you want to do in an efficient and interesting way.

On Music Genre Selection

The genres and subgenres of electronic music presented in this book are intended to be descriptive, rather than prescriptive, of common uses for Ableton Live and Max for Live. The genres in this book were chosen not only for their popular use at the time of writing but also for their value as vehicles for instructing the emerging Ableton Live user in advanced techniques. For example, a technical manual on the history of FM synthesis may not make compelling reading, but the heavy use of FM synthesis to recreate an existing musical style can help the user connect to the material.

The genres chosen not only demonstrate a wide variety of Live functions but also serve as vehicles for learning the history of electronic music, the original tools and methods that created each genre, and even a framework for understanding the technical evolution of pop music, which has developed in tandem with electronica from the 1970s onward.

In a few years' time, some of these genres may feel out of date in the same way that a book about jazz written during the 1930s may overemphasize styles later considered unworthy of canonization. We trust the reader will forgive our method of simply describing what is prevalent and useful in the here and now, rather than trying to force predictions upon you.

Book Design

This book is divided into 15 chapters that address concepts for composing music with technology in a number of styles. The book is structured as a step-by-step guide by which we'll complete activities. Each chapter culminates with an "On Your Own" assignment, which results in the creation of some creative work. We, the authors, will address the musical and technical concepts in each chapter. It is encouraged that the "On Your Own" assignments are revisited after the book is complete so as to produce different creative works for each assignment.

If you are an instructor using this book as the text for a semester course, we recommend that you cover about two chapters per week. The first five chapters address what we consider to be the core aspects of working with Live and Max for Live. New material builds upon previously learned concepts to some degree, so while skipping chapters is possible, students should be reminded to read the "Remember" section of each chapter to catch up on terms and features that may have been addressed in the chapter.

Basic Troubleshooting

The activities provided in this book have been tested, and you should not encounter any problems—in theory! As you move through this book, you're going to have to act as your own troubleshooting team if something goes awry. For each and every activity we do, there is a picture reference in the text and a working example available on this book's companion website (more about that website in the next chapter).

A few basic steps will help to make sure that you don't run into problems:

- Make sure you have the latest companion files for this book from the OUP website (URL provided in chapter 1).
- Save early and save often—ensure that you save your work frequently and that you keep your saved files organized. Don't accidentally overwrite files with the same name unless instructed to do so in the text.
- Follow the steps and make sure that you've followed the instructions exactly as written.
- Consult the pictures—as mentioned, a working example of each activity is available from the companion website.
- There are a few different versions of Ableton Live and a huge number of devices (instruments, effects, etc.). We have done our best to ensure that we are using devices that are available in your version, but sometimes versions change, software gets replaced or renamed, and you may not be looking at the same reverb effect as the one in this book. That's okay! This book is modular enough so that if you're missing an effect or a software instrument, you can substitute it for another one. We even suggest replacements in most cases. Some of the chapters require devices available in Ableton Live Suite. We'll note this in the text, but if you don't have it just download the trial while reading that chapter. The same goes for Max for Live.
- Restart the program. If you are still running into problems, save your work, restart the program completely, and reopen your work.
- Restart the computer. If your computer is being unresponsive, it is a good idea to shut it down, wait for a minute or so, and turn it back on (don't forget to turn it back on as this is considered to be an important step).
- Getting help—consult the *Help* resources within the software.
- If for some reason you still encounter an error, you should try to recreate the error on a different computer to identify problems with your machine. It's always possible that your volume is down, speakers unplugged, keyboard not working, and so on. Errors like this are best discovered in the privacy of your own home to minimize the amount of embarrassment experienced.
- The software manufacturers Ableton and Cycling '74 have support forums on their websites. However, you should refrain from posting your questions on this site until you have read through

this book and all of the reference files (including tutorials) included in the program. The users on the forum are helpful for matters that go beyond information that is clearly covered in the references provided here. If you're a student, it's also not a good idea to try to pay people on the forum to complete assignments for you. Users will generally ignore or even laugh at you, and they will likely refer you to the reference manuals. If you are reading this book as part of a course, the chances are strong that your instructor subscribes to the forums and will see your post.

- Be patient; some concepts are a little tricky, and you may have to reread something a few times before it sinks in. All in all, the concepts we introduce are not hard to learn, but be patient. Soon, you'll get the hang of it and will be writing your own interactive compositions in no time. Enjoy!

Acknowledgments

I would like to thank all of my colleagues at Worcester Polytechnic Institute (WPI) for their support and encouragement. To my colleagues in music technology, Frederick Bianchi and Scott Barton: thank you for your commitment to making music technology studies at WPI the most unique program I've seen. Thank you to Dean Karen Oates and my department head Kristen Boudreau for allowing and supporting our vision to make WPI an innovative place where books like this one can be written. Thank you to all of the students at WPI who have helped test-drive this book: Erica Bowden, Kyle Foster, Jesse Lehman, and Jonas McGowan-Martin.

To my friends and colleagues in the Kean University Conservatory of Music: thank you for helping to shape my views about how technology can facilitate musicianship. To my close friend and colleague Matthew Halper, thank you for your friendship through the years. I will always be grateful for our many conversations about composition, performance, education, theory, life, art, and the quality of slightly overdriven amp models. To my colleagues at the New Jersey Institute of Technology and Montclair State University: thank you for your support and insight throughout my time there. Thank you, Michael Halper, for your friendship, your thoughts on the Humeian *Is-ought,* and for doing some good work in that area with Scott Skeebo. To my colleagues in the Boyer College of Music and Dance at Temple University: thank you for your openness in spending time talking about my research ideas involving technology for music education and also your incredible enthusiasm. To Alex Ruthman and the music faculty at New York University (NYU): thank you for demonstrating the vast implications for technology in music. My continued thanks to David Elliot for your support, insight, and collegiality. Thank you also to David Cope, Peter Elsea, and Paul Nauert at University of California–Santa Cruz.

To my colleagues in the Technology Institute for Music Education (TIME) and the Association for Technology in Music Instruction (ATMI): thank you for your continued support and input about my work. My sincere thanks to Rick Dammers and Bill Bauer for making conferences interesting in a variety of ways.

This book, of course, could not be possible without Ableton, Cycling '74, the many members of the Ableton and Cycling '74 forums, and the numerous developers and artists throughout the world who contribute to this very unique community. Thank you to all users of the Modal Object Library and the EAMIR SDK. Thank you to Jonathan Bailey and Ben Senecal for your programming expertise and assistance in developing the Modal Object Library. And thank you, Annie Lennox and Jackson Browne, for everything.

To my fellow musicians, specifically, in *Clear Blue* and *Remnant*: thank you for your willingness (or unknowingness?) to create a performance opportunity in which we rely so heavily on technology. Thank you, also, for forgiving me for all of the times that I've stepped on the wrong pedal, left a backup running, forgotten to plug the charger in, upgraded plug-ins without testing, or triggered the wrong sample and totally delivered a deathblow to our live performance. I believe the concept is right. Besides, we will always have the studio version. To my bandmates in *Second Contact*: it's an honor playing really great music with you. There are so many things I want to say to you: most importantly, Queen's melodic writing, formal/structural development, sophistication of harmonic writing, pop accessibility, and unique blend of rock, musical theater, and neo-Romanticism are unparalleled by any band ever, objectively speaking, in my subjective opinion. Yes: neo-Romanticism. I'll thank you, friends, for not rolling your eyes while reading this.

To Norm Hirschy and Richard Carlin at Oxford University Press: my continued thanks to you and the rest of the team for your professionalism and expertise during this process.

To my co-author Will Kuhn and his family: thanks for making this happen. It's been fun planning, writing, rewriting, and editing with you. There's never a shortage of things that impress me about your creative ideas. I still feel strongly that we should have written this book in a comic book format with caption bubbles, but I suppose this will do.

Of course, I would be lost without the support of Raquel, her family, my family, all of my friends, and all of my pets. Thank you!

V. J. Manzo

. . . . .

I would like to first and foremost thank my wife Jennifer, my daughter Annelise, and my son Ethan, without whom my life would be hopelessly empty. I would also like to thank my close friends Brian, Davis, Laura, and John who have given me many years of friendship and support through this project.

I would like to thank the following electronic artists who started me down the path of electronic music making: Aphex Twin, FSOL, Daft Punk, The Prodigy, Moby, Imogen Heap, Bjork, Squarepusher, The Glitch Mob, and many many others.

To my colleagues and administrators at Lebanon High School: you encouraged me to build a new type of high school music program, and it has provided the template for bringing music to the masses for many schools for years to come. I would especially like to thank those people who made the initial year of Music Tech possible, especially David, who first uttered the phrase "Music Technology" when designing new courses back in 2006. Without you, this book would simply not exist.

To the students I have been fortunate to teach over the years: thank you for allowing me to experience music culture through your eyes and ears. Without your insight into current trends and your youthful energy I would not have been able to write this book. Grow up, make great things, and don't be evil.

To Norm Hirschy and Richard Carlin at Oxford University Press: Thank you so much for the opportunity to work on this project, and for your flexibility and help throughout the process.

To the folks at Ableton, Dennis DeSantis, Tony McCall, and Yukio Van Maren, who supported us during the early days of Live 9 and helped us craft an up-to-date book—your help in getting this project off the ground was incredible.

To my co-author V. J. Manzo: Thank you so much for taking me along on this ride. You are a true visionary and it is an honor to have worked on this project together. The graphic novel edition should be forthcoming, as well as the right-to-left-reading Manga version of this book.

Will Kuhn

About the Companion Website

http://www.oup.com/us/interactivecomposition

Oxford University Press has provided a companion website for *Interactive Composition.*

At this website, you will find chapter examples files that accompany each chapter in the book. You may download each chapter individually or all chapters collectively. To begin:

Download the *chapter examples* zip files to your computer.

The initial directions in chapter 1 provide explanation on where these unzipped chapter examples should be stored on your computer and how to access and use them. Each chapter will reference the contents of these chapter examples for activities demonstrated within the text and example illustrations that may be examined elsewhere. The authors Will Kuhn and V. J. Manzo created all examples unless otherwise stated.

The Basic Troubleshooting section above provides detailed steps for troubleshooting issues related to using Ableton Live.

Interactive Composition

Basics

I n this chapter, we will look at the ways that interactive composition can be facilitated using Ableton Live, a powerful digital audio workstation. The chapter also serves as an overview of the tools and functions available within Live and how they can be used to allow composition and performance. Even if you are already familiar with Live, you may find it useful to follow along as we discuss concepts related to interactive music-making using this tool.

Companion Site and Files

We assume that you have downloaded and installed the latest version of Ableton Live for your Mac or PC from *www.ableton.com*. One obvious difference between the versions of Ableton Live available for purchase (Live Intro, Live Standard, and Live Suite) is the library of samples, effects, and processing devices bundled within each version. If an illustration in this book uses content, such as a particular synthesizer sound or instrument, that is not available in your version of Live, you can substitute any other content you prefer. Remember that one objective of this book is to illustrate concepts of interactive composition as opposed to solely teaching how to operate a particular piece of software.

A companion website for this book has been created by Oxford University Press and is available at *www.oup.com/us/interactivecomposition*. The companion site features a number of content downloads related to this book, including the chapter example files. If you have not done so already, please download and unzip the chapter example files and store them on your computer for reference.

2

Basic Setup

Once you have installed Live, click the Live icon to open the program. The Live interface may seem intimidating at first glance, but in many ways it is a similar, yet enhanced version of traditional digital audio workstations (DAWs) you have likely encountered such as Logic, FL Studio, Pro Tools, and so on. One of the most important features within Live is *Info View*, which appears in the bottom-left portion of the program interface. This window, which provides a brief description of whatever your mouse is hovering over inside of Live, can be hidden or revealed by pressing the *?* key. It can also be enabled by selecting *View* from the menu at the top of the program and then selecting *Info View*.

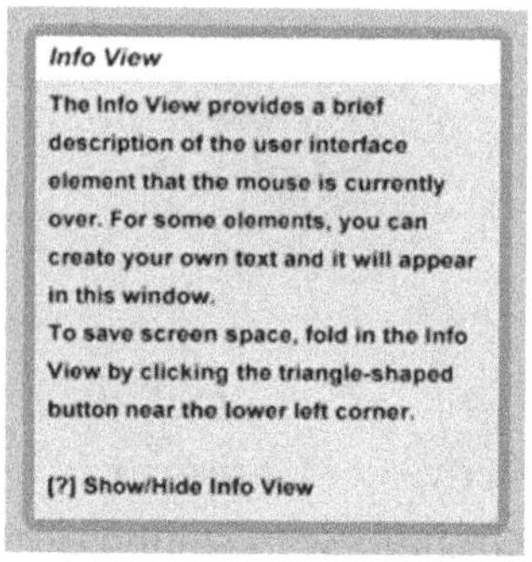

Info View

The Info View provides a brief description of the user interface element that the mouse is currently over. For some elements, you can create your own text and it will appear in this window.
To save screen space, fold in the Info View by clicking the triangle-shaped button near the lower left corner.

[?] Show/Hide Info View

FIGURE 1.1

Info View reveals a helpful description of whatever your mouse is hovering over.

1. Toggle to *Info View* by pressing the *?* key or selecting it from the *View* menu.

At the top-left side of the program is a menu of Browser items stacked vertically that, when clicked, allow you to see various content within the Live library including effects, synth instruments, loops, and more. These items are called *Devices* in Live. Notice that as you hover over these icons with your mouse, information appears in the *Info View* window.

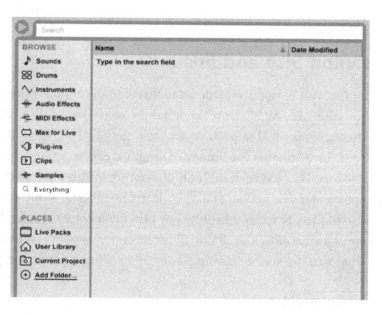

FIGURE 1.2

Browser reveals Live content when clicked.

Live Browser

The menus labeled *Sounds, Drums,* and *Instruments* allow you to see the software-based musical instruments available for use within Live's library. The menus labeled *Audio Effects* and *MIDI Effects* allow you to see the various effects that can be used in Live such as reverbs, delays, arpeggiators, and chord generators.

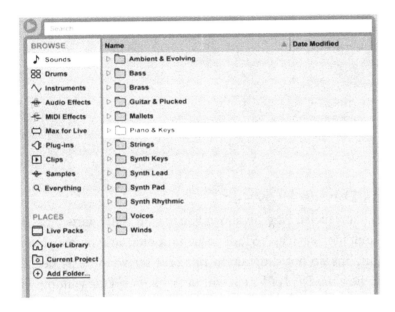

FIGURE 1.3

Live Device Browser shows the instruments, effects, and more bundled with Live.

2. Click on the various labels in the Browser.

The number of devices available for use within this library depends on your version of Live. However, the Live library can be expanded by downloading content directly from Ableton. The library may also be modified from the *Preferences* window by going to *Live>Preferences* (Mac) or *Options>Preferences* (Windows) from the top menu or by using the key command +, (Mac) or *ctrl+,* (Windows). From the *Preferences* window, the *Library* tab will allow you to see the location of your library on your computer as well as the devices you currently have installed. Additionally, you may *ctrl+click* (Mac) or *right-click* (Windows) a menu item from the Browser to import content from a previous version of Live.

Max for Live

The menu item labeled *Max for Live* represents an arsenal of tools for use within Live that draw from the power of Max/MSP/Jitter, a powerful programming language that can expand the palette of compositional and performance options available within Live.

4

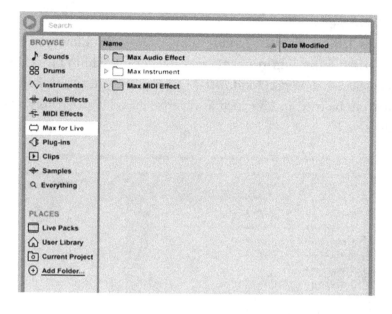

Plug-Ins Device Browser

The menu item labeled *Plug-Ins* allows you to view third-party plug-ins residing on your computer, such as VST, or audio unit plug-ins you may have installed. If these plug-ins do not show up in this browser window by default on your computer, view the *File Folder* tab within Live's *Preference* window. These plug-ins can be implemented into your projects just as easily as Live's devices.

Other Menus

The *Clips* menu allows you to see audio and MIDI files on your computer. These files, known in Live as *clips*, may include loops and other recordings.

The *Samples* menu is used to see small sound recordings on your computer called *samples*. These *samples* many times consist of only one note or beat in duration, but they can be used in a number of creative ways that we will discuss in future chapters.

You may search for devices and other content within the Live library and elsewhere by typing into the *Search* field at the top of the Browser.

Places

Live allows you to view files and other content on your computer within the *Places Browser*. These locations can be configured in a variety of ways to show commonly used file directories on your computer, such as a folder that contains all of your Live projects. The *Live Packs* location is reserved to point to the contents of the Live library on your computer. Note the words *Core Library* appear at the top of the Browser. This can be another way to view the content that is already accessible through the previously discussed menu items.

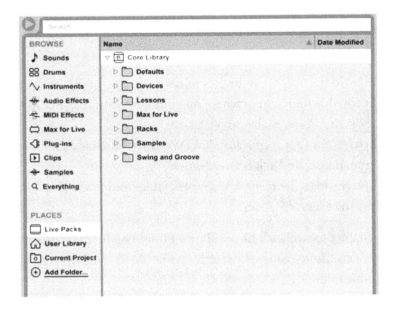

FIGURE 1.6

Live Packs menu item shows Live library files on your computer.

The *User Library Browser* location can be set to folders of your choosing. If you don't already have a folder on your computer to store your Live projects, please create that folder now.

3. First *ctrl+click* (Mac) or *right-click* (Windows) the *User Library* menu item and select *Add Folder*.
4. Create a folder on your computer named *My Live Projects*.
5. Select this folder as the *Places* location.

The folder *My Live Projects* will now be accessible from the sidebar menu area. As you create projects in Live, called "sets," you may save them to this folder for easy access.

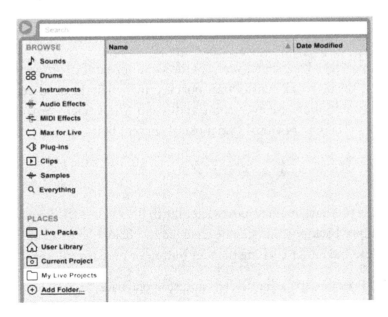

FIGURE 1.7

File Browser shows the newly created My Live Projects directory on your computer.

Adding Book Content

As mentioned earlier, this book has chapter examples and other content available through the Oxford University Press website. Once you have downloaded and unzipped the chapter examples file to your computer, please add this folder to the *Places Browser*.

6. Unzip the chapter examples folder from the OUP website and copy this folder somewhere on your computer, but not in the *My Live Projects* directory
7. *ctrl +click* (Mac) or *right-click* (Windows) the *User Library* menu item and select *Add Folder*.
8. Navigate to the chapter examples folder and select this folder as the *Places* location.

The chapter examples folder will now be accessible from the sidebar menu area. As you continue reading through this book, we will refer to various files located in this folder.

Working in Live

As you may already know, Live has two main views in which you may work: *Arrangement View* and *Session View*. These views may be toggled using the *tab* key or by clicking one of the two icons in the top-right portion of the program window. The views may also be changed from the *View* menu at the top of program.

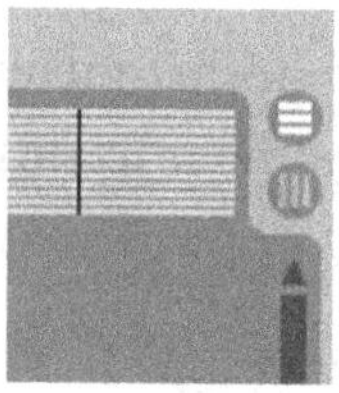

FIGURE 1.8

Icons to toggle between Session View and Arrangement View.

Arrangement View

We will begin looking at Live through *Arrangement View* since it more closely resembles the typical Digital Audio Workstation (DAW) layout.

9. Switch to *Arrangement View*.

Arrangement View shares many of the same appearance properties of typical DAWs. The playback control transport is provided in the dead-center of this view. By default, there are even some audio and MIDI tracks provided within Live, though there is, obviously, no musical content in this set yet.

FIGURE 1.9

Playback control transport.

10. Press the *play* button to begin playback.

As the playback marker moves laterally in the main track display, note that the initial playback position can be changed by clicking at other points within the timeline and either clicking the *play* button or pressing the space bar.

11. Press the space bar to start and stop playback.

12. Hold the *shift* key and press the space bar to start and pause playback.

MIDI and Audio Tracks

Live allows us to work with two basic types of media: MIDI tracks and audio tracks. It's also possible to work with video in novel ways, but for now our discussion will focus primarily on manipulating MIDI and audio. Notice that in the main track display, MIDI and audio tracks have been added to this set by default. To add more MIDI or audio tracks, choose *Create* from the top menu and add accordingly.

The MIDI protocol is a language that computers use to convey musical messages. Synthesizers as well as nearly all computer music software applications deal with MIDI in some way. What are these MIDI messages? In short, MIDI is a system for representing musical things like pitch, dynamics, and timbre with numbers.

To be precise, the numbers 0–127 are used to represent these musical things. The lowest MIDI note, 0, is the pitch C at five octaves below middle C. The number 1 is the C#/Db directly above that C, and so on. The MIDI note 12 is the C above the lowest C. Velocity is a measurement of pressure related to MIDI volume represented by the same numbers 0–127. A velocity value of 0 means that the note is off whereas the value 127 is the loudest volume that MIDI can produce. Therefore, the MIDI note 60 with a velocity of 127 could be described as middle C at a very loud volume.

When we record audio with microphones, the sound is sampled and stored at a very high rate to ensure that what was captured is an accurate representation of what the live sound actually sounded like. This results in very large audio files. One feature that is so great about MIDI is that MIDI files are essentially text documents containing a list of numbers that say, "These were the notes you played, this is how hard or soft you played them, and this is how long you held each note down." The resulting files are very small since the actual synthesis of those numbers into sound occurs within the DAW. Let's synthesize a MIDI file using the sounds given to us in Live.

13. Select the *Chapter Examples* menu icon from the *Places Browser* on the left.

FIGURE 1.11

MIDI and audio tracks in Live.

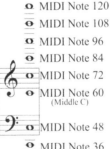

FIGURE 1.10

MIDI Note C as it relates to the grand staff.

14. Select the folder *Chapter 1* and expand it to reveal the file *piano riff 1.mid*.

15. Drag the file into the main track display area where the play-back marker resides.

Live will ask you if you want to import tempo and time signature information that is stored within the MIDI file, but for now, we'll select *No*.

16. Select *No* when Live asks you to import tempo and time signature information.

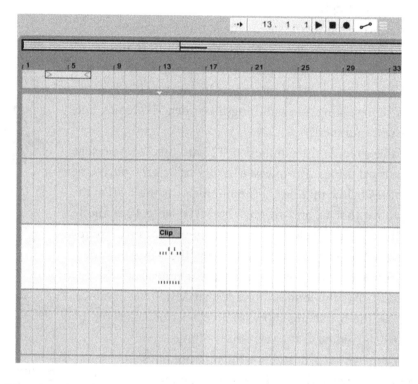

FIGURE 1.12

MIDI file represented in Live's track display.

If you've already tried to play this file by pressing the play button, you've probably realized that there is no sound. The reason is because, again, MIDI data is just a bunch of numbers that Live will interpret and synthesize with any sound of your choosing. Let's choose a sound so that these MIDI pitches can be heard.

17. Select the *Sounds* menu icon from the Browser on the left.

18. Expand the folder *Piano & Keys*.

19. Select the sound *Glass Piano.adg*. (Note: you may use any sound you like or have available.)

20. Click and drag this sound onto the track containing the MIDI file.

Notice that when you are selected on this MIDI track, the instrument device *Keys–Glass Piano* now appears at the bottom of the screen in Live's *Detail View* and that the MIDI track has been renamed to reflect this instrument. If you don't see this area, you can expand or contract *Detail View* using the arrow at the bottom right of the program screen or by choosing *View* from the top menu and selecting *Detail>Show*. Now that we have a sound to make sense of those MIDI numbers and map the data to an instrument timbre, let's play that file.

21. Click directly in front of the MIDI file.
22. Press *play* to begin playing the file.
23. Press the *stop* button after you have played the file.

Using Substitute Sounds for Missing Media

Suppose your friend makes a really great composition in Live and wants to send you the set so that you can see what he did. However, when you open the set, you are prompted with a message in the bottom *Status Bar* that says *Media files are missing*. This means that some of the media, perhaps recorded tracks or loops or even instrument devices, could not be found on your computer. There is no need to panic as Live will prompt you to search for the missing media. In the case that a file such as a vocal track cannot be found on your computer, you may need your friend to resend it. In the event that you do not have a particular Live instrument installed on your computer, you may ask your friend where he obtained the instrument. Or, you may use a substitute instrument by locating the track that contains the missing device, selecting a similar instrument device from your own local Live Library, and dragging it onto the instrument window within Live's *Detail View*.

If you open the companion files that accompany this book, you will most likely not encounter this issue. If you did, however, open the chapter example file for this chapter and are unable to load the Live instrument used, you may use the aforementioned steps to substitute for this missing media.

Now that we have some music working within Live, some of the processes you can perform with this file, referred to in Live as a *clip*, should be of no surprise. For example, you can copy and paste this clip by clicking on the clip title and selecting these options from the *Edit* menu at the top of the screen or with the key commands +*c* (Mac) or *ctrl+c* (Windows) for copy and +*v* (Mac) or *ctrl+v* (Windows) for paste.

24. Click on the *MIDI clip* to highlight it.
25. Copy the *clip* using one of the methods described above.
26. Click at another point in time along the *track display* and paste a copy of this *clip*.

Clip View

The contents of this clip as well as the way it functions within Live can be modified from within Live's *Clip View*. You can enter *Clip View* by double-clicking on the top title part of a clip. This will switch the bottom view from *Detail View* where we saw the MIDI track instrument to *Clip View*.

27. Double-click the *clip* to enter *Clip View*.

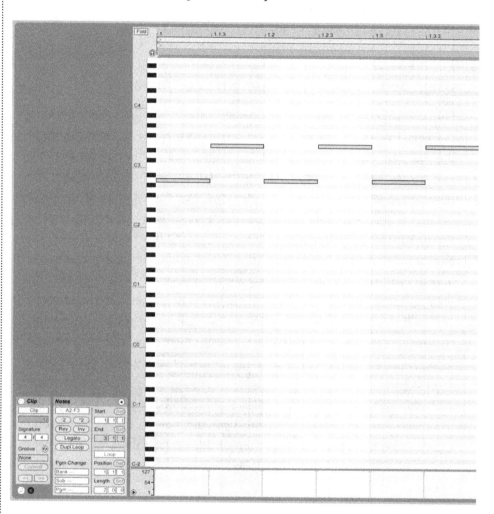

FIGURE 1.13

MIDI clip inside of Live's Clip View.

MIDI Pitch Editor

Since this clip is a MIDI file, *Clip View* allows us to see the pitches represented in Live's *MIDI Note Editor* (which some other DAWs refer to as a *Piano Roll Editor*). The *MIDI Note Editor* allows us to change the MIDI data within this clip and even add or delete MIDI notes. At the top left of this editor is a small circular icon with a tiny pair of headphones in it. Clicking on this circular *Preview* headphone icon will allow you to hear the MIDI data in the *MIDI Note Editor* when selected.

28. Click the circular headphone icon *Preview*. (Note: the icon will turn blue when enabled.)

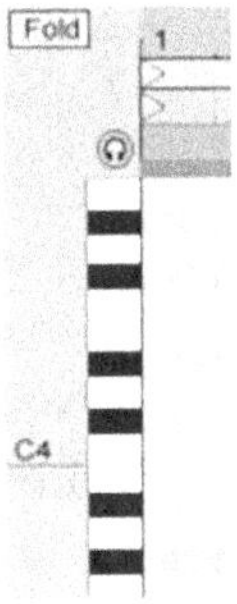

The horizontal bars inside of the *MIDI Note Editor* represent MIDI pitches across the vertical keyboard at the left. Clicking on these bars allows you to delete, reposition, and perform other manipulations on this clip.

FIGURE 1.14

The circular headphone icon allows you to preview MIDI and audio in Live.

29. Click on the MIDI bars inside of the *MIDI Note Editor*.
30. Reposition a few notes if desired by clicking on the note and dragging horizontally or vertically.

To lengthen or shorten a note:

31. Click on the edge of a MIDI bar so that your cursor turns into a bracket, then click and drag while holding the mouse down.

Notice that while resizing or relocating notes, the notes seem to snap into place when they approach or cross a bar line. This is because, by default, *Snap to Grid* is enabled in the *Options* menu. If you prefer to turn this option off and move your MIDI files more liberally along the bar lines, you may deselect *Snap to Grid* from the *Options* menu or use the key command *+4* (Mac) or *ctrl+4* (Windows).

32. Disable *Snap to Grid* using one of the methods described above and move one or more of the MIDI notes freely across bar lines.

To create new notes in the *MIDI Note Editor*, we will enter *Draw Mode*:

33. Press the *b* key on your computer keyboard and hover your mouse, now appearing as a pencil, over the *MIDI Note Editor*, clicking where you'd like to place a new note.
34. Press the *b* key again to allow your cursor to function normally. (Note that if you hold the *b* key, your cursor will function in *Draw Mode* only as long as you are holding the key down.)

MIDI Velocity Editor

Beneath the *MIDI Note Editor* is the *MIDI Velocity Editor*, which, as you may be guessing, will allow you to edit the velocity for each pitch above it. The velocity value for each pitch is represented as a vertical bar that can be increased or decreased by clicking on the top point of the bar and dragging up or down.

FIGURE 1.15

The MIDI Velocity Editor representing velocity values with vertical bars.

35. Click on the top point of one or more velocity bars and drag them up or down. (Note the numerical change for the MIDI velocity value reflected at the left side of the *MIDI Velocity Editor*.)

Note that selecting all of the notes shown in the *MIDI Note Editor* by choosing *Edit>Select All* or using the key command *+a* (Mac) or *ctrl+a* (Windows) will allow you to adjust the velocity for all notes in this clip simultaneously. This is also a great way to transpose all of the notes in a clip up or down for a number of semitones.

The small button labeled *Fold* located above the headphone *Preview* button will hide rows that do not contain MIDI clips. This can be used to make looking at data in the *MIDI Note Editor* a little easier. Be sure, however, to turn the *Fold* button off if you intend to move MIDI pitch bars from one note to another.

Loops

While the *MIDI Note Editor* screen is still open for this clip, notice the *Clip* and *Notes* boxes at the bottom left. These boxes allow different parameters to be set for the selected clip. We'll discuss this more in future chapters, but for now, one important aspect is that the word *Loop* is highlighted.

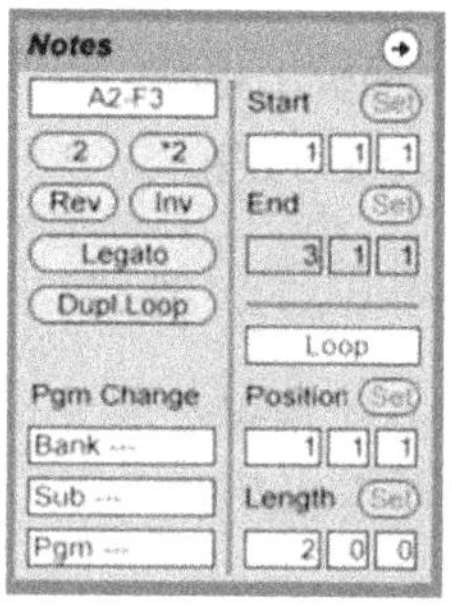

The selected clip will loop, that is, repeat itself, when the clip's length is dragged horizontally within the track display.

36. Select the clip within the track display.
37. Hold your cursor over the top-right edge of the clip until it appears as a bracket.
38. Click and drag the clip to the right to extend the loop over several bars.

The looped pattern refers to the data within the original clip. This is important because any changes you make to the original clip within the *MIDI Note Editor* will appear in all of the looped iterations of that clip. This is good if you decide to change a note or two in that clip later on. If you'd prefer that changes to the clips not appear in the looped iterations, simply copy and paste an instance of the clip on the same track.

39. Select the clip within the track display.
40. Copy and paste a copy of the clip to the right of the original clip.

FIGURE 1.16

MIDI clip is set to loop.

FIGURE 1.17

MIDI loop copied and placed alongside itself.

There are now two instances of this clip. Changes made in one clip will not have any impact on the other. This is a good technique if you make a drum loop pattern that you would like to make derivative patterns from later without destroying the original. For our purposes now, let's move this copied pattern to a new MIDI track and assign it a new timbre.

41. Select the copied MIDI clip within the track display.
42. Drag the clip to another track within the track display.
43. Double-click the track name for this new track to close *Clip View* and open *Track View*. (Note: you may also accomplish this from the *View>Detail* menu item at the top of the program.)
44. Select the *Sounds* menu icon from the Browser on the left.
45. Expand the folder *Piano & Keys*.
46. Select the sound *Keys–Tinefull Ambient.adg*.
47. Click and drag this sound onto the new track containing the copied MIDI clip.

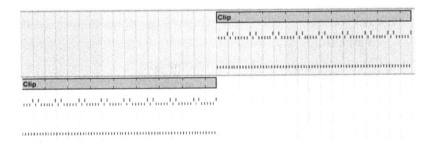

FIGURE 1.18

MIDI loop on different MIDI tracks.

We now have pitch material on two different tracks with two different timbres. Let's edit the MIDI clip on this track to create some basic counterpoint.

48. Double-click the newly copied MIDI clip to open *Clip View* revealing the *MIDI Note Editor*.

Among some of the more interesting compositional options one can explore within the *Notes* box are the buttons labeled *:2* and *⋆2*; that is, *Play at Double Tempo* and *Play at Half Tempo*, respectively.

49. Click the button labeled *:2* to change the MIDI values of the notes in Clip View so that they play at double speed.
50. In the track display, click at the beginning of this clip to move the playback marker to the front of it.
51. Press the *play* button to hear the same melodic pattern played at double speed.
52. Press the *stop* button when the track is done playing.

Notice that the second clip does, in fact, play twice as fast. Additional processes available through buttons within this box allow the MIDI data to be manipulated in other novel ways. Let's now move this track so that at least part of the clip begins playing in sync with the first clip.

53. Select the copied MIDI clip within the track display.
54. Drag the clip to the left so that at least part of the new clip is overlapping the original clip.
55. In the track display, click at the beginning of the original clip to move the playback marker to the front of it.
56. Press the *play* button to hear the same melodic pattern played at double speed.
57. Press the *stop* button when the track is done playing.

This is starting to sound interesting, but the volume of the newly created track could probably stand being reduced. To adjust the volume of a track:

58. Go to *View* from the topmost menu and ensure that *Mixer* is checked.
59. Go to the track name for this clip and locate the orange panel containing the number 0.
60. Click on this panel and drag your mouse down to decrease the volume to −3.
61. Press the *play* button to hear the changes.
62. Press the *stop* button when you are done.

FIGURE 1.19

Track mixer section contains volume, pan, activator, and other elements related to the track.

The mixer section of a track contains volume and pan-level controls, a track activator to mute tracks, a solo button to mute all other tracks, and other useful controls that we will discuss in the following chapters.

Adding Tracks

This set needs some bass and drum tracks. To create a new track, choose *Create* from the topmost menu and select *Insert MIDI Track*.

63. Create a new *MIDI track*.
64. Select the *Sounds* menu icon from the Browser on the left.
65. Expand the folder *Bass*.
66. Select the sound *Wobble Bass.adg*.
67. Click and drag this sound onto the new track.

Inserting a New MIDI Clip

There's currently no MIDI data on the *Bass-Wobble* track, so let's create a new clip and draw in some pitches using the *MIDI Note Editor*.

68. Select the track display for the *Bass* track and select a region by clicking and dragging your cursor to the right.

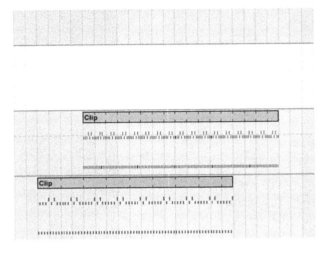

69. With the selection highlighted, *ctrl+click* (Mac) or *right-click* (Windows) the selection to show a contextual menu.
70. Select *Insert MIDI Clip* from the contextual menu.

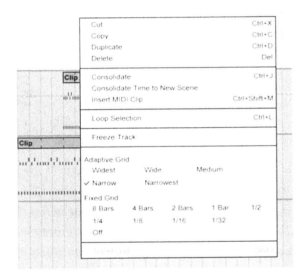

We now have a blank clip by which we can add bass notes. Note that the clip length is the same length as the region you highlighted. Of course, we can change this region length from *Clip View* as we saw earlier. Let's add some notes:

71. Double-click the clip to enter *Clip View*.
72. Within *Clip View*, click the circular headphone icon to allow MIDI note previewing while drawing MIDI notes.
73. From the vertical *piano roll* on the right-hand side of the *MIDI Note Editor*, locate the pitch marked *A0*.

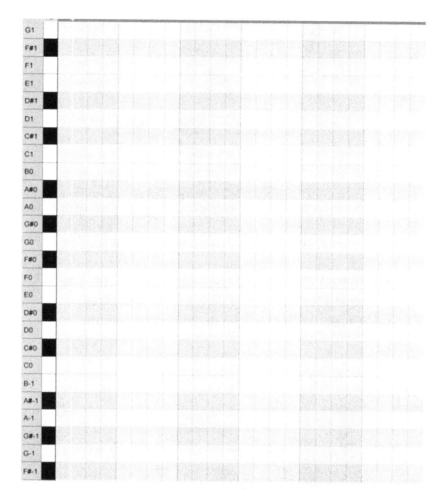

FIGURE 1.22

Pitches stacked vertically in the MIDI Note Editor.

74. Double-click in the first two squares directly to the right of the *A0* marking at the beginning of the MIDI clip. (Note: these two squares should fill up half of *bar 1* as delineated at the top of the *MIDI Note Editor*, leaving two squares empty.)

75. Skip the two adjacent squares in *bar 1* and click in the first and third squares of *bar 2*.

76. Play this set from the beginning to hear the changes, stopping playback when you are done.

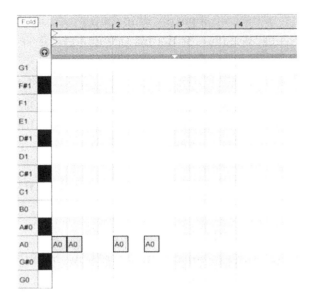

FIGURE 1.23

Bass figure drawn into the MIDI Note Editor.

The bass pattern provides a nice, low-end complement to the other clips in this set. However, as you have probably noticed, even though the bass clip is set to *Loop* in *Clip View*, the loop region itself is too large for the minimal amount of MIDI data we have entered. We can either write more notes to fit the length of the clip or adjust the size of the clip to the amount of notes we've written. Let's choose the latter.

At the top left of *Clip View*, note the two triangles stacked on top of each other just beneath the *bars/beats* numbers at the top. The top triangle is the *Loop Start* point. At the far right of the clip is the *Loop End* point. The length of the clip and, essentially, when and how it will loop depends upon the position of the *Loop Start* and *Loop End* points in *Clip View*.

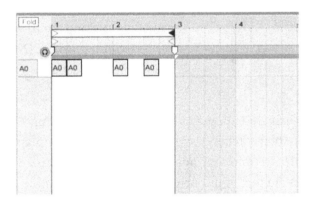

FIGURE 1.24

Adjusted loop region in the bass track's Clip View.

77. Click the *Loop End* point for this clip and drag it to the start of *bar 3* at the far left.
78. Press the *play* button to hear the change.
79. Press the *stop* button after you have played the track.

Notice that how the loop appears within the track display has now changed. Now that we have discussed how to do this, let's undo what we just did and save that process for another time when we need to use it.

The arrow beneath the *Loop Start* arrow is the *Start Marker* and controls from where in the loop region the track will begin playing. The reasons why you might want to reposition this marker will be addressed in future chapters; for now, we will leave this *Start Marker* in place so that this clip will play from the beginning.

Recording with a MIDI Keyboard or the Computer MIDI Keyboard
Let's now add a drum part.

80. Create a new MIDI track.
81. Select the *Drums* menu icon from the Browser on the left.
82. Select the sound *Kit-Core 909.adg*.
83. Click and drag this sound onto the new track.

If you have a MIDI keyboard connected to your computer, you'll be able to use it to play notes using this drum instrument as opposed to drawing them into clips like we've been doing.[1] If you don't have a MIDI keyboard, Live has provided a mechanism that allows you to use your computer keyboard to play MIDI notes. To enable this feature, go to *Options* from the top menu and check *Computer MIDI Keyboard*.

To preview MIDI playback on a MIDI track, using a MIDI controller or a computer keyboard, ensure that the track is selected and that it is armed for recording by selecting the *Arm Arrangement Recording* switch in the *Mixer* section of the track. The switch will appear red when the track is armed.

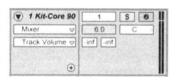

FIGURE 1.25

Arm a MIDI track for recording.

84. Ensure that the drum MIDI track is armed by clicking the *Arm Arrangement Recording* switch. (Note: ensure that the mixer section is visible in *View>Mixer*.)

If you are using a Computer MIDI Keyboard, you may use only certain computer keys to play pitches. For example, the keys *A–K* map to the pitches of the C Major scale. To transpose notes down or up an octave, use the keys *z* and *x*, respectively. Note that your current octave is shown in the *Status Bar* at the bottom left of the screen while you press the *z* and *x* keys.

FIGURE 1.26

Octave of Computer MIDI Keyboard shown in the Status Bar.

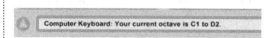

Computer Keyboard: Your current octave is C1 to D2.

The *Drum Rack* device shown in *Track View* shows a number of individual drums within a grid.

1. Note: If your MIDI controller is not working at the moment, we will discuss configuring it in the next chapter. Please read on. If you'd rather troubleshoot it now, you may open the *Preferences>MIDI Sync* menu to configure MIDI controller options.

Synthesized Sounds and Samples

The sounds, or instrument *timbres*, that are played with MIDI information generally fall into one of two categories: instruments that are primarily created *synthetically* by manipulating waveforms or frequencies to create new sounds or to emulate sounds that already exist; or instruments that are primarily created using recorded sounds, called *samples*. Of course there are also hybrid categories that combine both approaches.

In the synthesis approach to instrument creation, a spectrogram can examine the frequencies present when someone plays a note on the piano and then attempt to generate waveforms with oscillators to *synthetically* recreate that sound. When a MIDI key is pressed, the "synthesizer device" will understand the MIDI pitch that was pressed and generate a sound with those oscillators at a certain frequency based on the MIDI key/pitch that was pressed. Synthesis is now commonly associated with new, unique sounds as opposed to imitating existing sounds, especially given the increased popularity of the sampling approach.

In the sampling approach to instrument creation, instead of combining wave generators to imitate existing sounds, audio recordings are made of someone playing each note on the piano. Then, when a MIDI key is pressed, a "sampler device" will understand the MIDI pitch that was pressed and trigger an audio recording of the piano playing that same pitch. The sounds are incredibly realistic because they are recordings, or *samples*, of actual instruments. Early samplers, such as the *Birotron* or the *Mellotron*, used tapes to store the sample sound recordings. Now, software instruments feature sample libraries, consisting of several gigabytes, which contain audio recordings of many different instruments. Each sampled software instrument contains numerous recordings of each pitch at varying volumes played in different ways.

From the *Drum Rack* device, you may sample different sounds by clicking the small *Play* button in each of the grid cells. Notice that when you move your

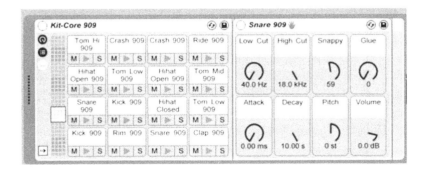

Individual drum samples within a Drum Rack device.

cursor over one of these cells, the *Status Bar* reveals which MIDI note must be played in order to trigger the sample. For example, the *Kick 909* sample is triggered with MIDI pitch *C1*. You may need to transpose down on your MIDI or computer keyboard to play this pitch. Once transposed to the correct octave, playing this kick drum on a MIDI keyboard will be with the note C; on a computer keyboard, it will be the *a* key.

85. Transpose your controller, if necessary, to the correct octave and play drum samples for this instrument.

Once you are able to get your controls working to play notes, recording them into the set is easy. With the drum track armed:

86. Using the keyboard to perform, determine a drum pattern to play that you feel fits with the musical material we already have in this set.
87. In the *track display*, click at the point in time where you would like to begin recording.
88. Press the *F9* key to begin playback/recording or click the *Global Record Button* in the transport dock at the top of the screen.
89. Press the *stop* button to end recording.

It is advised that you enable the *Metronome* while recording so that you

can keep in time by clicking the *Metronome* button at the top right of the screen (shown as two small circles). The icon will appear yellow when activated.

If you messed up a bit in the recording process, don't worry. You already have enough skills to correct timing and pitch problems in the *MIDI Note Editor* with *Clip View*. Let's take a closer look

at what you just recorded by opening *Clip View*.

90. Double-click the *Clip* title bar to open *Clip View*.

In this example, I can see with painful clarity that what I recorded does not line up with the bars and beats grid provided.

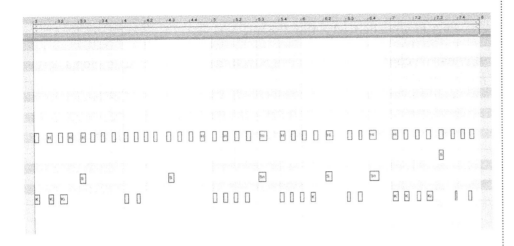

MIDI notes in the MIDI
Note Editor out of beat as
they were recorded.

At this point, I can manually reposition all of the notes to my choosing, or use a method called *Quantization* to nudge the MIDI notes to the nearest bar. To quantize this clip:

91. Highlight all of the notes within the clip
92. With the notes highlighted, *ctrl+click* (Mac) or *right-click* (Windows) the selection to show a contextual menu.
93. Select *Quantize Settings*" from the contextual menu.

The quantization process in Live can adjust the position of each MIDI note's start and end according to the beat spacing of the bars and beats grid. If you play a pattern of eighth or sixteenth notes and find that quantization does strange and unappreciated things to your notes, you may select different rhythmic values from the *Quantize To* pulldown menu in this box.

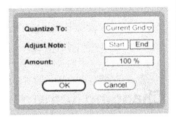

The Quantization Settings
box controls the ways that
quantization will function.

94. Click *OK* in the *Quantization* box to nudge the notes you playcd to the nearest bar and beat.

If this quantization process just ruined your recorded MIDI data, undo the process from the *Edit* menu and try the process again with different *Quantize To* settings.[2] Additionally, *ctrl+clicking* (Mac) or *right-clicking* (Windows) in *Track Display* or *Clip View* will also allow you to adjust the beat grid.

The drum clip I recorded is not long enough to cover all of the music I have in this set, so I am going to click the *Loop* button within *Clip View* in order to use this clip as a repeating pattern. If desired:

95. Adjust the region of the recorded drum pattern within the *MIDI Note Editor* by adjusting the *Loop Start* and *Loop End* points.
96. Enable the *Loop* button for this clip.

2. The *Global Quantization* button is located to the right of the *Metronome*.

97. Loop as desired within the track display.

As you continue on with this set, you may find it useful to loop a certain region of audio while adjusting volume, panning, or even notes in the *MIDI Note Editor*. To set the loop region to a specific clip:

98. *ctrl+click* (Mac) or *right-click* (Windows) the clip title bar for the drum MIDI track or another track.
99. From the contextual menu, select *Loop Selection*.

Notice that the loop region at the top of the screen now surrounds the length of clip you selected. This region can be adjusted from the *Arrangement Loop* settings at the top right of the program. Clicking the center icon called *Loop Switch* will loop the selection as it plays back. This is a very useful feature that will adjust balance, panning, and pitches or, as we will see in future chapters, instrument timbre qualities and effects.

100. Enable the *Loop Switch* and play the loop region, noticing how it loops.
101. Turn off the *Loop Switch* and notice how the track does not cycle back to the beginning as the playback marker reaches the end of the loop region.

Changing Tempo

At the top left of the program, near the *Metronome,* is a button that says *TAP* with the numbers *120.00* next to it. Changing this numerical value will change the tempo of this piece. The tempo, at *120* by default, is measured in *Beats Per Measure (BPM).* To change this number:

102. Click the number *120* in the *Tempo* box and scroll your cursor up or down to increase or decrease the tempo.
103. Play the file to hear the adjustment in tempo.

Additionally, you may click the *TAP* button repeatedly at the tempo of your choosing to impose that tempo value on your session.

Saving and Cleaning Up the Set

For now, we will close our discussion of Live's *Arrangement View.* In the next chapter, we will examine how Live's *Session View* functions. We will use the clips we've created in this chapter in our discussion of *Session View,* so let's quickly rename our clips so that our set is cleaner:

104. *ctrl +click* (Mac) or *right-click* (Windows) the clip title bar for any one of the MIDI tracks in the set.
105. Select *Rename* and rename the track with a more appropriate name such as *Keyboard Hook* or *Drum Pattern*.
106. Repeat this process for each clip in the set.

Note that you can use the key command +r (Mac) or *ctrl+r* (Windows) to rename anything in Live that can be renamed such as clips, tracks, and so on. Let's now save this set:

107. Click *File>Save Live Set*.
108. Save this project to the folder we created at the beginning of this chapter called *My Live Projects*.

Exporting Rendered Audio

Now that the project is saved, you may render the entire set as an audio file.

109. From the top menu, click *File>Export Audio/Video*.

There are a number of options that can be specified within this menu, including the audio settings and format. If it's not already apparent, the specific applications for changing these settings will become clearer later on in the text. Clicking *OK* will render the entire set as an uncompressed audio file.

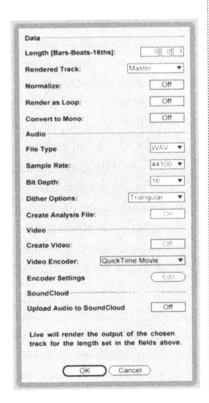

110. Click *OK* and specify a filename for your audio file.

FIGURE 1.34

Export Audio/Video window.

Note that highlighting a region in *Arrangement View* prior to selecting the *Export* option will allow only the highlighted region to be rendered. This is useful if you intend to render only specific loops or sections of your set, not the entire set.

On Your Own

Download a MIDI file from the internet and import it into Live. The MIDI file can be from anything you choose: a piece of classical music, a video game soundtrack, a popular song, or any other selection you might think of. Within Live, choose timbres to synthesize the MIDI data and address issues of volume balance within the instrument parts. Additionally, modify the MIDI data in interesting ways by changing pitches, adding instruments and pitches, copying musical segments, changing the overall tempo, and so on. Export the project as a *.wav* audio file.

Remember:

- *Info View* provides a brief description of whatever your mouse is hovering over and can be hidden or revealed by pressing the *?* key.
- The *Live Device Browser* allows you to see all of the effects, instruments, and utilities available for use within Live's library.
- Your *Preferences* for Live can be adjusted by using the key command +, (Mac) or *ctrl*+,(Windows).
- Live project files are called *sets*.
- *Arrangement View* and *Session View* may be toggled using the *tab* key.
- Add MIDI or Audio tracks by choosing *Create* from the top menu.
- MIDI is a system for representing musical elements like pitch, volume, and timbre with numbers.
- Show/hide *Detail View* by using the arrow at the bottom right of the program screen or by choosing *View* from the top menu and selecting *Detail>Show*.
- Loops and other media files in Live are called *clips*.
- Enter *Clip View* by double-clicking on a clip.
- Clicking on the circular headphone icon will allow you to preview the MIDI and audio data in Live.
- The small button labeled *Fold*, located above the headphone *Preview* button, will hide rows that do not contain MIDI clips.
- To resize the duration of a note, click on the edge of a MIDI bar so that your cursor turns into a bracket, then click and drag while holding down the mouse.
- Toggle *Snap to Grid* using the key command +4 (Mac) or *ctrl+4* (Windows).
- Press the *b* key to toggle *Draw Mode*.
- The length of the clip depends upon the position of the *Loop Start* and *Loop End* points in *Clip View*.
- The *track mixer* section contains volume, pan, activator, and other elements related to the track.
- To create a new track, choose *Create* from the topmost menu and select *Insert MIDI* or *Insert Audio Track*.
- To use your computer keyboard as a MIDI controller, go to *Options* from the top menu and check *Computer MIDI Keyboard*.
- Arm a track for recording by selecting the *Arm Arrangement Recording* switch in the *Mixer* section of the track.

- The *Status Bar* is shown at the bottom left of the screen.
- Press the *F9* key to begin playback/recording or click the *Global Record Button* in the transport dock at the top of the screen.
- Enable the *Metronome* by clicking the *Metronome* button at the top right of the screen (shown as two small circles).
- *Quantization* can be used to nudge MIDI notes to the nearest bar.
- The *Global Quantization* button is located at the right of the *Metronome*. Additionally, *ctrl +clicking* (Mac) or *right-clicking* (Windows) in *Track Display* or *Clip View* will also allow you to adjust the beat grid.
- Click the *TAP* button repeatedly at the tempo of your choosing to impose that tempo value on your session, or simply adjust the numerical value in the *Tempo* box.
- Use the key command *+r* (Mac) or *ctrl+r* (Windows) to rename anything in Live that can be renamed such as clips, tracks, and so on.
- Click *File>Export Audio/Video* to render the entire set as an uncompressed audio file.
- Highlighting a region in *Arrangement View* prior to selecting the *Export* option will allow only the highlighted region to be rendered.

2

Session View

n this chapter, we will examine Live's *Session View*, a unique way of working
with audio and MIDI tracks with real-time accessibility for composition and
performance. We will also examine the basics of audio recording within Live
and discuss the basics of applying audio effects to the signal source.

Session View

Up until this point, we've been working in Live's *Arrangement View*, which, in
many ways, functions like traditional DAWs by allowing users to record, mix,
and so on. Live's *Session View* provides a novel interface that allows you to interact with music material using a real-time performance approach. Let's examine
this view by opening the project from the previous chapter. If you don't have
this file handy, open the first file from the *Session View Project* in the *Chapter
Examples>Chapter 2* folder. This folder is accessible from the *Chapter Examples*
location on the left-side *Places* menu that we created in the previous chapter.

1. Open the file we made in the previous chapter or load the file
   Session View 1 from the folder *Chapter Examples>Chapter
   2>Session View Project*.

Before we look at *Session View*, let's export the clips we used in this project
so that we can work with them within *Session View*.

2. Select the *Places Browser* folder called *Current Project* at the left.
3. Click the clip title bar for any one of the MIDI tracks in the set
   and drag it to the right side of the *Current Project* Browser
   window.

4. Repeat the process for each MIDI clip in the set until all of the clips are listed in the Browser window.

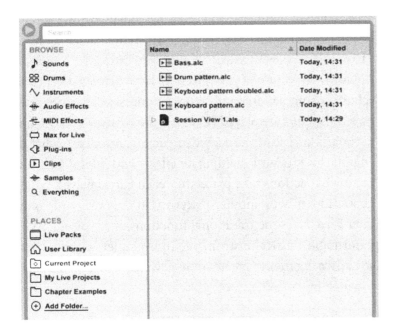

FIGURE 2.1

MIDI patterns as clips in the Current Project folder.

27

Now that we've made these clips, let's make a new set and build a *Session View* project from the ground up.

5. Choose *File>New* from the top menu to make a new set. (Note that you may be asked to save the changes you've made to the open document; choose *No*.)

Now that we have a blank set open, let's switch to *Session View* so that we can interact with these clips.

6. Switch to *Session View* from the top *View* menu, the *Selector* icon at the top right, or by pressing the *tab* key.

At first glance, you may not know what to do with *Session View*, so let's discuss the concept. Unlike *Arrangement View*, where the timeline moves forward on a linear plane playing the music material you placed therein, *Session View* allows you to load multiple clips into the various slots for each track in your set and play them whenever you'd like. To demonstrate this concept, let's navigate to the location where you saved the clips we made in the previous steps for this chapter.

FIGURE 2.2

Clip slots stacked for tracks in Session View.

7. From the *Places Browser*, navigate to the location on your computer where you saved the four clips made in previous steps. (Note—if you cannot access/find these clips, you may use the

demo clips located in the chapter examples folder: *Chapter Examples>Chapter 2>Demo Clips.*)

The basic concept behind *Session View* is that you can stack multiple clips for a single track in which each clip contains different musical ideas. This means that if you have one track with a drum sound, you can load a bunch of clips into each clip slot for each section of your piece: an intro drum pattern, a verse drum pattern, a chorus drum pattern, and so on. Of course, Live gives you total control over how these clips are played (Do I use the mouse to start/stop clips? Do I press a keyboard key? Can I use a video game controller?), what happens to them during playback (Can I manipulate effects and filters? Can I change the volume?), and what actions take place after each clip is played (Do they loop? Do they jump randomly to another pattern? Do they play only once?). In essence, *Session View* takes the traditional functions of a typical DAW and turns it into a performable musical instrument. To begin, let's double-click each clip you created earlier in order to create some new tracks within *Session View* with these clips loaded in.

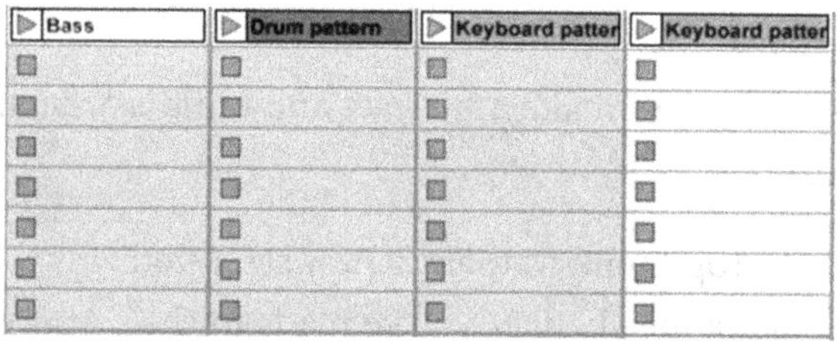

FIGURE 2.3

Clip slots loaded with clips on separate tracks.

8. Double-click each of the clips you created earlier from within the Browser at the right.

In Live, you can import audio from your computer into your session just by dragging it in. The files don't need to be in *.alc Clip* format; you can drag in *.wav* files, *.mp3* files, and other formats. However, a common process that occurs when importing files into Live is the *Auto-Warp Long Samples* feature, which can be toggled on or off in *Preferences*. We'll talk about *Warp* and *Preferences* later, but if you've skipped ahead and all of your samples are playing back at different tempos, read the *Help* file about turning off *Warp* or disable *Auto-Warp* from *Preferences*.

Notice that Live has created new tracks with each clip loaded into the first cell, known as a *clip slot*. The sounds we used earlier have been retained in these *.alc* format clips.[1] To play these clips:

1. Note: if we had imported MIDI files directly onto these clip slots by dragging them from the Browser onto new MIDI tracks, we would have to choose sounds to synthesize the MIDI data just as we did when we imported MIDI files onto tracks in the previous chapter.

9. Press the *Play* button triangle at the left of part of each *Clip Slot* to play the clip in that slot.

10. Press any of the *Stop* button squares on a track that is currently playing to stop the clip from playing. (Note—you may also use the square labeled *Stop Clips* at the button right on the *Master Track* to stop all audio clips from playing.)

When you click the *play* button for a clip, it begins playing looped. Each clip can play independent of the other clips on separate tracks. For example, you can press *play* for each clip, but then choose to stop, perhaps, just the drum clips or just the bass. In fact, we can make different configurations of clips on each row of cells and play all of the clips simultaneously.

FIGURE 2.4

Master Track at far right features the Stop Clips button to stop all clips simultaneously.

At the far right, you will see the *Master Track* complete with play buttons of its own.

Clicking one of these *play* buttons will play, or *launch*, all of the clips in the horizontal row, called a *scene*.

FIGURE 2.5

Master Track play buttons allow an entire row of clips to be played simultaneously.

11. Click the *play* button in *slot 1* of the Master Track to *launch* all clips in the first *scene*.

12. Click the *Stop Clips* button to stop playing the *scene*.

In essence, *scenes* can be thought of in relation to the structure divisions, or *form*, of a piece of music. Perhaps you would like to set up *scene 1* to be your *intro* by including just a few clips; maybe *scene 2* has new musical material within its clips that you'd like to use as your *verse; scene 3* can contain other musical material as a *chorus* section. The concept of organizing musical content into scenes can be helpful in creating some semblance of structure within the composition, even if the composition is largely improvised. Let's take a moment to copy clips from *scene 1* to other scenes.

13. Copy some, but not all, clips from *scene 1* to *scenes 2 and 3*. (Note: be sure to think about each scene as having unique structural differences despite the limited number of clips we are working with.)

14. *ctrl +click* (Mac) or *right-click* (Windows) the slot names for each scene on the Master Track and select *Rename* in order to label each scene according to its formal section (for example: scene 1 could be *intro*, scene 2 *verse*, scene 3 *bridge*, etc.).

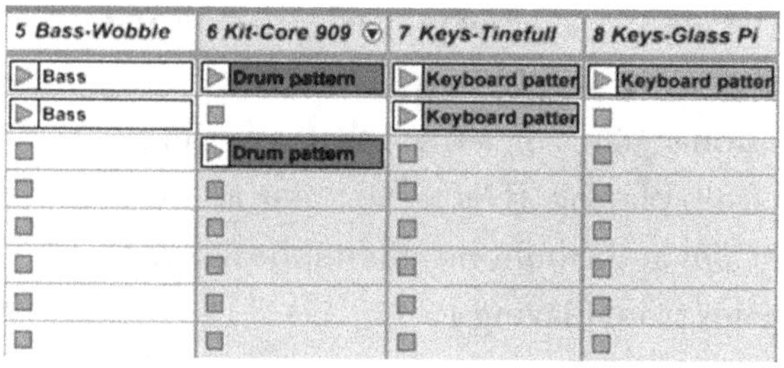

5 Bass-Wobble	6 Kit-Core 909 ⊙	7 Keys-Tinefull	8 Keys-Glass Pi
▷ Bass	▷ Drum pattern	▷ Keyboard patter	▷ Keyboard patter
▷ Bass	☐	▷ Keyboard patter	☐
☐	▷ Drum pattern	☐	☐
☐	☐	☐	☐
☐	☐	☐	☐
☐	☐	☐	☐
☐	☐	☐	☐
☐	☐	☐	☐

FIGURE 2.6

Multiple scenes representing the formal structure of this composition.

15. Launch each of the scenes you've just created.
16. Stop the scenes when you are done.

Did you notice that when you pressed the *play* button to launch a scene, it began playing on beat when the previous scene ended and not necessarily at the exact moment when you pressed the *play* button? The way that Live knows what beat to come in on is determined, once again, by the quantization menu at the top left of the program to the right of the metronome. If set to *1 bar*, the selected scene will begin playing *1 bar* after the previous scene has ended. If set to *none*, the selected scene will begin playing instantly when the play button is pressed.

17. Set the quantization menu value to *none*.
18. Play different scenes, taking note that the alternation occurs immediately.
19. Reset the quantization menu value to *1 bar*.

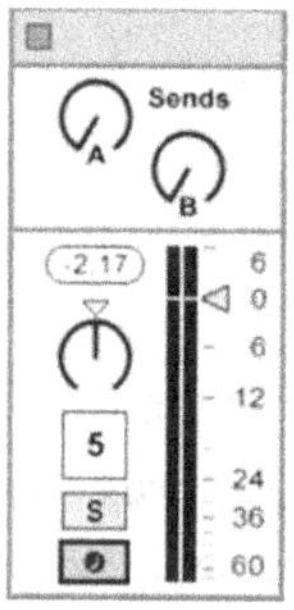

FIGURE 2.7

The session record button for a MIDI track is enabled to allow MIDI controller throughput.

Recording and Editing Clips

In the same way that we record and edit content on tracks in Live's *Arrangement View*, we are able to perform these operations and more within clips in *Session View*. Similar procedures for recordings apply in this context: select a track to record to, arm session recording for the track, and click the record button. In fact, as you may have noticed, if you arm a MIDI track for recording, you can use your MIDI keyboard or your computer keyboard to play notes using that instrument timbre.

FIGURE 2.8

Empty clips show a track with stop buttons on empty clips on the left and a record-enabled track with armed empty clips on the right.

In *Session View*, when a track is armed for recording, the appearance of the empty clip slots change from square *clip stop* buttons to circular *record* buttons. Clicking one of these *record* buttons for a given clip will record into that clip.

20. Select a MIDI track and arm it for recording by selecting the *Arm Session Recording* button on that track's mixer section.
21. Select an empty clip on that track and click the circular record button, then begin playing some notes on your MIDI controller or computer keyboard. (Note: you may find it helpful to turn on the metronome while doing this or even launching a scene.)

22. Press the *stop* button at the top or the *Stop Clips* button at the
    bottom right when you are finished recording.

Editing the clip you just recorded is just as easy to do in *Session View* as it
is in *Arrangement View*. Simply double-click the clip in order to open *Clip View*.

23. Double-click the recorded MIDI clip to reveal the *MIDI Note
    Editor* within *Clip View*.

From within *Clip View*, you should already be familiar with the types of
edits you can perform on this MIDI data. If necessary, disable the *Fold* button
and enable the *Preview* headphone button to aid in this endeavor as we did in
the previous chapter.

24. Edit the recorded MIDI data as desired (this may include
    adjusting the clip length and loop section).

For the sake of variety, instead of continuing to record MIDI, let's look at
recording audio from a microphone into an audio track.

Recording Audio

Recording audio from a microphone can be accomplished just as easily as recording MIDI and it will give our tracks the added benefit of containing "real"
sounds, such as a track of your own voice or a guitar riff. In order to get started
recording from a microphone, we need to make sure that your microphone is
configured properly to work in Live, so let's check the *Audio* settings within
Preferences.

25. Go to *Live>Preferences* (Mac) or *Options>Preferences* (Win-
    dows) and select the *Audio* tab.
26. Select your computer's soundcard from the *Audio Device* menu
    if it is not already selected.

It may be necessary to change your audio driver by selecting it from the
Driver Type menu in order to reveal your soundcard; this is sometimes necessary with ASIO soundcards on Windows or audio interfaces that have specialized drivers.

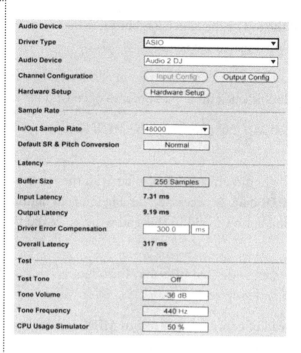

Audio Channels

Depending on the type of soundcard you have in or connected to your computer, you will be able to record audio using a number of input streams known as *channels*. For example, if your computer has a built-in microphone, you can typically record two audio channels simultaneously, as a pair, or each channel independently. The pair of audio channels is referred to as a *stereo* pair, meaning the microphone can capture sound as a combination of two audio channels: one (*mono*) channel occupying sound captured from the left side of the microphone, and one occupying sound captured from the right side of the microphone.

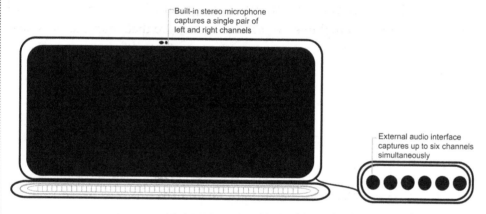

The more channels your audio device has, the more tracks you can record simultaneously. If you want to record yourself singing and playing guitar, you would probably want to connect a microphone to one channel to record voice and use another channel to record your guitar, either by placing a microphone in front of it or by plugging it directly into the audio device if possible. Recording each piece of a brass ensemble would require many more microphones and an audio device that can support recording multiple channels of audio simultaneously. If your soundcard only allows one channel to be recorded at a time, you can always record a track and then record another part afterward as we did in the previous chapter; this is called *overdubbing*.

To view the available channels you can use for recording, select the *Input Config* button within *Audio Preferences*.

27. Select the *Input Config* button within the *Audio Preferences* screen.

1 (mono) & 2 (mono)	1/2 (stereo)

FIGURE 2.11

Input channel configuration within the Audio Preferences menu.

Depending on your audio device, the *Input Config* screen will allow you to record with a single stereo (two-channel) stream of audio or a single separated channel from the stereo pair (left or right) on a track. Enabling both the stereo pairs and the individual channels for recording gives the most flexibility for recording.[2] For example, in a recording session, you may want the flexibility to use microphones on channels 1 and 2 to record a stereo piano track from two different angles, and then use just one of those microphones to overdub a vocal track on top of that piano track. For now, enable all of the inputs available as you can always change this later.

28. Enable both the stereo inputs for channels 1 and 2 as well as the individual channels 1 and 2.
29. Click *OK* and close the *Audio Preferences* menu.

Returning, now, to Live's main window, we can configure the tracks to show the various input and output options available while recording by enabling the *In/Out Section* via the small, circular *IO* button at the right of the Master Track's volume slider.

FIGURE 2.12

In/Out Section enabled for tracks by clicking the IO button near the Master Track.

With the *In/Out Section* enabled, each track now shows an *Audio From* menu as well as an *Audio To* menu. The concept of signal flow from the microphone to the computer can be confusing, but here is how it works for the most part:

FIGURE 2.13

Basic signal-flow diagram explaining how audio is transferred to the computer.

A microphone is connected to the computer on a channel of the soundcard/audio interface. The audio interface is connected to the computer via a cable such as USB or FireWire; in the case of built-in microphones, the microphone is actually part of the computer. Within the computer, the program Live has options to receive and record the audio signal from the channels of these soundcards/audio devices and represent that audio on tracks. In Live, the specific channels of input are determined by the *Audio From* menu.

---

2. Enabling more channels for recording allows greater flexibility but also uses a bit more of your computer's computational power.

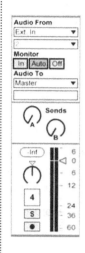

FIGURE 2.14

In/Out Section of an
Audio Track.

30. If an audio track is present in your set, examine the menu labeled *Audio From* and select *Ext. In.*[3] (Note: If no audio track is present in your set, choose *Create>Insert Audio Track* from the top menu, then follow the previous step.)

For our purposes, the audio track will receive external input from one of the audio channels that our audio device supports. The specific channel you choose, of course, should be the one that has a microphone connected to it; a microphone connected to channel 1 on your audio interface means that this track's input should be set to receive *Audio From* channel 1. In Live, it's also possible for tracks to receive audio from other tracks, but we won't discuss that concept now.

Continuing through the signal path, the audio track is set, by default, to send *Audio To* the *Master Track*. As you know, the *Master Track* is the "end of the line" for our computer's involvement in this process. You can control the output volume and a few other things on the *Master Track* but, after that, the signal goes back out to the soundcard/audio device and then to the speakers, where it is heard with our ears.

Before we arm the track for recording and press the record button, the issue of *Monitoring* should be addressed. In other words, would you like to hear what you're recording while you're recording it? The answer is commonly yes. Notice the *Monitor* section of the track shows the options *In, Auto,* and *Off.* Here's the difference between the three: The *Off* button turns off monitoring—while recording, you can't hear what's coming through the microphone. The *In* button allows the audio signal to constantly come through the microphone to the track even when the track *is not* armed for recording. The *Auto* button only allows the audio signal to come through to the track when it *is* armed for recording. With both of the last two options, you should consider using headphones while recording so that the sound of the other tracks in your set coming through the speakers is not accidentally captured by the microphone; this phenomenon is known as *bleed.*

3. Note that *Audio From* on Audio Tracks is different from *MIDI From* on MIDI tracks, but they conceptually function the same way to record data.

Let's now record some audio from our microphone on an audio track.

31. Select an *audio track* in your set.
32. Arm the track for recording by hitting the *Arm Session Recording* button. (Note: Be careful that your microphone is not too close to your speakers or else loud "feedback" squeals will occur as the microphone attempts to capture itself. The use of headphones will help prevent this.)
33. Ensure that *Audio From* is set to *Ext In* and that the *Input Channel* menu beneath it is set to receive on the channel your microphone is connected to. (Note: for built-in microphones, this is commonly channel 1 or 2 or the stereo pair of 1 and 2.)
34. Ensure that *Monitoring* is set to *Auto*.
35. Ensure that *Audio To* is set to *Master*.
36. Select an empty clip slot on the audio track to record to.
37. Say or sing a few words into your microphone to ensure that the computer is receiving audio. You will see the meters within the *track volume* light up as you speak.
38. Click the circular *Record Button* on that clip and begin speaking or singing something.
39. When you are done recording into the clip, click the *stop* button on another clip slot or simply click the *play* button on the same clip.

You should now have an audio recording in the selected clip slot. As you may have guessed, recording audio in *Arrangement View* is done the same way; this is, of course, more like the traditional approach to using a DAW. Take a moment and copy this clip to one or more scenes in your set.

40. Copy this newly recorded clip to one or more of the clip slots in your existing scenes or create new scenes.
41. Record more clips if desired.

Sampling Rate and Bit Depth

In recording, the term *samples* does not refer to sampling in the sense that a MIDI note may trigger back some "sampled" (prerecorded) audio file (like using the woodwind samples in a MIDI instrument). Instead it refers to a rate by which an audio signal—for example, you singing the note A, which is a continuous flow of audio—can be broken down into "discrete" and evenly spaced series of signals. In digital audio, each of the discrete signals is given numerical values to represent the overall continuous signal that was broken down. Each of these values is referred to as a *sample*.

There are different numerical rates by which someone can sample audio. For example, many computer soundcards can record 44,100 samples per second. This means that for a one-second recording of you singing the note A, there are 44,100 samples representing that one second of continuous audio. Some more advanced soundcards have the ability to use more samples per second in the sampling process.

The *sampling rate* is different from a *bit depth*, which refers to the amount of binary digits (or *bits*, for short) that can be used to represent the data being recorded. For example, as you may know, "binary code" refers to a counting system using only the numbers 1 and 0 where 1 represents that something is in the state of being "on" and 0 represents that something is "off." The more 1s and 0s you string together, the longer the number will be and the more information your number will contain—information that is used to describe something, such as amplitude, in computer terms. For example, the binary "word" *1011101011110001* represents many more "on/off" states than the word *1011*. The longer binary word can represent something better than the shorter one simply because it has more numbers (binary digits or *bits*) to work with.

When a binary word is 16 characters long, it is said to be *16-bit*; 32 characters is *32-bit*, and so on. A *1-bit* word has only one character and two possible states: 1 or 0. A *2-bit* word has two characters and four possible combinations of 1s and 0s. An *8-bit* word has eight characters and can represent 256 possible values given the combination of 1s and 0s. The reason that MIDI uses the numbers 0–127 is because the protocol dedicates 7 bits to representing things like pitch and velocity; 7 bits yields 128 possible combinations of 1s and 0s.

All of this to say: recording something at *24-bit* means that you are using more numbers to digitally represent the recorded analog signal when it is converted from analog to digital than if you recorded it at *16-bit*. The sampling rate refers to how frequently you will take "snapshots" (samples) of a continuous audio signal. Whew!

Adding Effects

Unlike MIDI files where we can drag various instruments onto our MIDI track to achieve different instrument timbres, we are limited, in some ways, by working with recorded audio. For instance, if you record a MIDI pattern, you can easily play that pattern back with a piano sound or a trumpet sound with a few clicks; you can even quickly change the notes if you played a wrong one. If you record yourself singing, you may have a more difficult time making your voice sound like Pavarotti or Ronnie James Dio. However, even though we can't add MIDI instruments to audio tracks, there are a number of effects and other useful processes that we can add to audio tracks. This book will cover many of those effects as they relate to stylistic creative endeavors, but for now, we will discuss the concept of adding just a few effects to an audio track.

42. Select the *Audio Effects Browser* from the left side of the program.

The effects listed in this Browser are depicted in folders; each folder contains presets that exemplify the versatility and overall "coolness" of each effect. For the audio clip we just made, let's begin by adding a delay.

43. From the *Audio Effects Browser*, select *Ping Pong Delay*. (Note: again, you may substitute this effect for another if desired or if the effect is unavailable.)
44. Drag the effect from the browser onto the *audio track* containing the recorded clip.

Notice that the effect is shown in Live's *Device View* in the same manner that instruments are shown for MIDI tracks.

45. Press *play* on the clip to hear the delay effect.
46. Press the *stop* button when finished.

FIGURE 2.15

Ping Pong Delay shown for the audio track in Live's Device View.

A *delay* is a copy of the original sound file played at an offset time as the original sound file. In some ways that we will discuss later, most effects are delays, but for now know that the *Ping Pong Delay* is an effect that combines several delays of the audio on the track.

All of the effects that we'll discuss have a number of parameters that can be adjusted. Some will have the option to *Sync* some sort of timing function (such as the amount of time between delays of the signal) to Live's metronome time. A description of each parameter within a given effect is viewable from the *Info View* box at the bottom left of the program when you hover your mouse over a parameter knob.

47. Hover your mouse over the *Dry/Wet* parameter knob.

The *Dry/Wet* of the effect is probably the most important effect parameter because it controls how much of the effect you would like to apply to the audio clip.

48. Press *play* on the clip to hear the delay effect.
49. Decrease the *Dry/Wet* parameter knob to 0% while the clip plays.
50. Increase the *Dry/Wet* parameter knob to 100% while the clip plays.
51. Return the *Dry/Wet* parameter knob to 50% and stop the clip.

Notice that you hear more or less of the effect by changing the *Dry/Wet* parameter knob. If you want to turn off the effect completely, simply click the *Device Activator* button at the top left of each effect. This will allow audio to pass through to the *Audio To* output destination, bypassing the audio effect altogether. Let's deactivate the delay and add a new effect next to this delay.

52. Click the *Device Activator* button at the top left of the *delay effect* to deactivate it.
53. From the *Audio Effects Browser*, select *Chorus*.
54. Drag the *Chorus* effect from the Browser to the right[4] of the *delay effect* that is present on the audio track containing the recorded clip.
55. Press *play* on the clip to hear the *Chorus* effect.
56. Decrease the *Dry/Wet* parameter knob to 0% while the clip plays.
57. Increase the *Dry/Wet* parameter knob to 100% while the clip plays.
58. Return the *Dry/Wet* parameter knob to 50% and stop the clip.

The *Chorus* effect, in essence is like a very short delay between the original signal and the one after it. Additionally, the delayed version of the signal is slightly out of tune from the original, which produces that somewhat warbled sound. Increasing the modulation amount via the *Amount* parameter will increase the out-of-tune aspect of this chorus.

In case you're wondering: yes, the order of the effects in the "signal chain" does make a difference. If we activate the delay effect, the signal path for this clip will be (1) delay and (2) chorus. The delayed signal will have the *Chorus* effect applied to it. The other way around, the signal will be chorused and that signal will then be delayed. It may seem like the same thing either way, but as

---

4. On older versions of Live, if you are not careful to place the effect next to the existing effect and not on top of the effect, you will replace the existing effect.

you continue to learn more about effects, you will notice that the order in which you apply them within the path of the signal chain will make a noticeable difference.

59. Activate both effects.
60. Press *play* on the clip to hear the clip with both effects applied to it.
61. Click on the *Device Title Bar* for the delay effect and drag it to the right of the *Chorus* effect.

There is a subtle difference in the sound as a result of the ordering of these effects. As noted, the order of the effects will make a noticeable difference as we continue. For now, let's save our discussion of effects for later and discuss ways to interact with the clips in our set.

Key and MIDI Mapping

Not only is Live a novel DAW environment because of *Session View*, but it provides numerous approaches to interact with the computer in ways that far surpass other audio environments. One approach is the way that you can map most buttons, parameters, knobs, and more to MIDI buttons, sliders, knobs, and more. In fact, you can also map Live buttons to the keys on your computer keyboard. Imagine playing clips or scenes just by pressing the number keys on your computer keyboard! Let's get started with mapping.

In the top-right corner of the screen are a number of buttons and indicators. Among them, the *CPU Load Meter* can help you keep track of how much you're taxing your computer's processors and the MIDI track indicators.

The buttons marked *Key* and *MIDI* allow you to map Live control buttons, sliders, and knobs to computer keys and MIDI controls. Let's begin by mapping some scenes to be controlled by the number keys on our computer keyboard. From within *Session View*:

62. Select the button at the top right marked *Key* to enter *Key Map Mode*.

Here's the not-so-tricky part: decide what controls you'd like to map, such as *clip play* buttons or *scene play* buttons, device activators, and so on, and then decide which computer keys you'd like to map them to.

63. With *Key Map Mode* enabled, click the first *Play* button for scene 1.

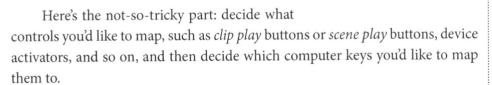

39

FIGURE 2.16

Indicators and buttons at the top right of the screen.

FIGURE 2.17

Key Map Mode enabled.

64. Press the *1* key on your computer keyboard. (Note: at the left of the program window, you will see a list marked *Key Mappings* begin to populate as you assign keys to Live parameters.)

65. Select the button at the top right marked *Key* to exit *Key Map Mode*.

That's it, believe it or not. Once you've exited *Key Map Mode*, press the *1* key on your computer keyboard to launch scene 1.

FIGURE 2.18

Scene 1 mapped to launch when the 1 key is pressed.

66. Press the *1* key on your computer keyboard to launch scene 1.

67. Stop the scene when you are done.

Take a moment and map the other scenes to the remaining number keys. Be careful, however, because some of the computer keys are mapped to other things when *Computer MIDI Keyboard* is enabled.

68. Enter *Key Map Mode*.

69. Map other scenes, clips, and stop buttons in your set to the number keys *2–9*.

70. Exit *Key Map Mode*.

71. Use the number keys *1–9* to perform your set.

How fun is that?! Let's, now, map our MIDI controller to other parameters such as *Dry/Wet* knobs and track volume sliders. In order to do this, we must first make sure that our MIDI device is configured properly to be used as more than just a note-playing instrument.

72. Go to *Live>Preferences* (Mac) or *Options>Preferences* (Windows) and select the *MIDI Sync* tab.

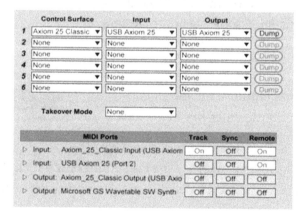

FIGURE 2.19

MIDI devices in the MIDI Sync tab of the Preferences menu.

From this menu, you should be able to see your MIDI device. Note that in order to *Track* with this MIDI device, meaning "record notes into tracks," you must enable the *Track* button on the *Input* device. In order to use this MIDI device to control parameters in Live, you must enable the *Remote* button *Input* device.

73. Ensure that both the *Track* and *Remote* buttons are enabled for your MIDI controller.
74. Close the *Preferences* menu.

The same procedures apply for mapping Live parameters to MIDI controls as they did for mapping computer keys. If your MIDI controller has knobs or faders on it, let's map those to control the volume of some of the tracks.

FIGURE 2.20

MIDI Map Mode enabled.

41

75. Select the button at the top right marked *MIDI* to enter *MIDI Map Mode*.
76. With *MIDI Map Mode* enabled, click the *volume slider* for one of the tracks in your set.
77. On your MIDI keyboard or controller, move the *MIDI control* that you'd like to map to this volume slider. (Note: at the left of the program window, you will see a list marked *MIDI Mappings* begin to populate as you assign MIDI controls to Live parameters.)
78. Select the button at the top right marked *MIDI* to exit *MIDI Map Mode*.
79. Play your set and use the MIDI control to change the track volume.
80. Repeat this process with other MIDI controls for other Live parameters. (Note: if a device, such as an effect or an instrument, is unseen, exit the *Map Mode* and select the track containing that device. Then, reenter *Map Mode*.)

You have now created a performable DAW-type interactive instrument. Designing a system like this is one basic concept of performing interactive music.

Record to *Arrangement View*

Performing interactively in *Session View* is one of the most appealing aspects of Live that sets it apart from most other DAWs. An additional feature in *Session View* is that your interactive performance can be recorded linearly into *Arrangement View*. This allows you to edit your live performance later on in *Arrangement View*.

To record your *Session View* performance, simply click the *Arrangement Record Button* next to the *Play* and *Stop* buttons within the transport controls at the top of the screen.

FIGURE 2.21

Arrangement Record Button enabled within Session View.

81. In *Session View*, click the *Stop All Clips Button* at the bottom right of the program above the *Master Track*. This will stop all clips from playing.

82. Click the *Stop* button at the top of the screen twice to reset the playback position to 1.1.1. This position corresponds to the linear position within *Arrangement View*, specifically the first bar, beat, and beat division.

83. Click the *Arrangement Record Button*.

84. Perform clips and slots as desired, then click the *Stop* button.

Your performance is recorded verbatim into *Arrangement View*.

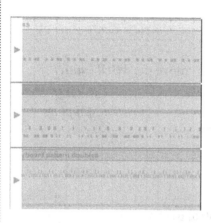

85. Switch to *Arrangement View* to see your recorded performance.

With your *Session View* performance now recorded into *Arrangement View*, you can produce the tracks as you would any other by making edits, adding effects, and so on. Let's now save this set:

86. Click *File>Save Live Set*.

87. Save this project to *My Live Projects*.

FIGURE 2.22

Session View performance being recorded in Arrangement View.

On Your Own

Compose a number of short MIDI clips, record a number of short audio clips, and get some sound files from the internet. Organize the musical material into several clip slots and scenes. Try out some effects and add them to the tracks. Map the scenes and other parameters to a MIDI controller and/or your computer keyboard. Record the performance into *Arrangement View* and overdub some additional recorded tracks within *Arrangement View*. (Note: you will have to set up an audio track in *Arrangement View* just as we did in *Session View*. Export the project as a *.wav* audio file.)

Remember:

- Switch to *Session View* from the top *View* menu, the *Selector* icon at the top right, or by pressing the *tab* key.
- *Session View* takes the traditional functions of a typical DAW and turns it into a performable musical instrument.
- The cells for each track in *Session View* are known as *Clip Slots*.

- Press the *Play* button triangle at the left of part of each *Clip Slot* to play the clip in that slot.
- Press any of the *Stop* button squares on a track that is currently playing to stop the clip from playing.
- Use the square at the button on the right, labeled *Stop Clips*, to stop all audio clips from playing.
- A horizontal row of clips in *Session View* is called a *scene*.
- In *Session View*, when a track is armed for recording, the appearance of the empty clip slots change from square *clip stop* buttons to circular *record* buttons.
- The more channels your audio device has, the more tracks you can record simultaneously.
- *Overdubbing* is when you record a track and then record another part "on top of it."
- Use headphones while recording so that the sound of the other tracks in your set are not accidentally captured by the microphone.
- A description of each parameter within a given effect is viewable from the *Info View* box at the bottom left of the program when you hover your mouse over a parameter knob.
- You will hear more or less of the effect by changing the *Dry/Wet* parameter knob.
- The buttons marked *Key* and *MIDI* allow you to map Live control buttons, sliders, and knobs to computer keys and MIDI controls.
- Some of the computer keys are mapped to other things when *Computer MIDI Keyboard* is enabled.
- Refer to the *MIDI Sync* tab in the *Preferences* menu to configure your MIDI controller.
- If a device, such as an effect or an instrument, is unseen, exit *Map Mode* and select the track containing that device. Then, reenter *Map Mode*.
- Click the *Stop* button at the top of the screen twice to reset the playback position to 1.1.1.
- Click the *Arrangement Record Button* to record a *Session View* performance to *Arrangement View*.

3

Introduction to Max for Live

I n this chapter, we will look at using Max for Live, the add-on for Live that allows users to incorporate the powerful graphical programming language Max/MSP/Jitter into their Live sessions. We will discuss the advantages of using Max for Live, which include creating custom MIDI effects, instruments, and audio effects for use in Live.

In order to make use of Max for Live, you must install it on your computer; it is bundled with Max/MSP/Jitter. A 30-day demo version of Max for Live is available through www.ableton.com and www.cycling74.com. If you've not done so already, visit www.cycling74.com and download and install Max/MSP/ Jitter.

In 2008, Cycling '74, the developers of the graphical programming software Max/MSP/Jitter ("Max"), collaborated with Ableton to create the product Max for Live (M4L). Max for Live is an implementation of the Max/MSP/Jitter programming environment that is accessible directly from within Live, and it allows you to write a Max program for MIDI, audio, or visualization for use inside of Live. In this book, and in this chapter, we will look at ways to create Max for Live plug-in files, called *patches*, which will give us advanced and customized control of the MIDI or audio we send through these patches.

Please note that this book is not a guide to using Max or to developing sophisticated musical applications within Max as much as it is a guide to incorporating basic Max concepts inside of Live using Max for Live. Users looking for the former type of guide should consult the tutorials within the Max *Help* menu or the numerous books and tutorials written about Max, including the co-author's own book *Max/MSP/Jitter for Music* (Manzo 2011c).

Why Would I Want to Start Programming?

Although Ableton Live is very flexible in terms of customization to fit your performance and compositional needs, it is likely you will notice some particular uses that aren't immediately accessible; these may include a particular audio or MIDI effect that you'd like to create, the implementation of a new musical instrument design for performance, or some unique way of generating or composing. For these purposes, a little insight into the basic programming techniques used in Max can be the catalyst for unparalleled creativity.

Unlike traditional text-based programming languages, Max is a visual programming language in which data flows from one programming function to another. For example, think about the signal chain involved in recording on your computer using a microphone:

As we can see in Figure 3.1, sound received in the microphone is transmitted through a cable to the soundcard. Another cable transmits

FIGURE 3.1

Signal flow diagram.

the data from the soundcard to the computer. Finally, cables are used to transmit the data to the speakers. In Max, each component in the figure would be referred to as an *object*, a programming function with a particular purpose. Data in the form of MIDI numbers, audio, video, text, and more are transmitted between objects through the use of connecting cables called *patch cords*.

As we begin to program in Max, it is important to think about each procedure involved in the process we hope to achieve. For example, playing a G chord on the guitar might seem like a single task, but in the programming world the task needs to be broken down into smaller steps. If you've ever tried to teach someone to play the guitar, you might be aware that the single directive "play a G chord" requires several smaller steps: proper posture and positioning of hands on the guitar, moving fingers to the appropriate frets and strings, and so on. While programming, each step in the task likely requires one or more objects in order to produce the desired overall function of the program you wish to write. The more familiar you become with Max, the easier it will be to mentally group your ideas into smaller, more manageable steps to be programmed.

Writing a MIDI Program

We will begin exploring Max for Live by creating a simple MIDI effect that adds a Perfect 5th to every MIDI note received from our MIDI keyboard.

45

1. From the left-side Browser, select the *Max for Live Browser*.
2. Select the arrow to the left of *Max MIDI Effect*.

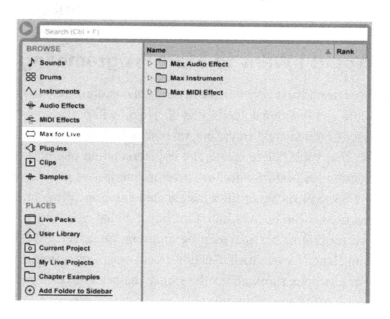

FIGURE 3.2

View of leftmost Browser showing Max MIDI Effect in Device Browser.

3. Double-click *Max MIDI Effect*.

Double-clicking *Max MIDI Effect* loaded a new MIDI track into your session containing an effect labeled *Max MIDI Effect* viewable from the *Detail View* window at the bottom of your session.

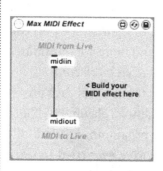

FIGURE 3.3

View of Max MIDI Effect patch loaded on MIDI track.

The effect interface window shows the words *MIDI from Live* and *MIDI to Live* separated by two rectangular boxes, called *objects*, connected by a solid black line, the patch cord. These objects reflect that concept in this effect: MIDI data will be received in the top object, the *midiin* object, from Live, and sent directly back to Live via the bottom object, the *midiout* object. This is not the most exciting MIDI process ever conceived; in fact, all it does is route MIDI data through unchanged. This is, however, a good starting point for building a cool effect. At this point, we can't hear the MIDI data being synthesized, so let's add an instrument to this track.

4. From the *Instrument Browser*, select *Instrument Rack>Piano and Keys*.
5. Click the arrow on the left and find *Dance Dot Org.adg* (if you do not have this instrument installed on your computer, any similar clean, pitched instrument will do) .
6. Click and drag the device name to the right of the *Max MIDI Effect* or simply double-click the device name.

Once again, this Max patch receives MIDI data from Live and sends it straight out to the next device in the chain, which is the instrument.

7. Play a few notes on your MIDI input device to ensure that data is being sent through Max to the instrument. (Note that the Max patch shouldn't be doing anything special in terms of processing or filtering at this point.)

FIGURE 3.4

Devices displayed in Live's Detail View.

With Max for Live, you can edit the objects in this effect and add new ones by clicking the third icon from the right, labeled *Edit*, at the top of the effect's *Device Title Bar*. Clicking the *Edit* button will open the program Max and allow you to edit this effect as if it were a Max patch utilizing all of the objects included in the Max programming language.

8. Click the third icon from the right of the *Max MIDI Effect*, labeled *Edit*, at the top of the effect's *Device Title Bar*.

Outlets, Inlets, and Patch Cords

In Max, data is transmitted from object to object through the use of patch cords—the black cable connecting the *midiin* object to the *midiout* object. If you look closely at each of these two objects, you will notice that there is a small shaded spot where the patch cord is connected; these are called outlets (on the underside of objects) and inlets (on the top side of objects). Data is transmitted and flows from one object's outlet to another object's inlet. In fact, if you hold your mouse over the outlet of *midiin*, you will notice a red circle around the outlet and a small window that describes the data coming from that object's outlet. In the case of *midiin*, the data coming from its only outlet is *Raw MIDI Messages*. The inlet of *midiout* accepts *Raw MIDI Messages*.

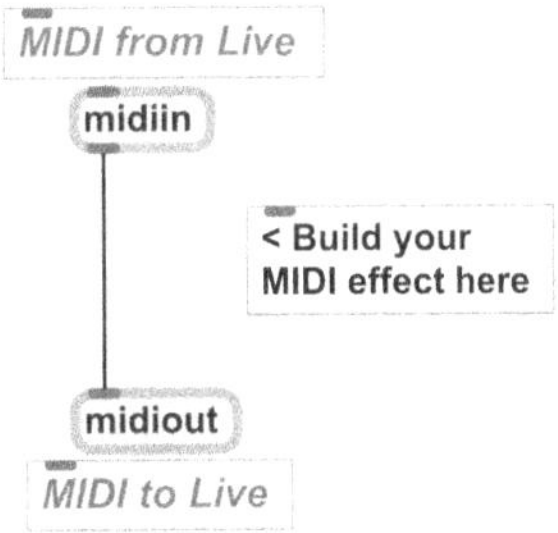

FIGURE 3.5

View of default Max MIDI Effect patch loaded in Max.

Segmented Patch Cords

Before we begin adding objects to our patch, we recommend that you go to the menu item at the top of the Max for Live window marked *Preferences* (Mac) or *Options* (Windows) and make sure that *Segmented Patch Cords* is checked by switching to the *All* tab and scrolling to the *Patching* section. *Segmented Patch*

Cords is an option that causes a patch cord to be created when you click on the outlet of an object. The cord will travel wherever your mouse does and will not disappear until you click on the inlet of another object or press the *esc* key. We have found that this option is easier for beginners to work with, so if *Segmented Patch Cords* is not checked, consider clicking on the menu item to enable it. You can always disable it later. To connect objects with the option unchecked, you have to hold down your mouse from the time you click on an object's outlet until your mouse is over another object's inlet.

Adding Objects

Currently, raw MIDI data is coming into our patch through the *midiin* object. This data includes what pitches were played, how hard they were played (called "velocity"), the particular MIDI timbre used (called "a program"), pitch bend data, and more. Since our goal is to take just the MIDI pitches and add a Perfect 5th to them, we need some way to parse the MIDI data received from the *midiin* object. One such object is called *midiparse*.

9. Create a new object box by pressing the *n* key on your computer keyboard.
10. Type the word *midiparse* in the new object box.
11. Hit the *enter/return* key.

If you've accidentally clicked away from the new object box without typing in the word *button*, you can double-click the object box to allow text to be entered once again. Ignore the *Device Vertical Limit* comment in the patcher at this time. We will address this shortly.

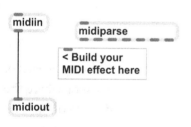

Notice that once the object has been instantiated, it can by moved around within the patch. Now, let's connect the *midiparse* object to receive data from the outlet of the *midiin* object. In order to do this, we'll need to disconnect the patch cord connecting the *midiin* object from the *midiout* object, either by clicking on the cord and pressing the delete key or by clicking the connection at the inlet of *midiout* and dragging the cord to the inlet of *midiparse*.

12. Highlight the patch cord connecting the *midiin* object from the *midiout* object by clicking on the cord and pressing the *delete* key.
13. Connect the outlet of *midiin* to the inlet of *midiparse* by clicking on the outlet of *midiin* and then clicking the inlet of *midiparse*. (Note: as you move your mouse over an inlet or an outlet, a red circle helps you see which inlet/outlet you are looking at;

FIGURE 3.6

New midiparse object added to Max patch.

something helpful when working with objects that have more than one inlet/outlet.)

Since *Segmented Patch Cords* was selected earlier, the patch cord will follow your mouse once you click without your having to hold the mouse button down while dragging the cord to an inlet. Patch cords always connect from outlets to inlets and never the other way around. Keep in mind that if you click on an object's outlet, the patch cord will follow your mouse until you connect it to another object's inlet or press the *esc* key.

14. Reposition the *midiparse* object beneath *midiin*.

FIGURE 3.7

Midiparse receiving MIDI data from midiin.

The *midiparse* object separates the raw MIDI data received from the *midiin* object. Hold your mouse over each of the outlets of *midiparse* to see the type of MIDI sent from each outlet; for example, the last outlet of *midiparse* outputs the MIDI channel number of input received from *midiin*. If you'd like more information on this or any object in the Max language, you can open up the *Help* file for each object[1] by *ctrl+clicking*[2] (Mac) or right-clicking (Windows) on the object and selecting *Open Help* from the contextual menu. You may also open *Help* by holding down the *alt/option* key and clicking on an object.

15. Open the *Help* file for the *midiparse* object.

Help Patchers

In the *Help* file for an object, a description of the object is given along with fully working examples of how the object may function within a patch. The interesting thing about *Max Help* files is that they too are Max patches. You may have noticed that you are unable to move the objects in the *Help* file. The reason is because this patch is currently "locked" and cannot be edited.

Patching Mode

Up until this point, we've been working in what Max calls *Patching Mode* or *Patching View*. In Patching Mode, you can create new objects, move them around, resize them, and connect them to each other. By going to the *View* menu at the top of the screen and unchecking the item marked *Edit*, the patch will become locked, that is, the patcher will function as a program and cannot be edited in any way until the patch is unlocked again. You can lock and unlock a patch by clicking the small *Lock* icon in the bottom left of the patcher window or by using the key command +*e* (Mac) or *ctrl+e* (Windows). You can also +*click*

---

1. In an unlocked patch.

2. Mac users will have to use *ctrl+click* if right-clicking has not been enabled in *System Preferences* or if their mouse or touchpad does not support right-clicking capabilities.

(Mac) or *ctrl+click* (Windows) any white space in the patch to toggle lock modes.

Unlocking the *Help* patch for *midiparse* allows you to copy working bits of code from the *Help* patch into your own patches. In essence, you can construct entire Max programs by copying working code from the *Help* files. To find out more information about an object including all of the available messages you can send to it, click on the *Reference* link accessible by click the *?* tab within an object's *Help* file. It's also useful to look at similar or related objects in the *See Also* portion of that tab.

Hold your mouse over the first outlet of *midiparse* to learn that this outlet outputs a pair of MIDI numbers in a list representing pitch and velocity. In order to accomplish our goal of harmonizing MIDI notes with a Perfect 5th, we'll need to now separate the MIDI pitch value from the MIDI velocity value for data received at this inlet. To break up this list into two separate values, we'll use the object *unpack*.

FIGURE 3.8

Pitch and velocity pairs from midiparse are unpacked into separate list items.

16. Create a new object called *unpack* beneath *midiparse*.
17. Connect the first outlet of *midiparse* to the inlet of *unpack*.

When MIDI data is received from the *midiin* object, that is, from Live, the pitch and velocity messages will be parsed with the *midiparse* object and then separated from each other using the *unpack* object. In this case, the pitch and velocity values will be sent through the outlets of *unpack*. In order to actually see these values, we'll need to use the *number* object to display the MIDI numbers received from *unpack*'s outlets.

The *number* object, also called a *number* box, is such a common object in Max that it has its own key command shortcut, the *i* key, for putting the object in your patch. Think of the *i* as short for *integer* as opposed to the other types of numbers we'll deal with in Max: floating-point numbers and numbers with a decimal point.

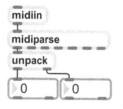

FIGURE 3.9

Separate pitch and velocity items are displayed using number objects.

18. Create two *number* objects.
19. Connect each outlet of *unpack* to the inlet of each *number* box.

At this point, playing notes on your MIDI keyboard should cause the MIDI pitch and velocity values to be displayed in the *number* boxes. Notice that if you play the note middle C at a very loud volume, the left number box will display the number 60 (MIDI pitch 60 representing middle C) and likely some number greater than 100 in the right number box (representing a MIDI velocity value from 0–127 based on how hard you played the note middle C).

Aligning

You may have noticed that the patch cords in the above example look more segmented than yours. This is accomplished by clicking at different points in the patch between where you initially clicked and where the patch cord connects to another object's inlet. It can also be accomplished by highlighting the patch cord by *ctrl+clicking* (Mac) or *right-clicking* (Windows) after it's connected to some objects and selecting *Align,* or by using the key command *+y* (Mac) or *ctrl+shift+a* (Windows).

You can also align highlighted objects using the same key command.[3] You can highlight multiple objects, either by holding the *shift* key and clicking the desired objects or by drawing a marquee around them with the mouse. To highlight patch cords while you are drawing a marquee, hold the *alt/option* key.

Simple Math

Our goal is to harmonize incoming MIDI pitches, which, in essence, means adding notes. Since MIDI represents notes numerically, achieving harmony is simply a matter of addition. For example, if you want to add a Major 3rd to all incoming notes, simply add four half-steps (+ 4) to each MIDI note played. Adding an octave to incoming notes would be adding 12 to each MIDI note. To add in Max, we will use the + object.

The + object takes numbers received in its left inlet and adds the number received in its right inlet. However, we can also supply the + object with an *argument* to specify a default number for which to add to numbers received in the first inlet. Arguments are used to set or change variables for an object and are related to the types of data and messages the object deals with. In most cases, specifying an argument replaces some default value, if the object had one, with a new one. In this example, that argument number is then added to all numbers received in the + object's first inlet.

20. Create a new object called **+** with the argument **0**.
21. Connect the first outlet of the *number* box, receiving from *unpack*'s first outlet to the first inlet of **+ 0**.

Note that this is an object called **+** with an argument **0**; that is, [**+ 0**] with a space in-between. There is no object called *+0*, and typing in such an object will result in an error clearly visible in the *Max Window* by using the key command *+m* (Mac) or *ctrl+m* (Windows).

---

3. This option is best used for objects positioned along the same plane. Highlighting everything in the patch and clicking *align* could make a mess.

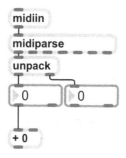

FIGURE 3.10

Pitch values are connected to a + 0 object where numbers can be added to them.

This patch currently will currently transpose MIDI notes up 0 semitones by add the number 0 to incoming MIDI pitches. Obviously, our long-term goal is to allow this patch to harmonize MIDI data (with a Perfect 5th), so we should build in some flexibility in terms of what intervals we will use in the harmonization. To do this, we will need to be able to change the argument of + from 0 to some other number (0 for unison, 1 for minor second, 7 for Perfect 5th, 12 for octave, etc.). A number received in +'s second inlet changes the value of the argument, that is, the number being added to the one sent to the first inlet. We can therefore insert a *number* box and connect it to the second inlet of +.

Formerly in Max, using the object *number* would have been sufficient for this task, but, since the creation of Max for Live, a number of objects were written as substitutes for standard Max objects like *number*. These substitute objects are named with the prefix "*live.*" and, in addition to looking a little different, allow number values to be stored within the M4L patches even after restarting Live, something not immediately possible with some objects like *number*. Since we want the harmonization setting we select to be present when we open the Live session later, we've use the *live.numbox* object in place of the *number* object.[4]

22. Create a new object called *live.numbox*.
23. Connect the first outlet of *live.numbox* to the second inlet of + 0.

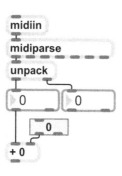

FIGURE 3.11

The value added to the incoming pitch numbers is determined by the value in live.numbox.

Changing the number value in *live.numbox* will ultimately change the interval used in harmonizing MIDI notes. This patch is just about done at this point; all we have left to do is repack our new "added" pitch with its velocity value, and reformat the MIDI message. We used *unpack* to break apart the list containing the pitch and velocity values, so let's use the *pack* object to pair the modified values together again.

24. Create a new object called *pack*.
25. Connect the outlet of + **0** to the first inlet of *pack*.

The previous steps connected the modified pitch values to the *pack* object. Now, let's connect the velocity values.

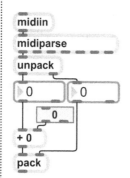

FIGURE 3.12

The modified pitch value and the original velocity value are repacked into a list.

4. For a list of Max objects and their M4L equivalents, see the patch *M4l_equivalents.maxpat* in the chapter examples folder.

26. Connect the first outlet of the *number* box receiving from *unpack*'s second inlet to the second inlet of *pack*.

In order to finish formatting the MIDI message in a way that makes it suitable to send to the *midiout* object, we'll use the *midiformat* object.

27. Create a new object called *midiformat*.
28. Connect the outlet of *pack* to the inlet of *midiformat*.

Our modified pitch and velocity messages are repacked into a list using *pack* and are formatted into a MIDI message using *midiformat*. Note that if you hold your mouse over one of the outlets of *midiparse*, then over the same outlet number of *midiformat*, the hint that pops up reveals that the same MIDI data is sent/received at that connection. Since none of the other MIDI data from the *midiparse* objects outlets have been modified, we can simply connect them directly to their correlating inlet of the *midiformat* object to finalize our formatted MIDI message.

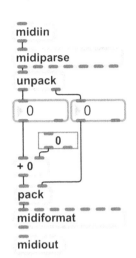

FIGURE 3.13

Pitch and velocity pairs from pack are formatted into a MIDI message with midiformat.

29. Connect the remaining unused outlets of *midiparse* to the correlating inlets of *midiformat*.

Let's take a quick moment to save this patch:

30. Click *File and Save* and save the file as *Adding_Notes.amxd*.
31. Close the Max patch window.

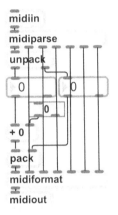

FIGURE 3.14

Remaining MIDI messages are formatted with midiformat.

At present our patch, with the addition of the + object, simply transposes incoming pitches up some degree of semitones (specified via *live.numbox*).

32. Play a few notes on your MIDI input device. From Live's *Detail View*, changing the value in *live.numbox* will change the value of transposition for the MIDI notes you play. To change these values, click on the *live.numbox* object and enter a numerical value followed by the *return/enter* key.

In order to combine the transposed value with the original value, we'll need to connect the first outlet of *midiparse* to the first inlet of *midiformat*.

33. In Live's *Detail View*, click the third icon from the right of the Max MIDI Effect, labeled *Edit*, at the top of the effect's *Device Title Bar* to open the Max patch once again.

Connecting the first outlet of *midiparse* to the first inlet of *midiformat* sends the played MIDI values to the *midiout* object simultaneously with the transposed value.

34. Connect the first outlet of *midiparse* to the first inlet of *midiformat*.

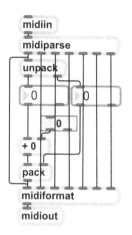

The patch is done at this point. You may have noticed, however, the small comment box that says *device vertical limit*. This refers to the space visible within Live's *Detail View*. Obviously, our patch is too big to display all of the content, but luckily Max patches have an option called *Presentation Mode* to help us build a nice-looking interface.

FIGURE 3.15

MIDI data is sent to Live via the midiout object.

Presentation Mode

There are certain parts of your patch that your users don't really need to see. In fact, the most useful part of the patch, from the user's perspective, is the number in the *live.numbox* since it controls the degree of harmonization. In the previous version of Max, in order to modify your patch's interface, you would have had to hide less useful objects. While this option is still available, it has been improved upon with the addition of *Presentation Mode* or *Presentation View*, an additional layer in Max designed to be used for developing an interface for patches. When objects are added to the *Presentation Mode* layer, they can be moved around and reorganized without disrupting their place in the *Patching Mode* layer—the layer we've been working in thus far.

35. Highlight the *live.numbox* object.
36. *ctrl+click* (Mac) or *right-click* (Windows) one of the highlighted objects and select *Add to Presentation*. You will notice that the object will then become bordered with a glowing red color.

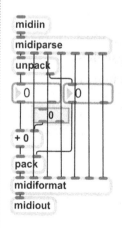

To enter *Presentation Mode*, click the *Presentation Mode* icon on the bottom menu, go to *View and Presentation* from the top menu, or use the key command +*alt/option+e* (Mac) or *ctrl+alt+e* (Windows). From within *Presentation Mode*, rearrange the objects in a way that you feel makes for accessible use. When you are satisfied, you may return to *Patching Mode*. Any objects made while in *Presentation Mode* are automatically added to the presentation.

FIGURE 3.16

The live.numbox object is added to Presentation Mode.

37. Toggle between *Patching Mode* and *Presentation Mode*.

Commenting

It is a good idea to make comments within a patch while you are writing it. As patches become larger, they can become difficult to read, and if you haven't opened the patch in a while it is easy to forget what you did and how certain parts of it function. The *comment* object, also called a *comment* box, allows you to type directly into your patch and document it. The *comment* object is such a common object in Max that it has its own key command shortcut, the *c* key, for putting the object in your patch.

Enter *Presentation Mode* and:

38. Create a new object called **comment**. (Note that since this object was created in *Presentation Mode*, it is automatically added to the *Presentation Mode*.)
39. Enter the text **add interval** in the **comment** box and position it next to the *live.numbox* object.

```
7    add interval
```

FIGURE 3.17

View of patch in Presentation Mode.

Inspector

We need to set this patch so that it opens up in *Presentation Mode*. To change properties about this patch, go to the *Patcher Inspector* by *ctrl+clicking* (Mac) or *right-clicking* (Windows) an empty area of the patch and select *Patcher Inspector* from the contextual menu in an unlocked patch.

You can also change properties for objects in the same manner. In an unlocked patch, with an object highlighted, you can also use the key command +i (Mac) or ctrl+i (Windows), or click the *Inspector* icon located at the bottom of the patch window. Another method of getting to *Inspector* is to hold your mouse in the middle of the left side of the object and click the *pinwheel* icon when it appears.

40. *ctrl+clicking* (Mac) or *right-clicking* (Windows) an empty area of the patch and select *Inspector* from the contextual menu.

From the *Inspector* menu, you can select tabs for editing the object's properties such as the colors and general behavior of the patch. The tab *All* contains all of the property options of the other tabs.

41. Check the checkbox labeled *Open In Presentation*.
42. Close *Inspector*.

Once again, save your patch. You can now close the Max patch window. Notice that the *Presentation Mode* of the Max patch is viewable from within Live's *Detail View*.

43. Set the *live.numbox* value to 7, a Perfect 5th, and play single notes and chords.

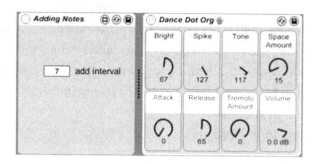

56

Wrap-Up

For future discussions in this book, we will not go into this much detail explaining patches. A discussion in this manner was necessary for our brief "crash course" in Max, which involved understanding the concepts of dataflow programming and some of the basic objects and techniques that are frequently used. As mentioned, further information about Max programming can be found in the resources listed above. It would be helpful to open the *Help* patch for each Max object mentioned in this and all chapters of the text. Then examine how each object works and refer to the *See Also* menu for related objects.

On Your Own

- Read the *Help* file for each of the new objects introduced in this chapter.
- Begin reading through the Max tutorials bundled with Max/MSP/Jitter.
- Write a patch that adds two intervals to MIDI pitches played on your MIDI keyboard.

Ambient

Ambient is a musical style that grew in popularity in the 1960s and 1970s. The genre has similarities to minimalism and is sometimes referred to as "background music." The term "furniture music" (Gillmor 1988) is often used to describe the ambient style, in which the music plays a subservient role for the listener as opposed to being the focal point. Ambient music is often void of musical elements that appear in other styles, including time-based elements (such as a steady beat), a sense of formal sections, and structures of measures. The instruments in ambient music tend to employ longer, sustained gestures as opposed to faster ones, though it isn't beyond the scope of the style to include rapid, minimalist gestures, often diatonic, among the layers of sound.

Getting Started

Let's begin composing a piece in the ambient style by selecting an instrument ideal for playing back sustained notes. Since the ambient style treats time elements differently than other styles, we will choose an instrument whose timbral qualities vary to some extent over time.

Setting the Synth Pad

Ableton Live's *Instrument Rack* allows us to browse for instruments in the typical synth categories *lead, bass,* and *pad.*

    1. Open Live and ensure that you are in *Session View.*

2. From the left-side Browser, select *Instruments>Instrument Rack>Pad*.

3. Click the arrow to the left of *Pad* and select *Sadness Pad*. If you do not have this instrument installed on your computer, search for *pad* at the top of the Browser and choose another *pad* instrument.

4. Drag this device onto the main *Device Drop Area* to create a new MIDI instrument track with this sound.

5. Double-click the track title to reveal this device's properties in *Device View*.

6. Click the *Record* button on the track to *Arm* it for recording.

7. Ensure the *Computer* MIDI *Keyboard* is checked in the *Options* menu at the top of the program toolbar.

8. Audition this instrument and others in the *Synth Pad* category by playing notes with your computer keyboard keys (for example, press the keys *A–K*).

9. Press the keys *Z* and *X* to drop or raise the *Computer* MIDI *Keyboard* pitch in octaves until the current octave displays *current octave C2 to D3* in the status bar.

10. Hold the *A* and *H* keys to produce the interval of a major sixth.

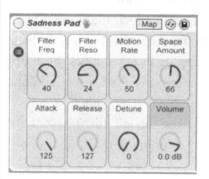

FIGURE 4.1

Sadness Pad instrument in Device View.

Notice the parameter settings for this device. An instrument with a larger *attack value* will take more time, often measured in milliseconds, to fade in while an instrument with a larger *release value* will continue to sustain and decay for some measure of time, often in milliseconds, after your fingers have left the keyboard. One aim of achieving an ambient sound is to adjust the *attack* and *release* settings so that a note or chord sustains long enough when switching to other notes; another is that the sound of the new notes fading in, determined by the *attack value*, blends with the sound of the previous chord decaying, determined by the *release* value. Notice that for the instrument *Sadness Pad*, the *attack* and *release* dials have been set to the maximum position.

11. Hold the *A* and *H* and other keys while adjusting the parameters for this instrument.

Artist Profile: Brian Eno

Brian Eno is an English composer who specializes in the ambient style. Like many composers in the genre, Eno has used musical material in novel ways to create soundscapes. In the ambient style, greater emphasis is placed on creating a musical environment with subtle sonic changes rather than the formal development of themes typical in Western music. Whereas traditional composers used conventional notation to create, Eno uses the studio as a tool to assist his creative process of exploring changes in timbre that evolve over time.

Suggested Listening

Brian Eno: *Ambient 1: Music for Airport*

Squarepusher: *Vacuum Garden*

Aphex Twin: *Selected Ambient Works Volume II*

Adding a reverb effect will help ensure that notes are sustained until the new notes fade in. It will also help to create a sense of depth for the instrument.

12. From the Browser, select *Audio Effects>Reverb>Room*.
13. Click the arrow to the left and find *Wooden Room*.
14. Double-click this device to add it to the *Sadness Pad* instrument track or simply drag the device name to the right of the *Sadness Pad* device window in *Device View*. If you cannot see the end of the device chain, click and slide on the *Device View Selector* at the bottom right of the screen.
15. Audition this effect by playing notes on your MIDI keyboard while increasing the *Decay Time* dial for added sustain.

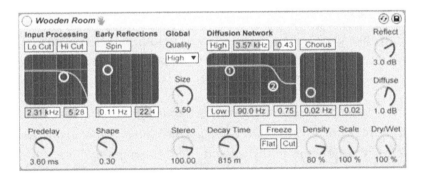

FIGURE 4.2

Wooden Room reverb effect with Decay Time parameter increased.

This instrument would be better suited for playing sustained notes and chords than fast, rhythmic musical gestures. It can also play "taller" chords across several octaves, such as ninth chords or other chords that are somewhat unstable harmonically because of added tones beyond a simple major or minor triad (root, third, fifth). Added chord tones can increase color and weaken the sense of resolve while sustaining a chord. In ambient music, we don't want the listener to feel like any one chord gives a sense of finality in terms of the piece concluding. Thus you should choose chords, pairs of notes, and even single notes that are open-ended. Closed, root-position triads may not be ideal for the timbre you've created.

16. Practice playing some notes with this instrument, deciding on a few notes or chords that you like.

Another way to further ensure that this instrument has an eternal quality is to record a loop length for playback. Let's make this instrument last for at least 16 measures.

17. Select the first empty clip slot on the *Pad-Ambient* track.
18. Click the *Record Button* to the left of the clip slot to begin recording as you play on your MIDI keyboard or computer keyboard. Alternately, double-click the empty clip to open the MIDI note editor and draw in MIDI notes.

Listen to what you have recorded and make sure that you are satisfied with how your performance works with this particular instrument. Make further changes if necessary.

Other Instruments

Continuing with Satie's idea of "furniture music," let's now add some other instruments to contrast with the sustained instrument already in place. This process, of course, will vary greatly based on the compositional mood you're going for. Here are a few examples of directions you could take that are common in the ambient style.

Calm Piano

Brian Eno often used a piano with a spacey, smooth, and eternal quality of playing. Let's start with a basic grand piano. To make this piano sound like it will go on forever we need to give it some reverb.

19. From the top menu, choose *Create>Insert MIDI Track*.
20. From the Browser, select *Instruments>Simpler>Piano and Keys*.
21. Click the arrow to the left and select *Grand Piano*.
22. Double-click this device to add it to the session or simply drag it onto the main area.
23. Ensure that the track is *Record Enabled* and audition it using the *Computer* MIDI *Keyboard*.

Let's now add a reverb device to this instrument.

24. From the Browser, select *Audio Effects>Reverb>Hall*.
25. Click the arrow to the left and find *Spacious*.
26. Double-click this device to add it to the *Grand Piano* instrument track or simply drag the device name to the right of the *Grand Piano* device window in *Device View*.
27. Audition this effect by playing notes on your MIDI keyboard while adjusting the *Wet/Dry* dial to control the amount of the effect (*wet*) that will be applied to the *dry* piano signal.

You may find that playing a few diatonic notes in the middle or upper register of the piano creates a serene mood. Depending on the tonality of your sustained layer and your overall compositional goals, you may find that playing clusters of notes a semitone apart from each other creates a darker, heavier, and more dissonant mood.

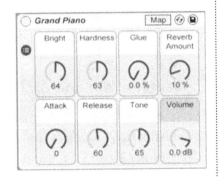

FIGURE 4.3

Device View of piano.

Dissonant Piano

Using the same piano instrument and reverb, let's make this layer sound a bit darker by adding the redux effect before the reverb in the device chain.

28. From the Browser, select *Audio Effects>Redux*.
29. Click the arrow to the left and find *Mirage*.
30. Double-click this device to add it to the right of the *Grand Piano* instrument track.
31. In *Device Detail View*, drag the *Mirage* effect before the *Spacious* reverb effect in the signal chain.

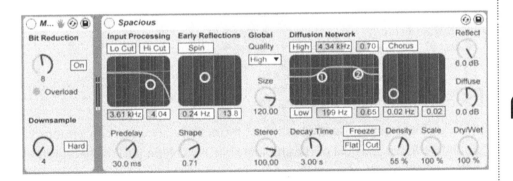

FIGURE 4.4

Device View with two effects loaded on the piano instrument.

Redux, sometimes referred to as a *bit crusher* in other programs, lowers the audio quality digitally by affecting the sample rate and bit depth of the instrument track it's loaded on. You can lower the bit depth (which makes the audio sound choppy under 8-bits) or the sample rate (which lowers the overall pitch range and contrast of the recording). Lowering the sample rate will also lower the maximum frequency that's able to play, which, in effect, adds a lo-fidelity, low-pass filter to the instrument sound.

Audio effects, as they appear in the signal chain for this instrument, work in sequence. If you place redux after the reverb effect, the piano will get a beautiful reverb added to it, and then it will get reduced in quality by redux. While this would produce an interesting sound, it would not be very ambient as it would be hard for this sound to blend into the background. In the way we've placed the effects, the piano is first crushed by redux and then the sound is beautifully reverberated in high-definition quality. This produces an instrument that achieves both eeriness and ambience.

Sample Rate and Bit Depth

When recording or playing back digital audio, there are two properties we must consider: *sample rate* and *bit depth*. The *sample rate* is how many times per second the computer is either capturing or playing back audio. CD-quality audio does this at a rate of 44,100 times per second, commonly referred to as 44.1 kHz. Most modern audio systems can record at a sampling rate of at least 96,000 samples per second, or 96 kHz. The higher the rate at which you sample while recording, the more frequency information you will capture from your sound source.

The *bit depth* refers to the amount of binary digits (bits) used to represent the audio. When audio is converted from an analog sound source heard with our ears into a digital one captured by a computer, the more numbers used to represent the audio during the conversion will determine how similar the digital representation of the sound source is to the original analog one. A 16-bit recording system is capable of using more numbers to represent the sound source than an 8-bit system. The higher the bit depth, the more accurately your digital recording will represent your original analog sound source.

Form

While ambient music usually has no set form, there are a few conventions we can follow. Since one goal of the ambient style is to blend into the background, limiting the overall amount of activity for each instrument is common. Each instrument should be given some time to breathe before new notes are played. The musical ideas can be reused or "through-composed" with new material added throughout.

Generating Ambient Music Automatically

The ambient style sometimes employs techniques in which music is *generated* based on certain criteria. The pitch material might be a repeated ostinato, an arpeggiating chord, or random notes within the same key. With these generative techniques, the human role lies more in the control of these processes—turning one or more of these processes on and off, varying the tempo and pitch material, and so on. Let's create an M4L instrument that randomly generates MIDI pitches and some controls to interact with this process. A pitched percussive instrument timbre, such as a marimba with its short attack, will be an appropriate timbre to contrast with the slow attack of our sustained synth instrument.

32. From the top menu, choose *Create>Insert MIDI Track*.
33. From the Device Browser, select *Instruments>Instrument Rack>Mallets*.
34. Click the arrow to the left and find *Brushed Bell Hits Bells*.
35. Double-click the device to add it to the newly created MIDI track.
36. From the Browser, select *Max for Live*.
37. Select the arrow to the left of *Max MIDI Effect*.
38. Double-click *Max MIDI Effect* to add it to the new MIDI track before the *Brushed Bell Hits Bells* synth device.
39. Play a few notes on your *Computer* MIDI *Keyboard* to gain a sense of how this timbre can function within the ambient style.

Now that our instrument is set up, let's create a Max patch that generates random pitches.

40. Click the *Edit* button on the *Max MIDI Effect* device visible in the *Detail View* panel. This will open Max and allow you to edit the patch.

The default objects, *midiin* and *midiout,* allow MIDI data to route from Live to the *Bell* synth device. We're going to be generating pitches directly from the Max patch itself, so we essentially don't need to have MIDI data route into the *Bell* synth device. But we'll leave these devices in place so that if we later decide to use our MIDI keyboard with this track, the MIDI data will be able to route properly through the Max for Live patch into the *Bell* synth. If we did not leave these objects in the patch, MIDI data would not be allowed to enter the Max for Live patch and, as such, would never reach the *Bell* synth.

41. Leave the default objects in place.

We'll be starting this patch from scratch:

42. Create a new object (press *n*) called *random*.

The *random* object takes a number as its only argument and randomly generates a number between 0 and one less than the argument when it receives a bang in its inlet.

43. Give this *random* object the argument *128*. (Note: if you already clicked away from the object, double-click it in order to, once again, enable typing within the object box.)

Be sure to put a space in between the word *random* and the argument *128* or else Max will look for an object called *random128* that does not exist.

44. Create a new *button* (press *b*)
45. Connect the outlet of *button* to the first inlet of *random 128*
46. Create a *number* box (press *i*)
47. Connect the outlet of *random 128* to the inlet of the *number* box.

FIGURE 4.5

Outputs of random numbers 0–127 when a bang is received.

Do you remember that kid you went to grammar school with who asked you to count to ten, and when you started counting "one, two, three" he stopped you and laughed, as he declared, "No! You forgot the number zero!" I'm sure you remember that kid, or maybe you were that kid. Well, in Max, we almost always start counting at the number 0, not the number 1. With the argument *128*, the *random* object will randomly output a total of 128 possible numbers starting at 0, which means that the range of numbers being randomly generated from *random* will be 0–127.

48. Lock your patch and click the *button* to see random numbers 0–127.

MIDI Values

Remember, MIDI is a computer protocol for representing musical elements like pitch and volume with numbers. In particular, MIDI is a bunch of messages in which a total of 128 numbers, the numbers 0–127, are used to represent these elements.

Synthesizing MIDI Numbers

With the above objects, we are able to generate random numbers, which is not a very musical task. However, since MIDI uses numbers to represent pitches, there's no reason why we can't use these random numbers as pitches. We would then hear each random number as a random pitch. In order to accomplish this, we need to format those pitches into a MIDI message that includes some information about the velocity of the random pitch and how long the note will sound. An easy way to format this is with the *makenote* object. The *makenote* object takes two numbers as arguments to specify a default velocity (first argument) and default duration (second argument), which will be associated with the random pitch value. The duration value is how long, in milliseconds, the note will last until *makenote* sends out a velocity *0* value to turn the note off. Unlock your patch and:

49. Create a new object called *makenote* with the arguments *100* and *500*.
50. Connect the first outlet of the *number* box to the first inlet of *makenote 100 500*
51. Create two *number* boxes.
52. Connect each outlet of *makenote 100 500* to the inlet of the two newly created *number* boxes, respectively.
53. Lock your patch and click the *button*.
54. Unlock the patch.

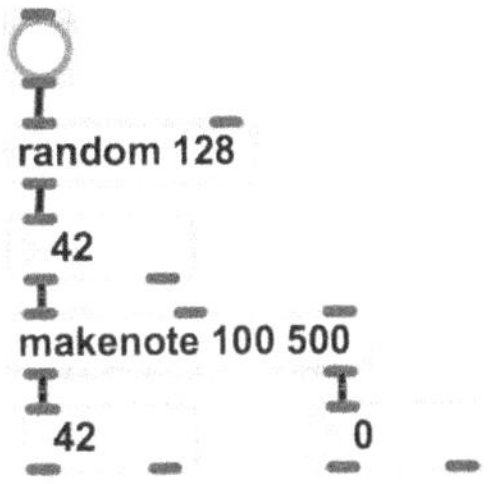

FIGURE 4.6

Formats a MIDI message using the random number as pitch.

You've likely notice that although we see the numbers change, there is no sound. Remember, up to now we've only organized a bunch of messages; we haven't included an object to allow us to hear the note through our computer's soundcard. With the objects we've assembled thus far, clicking on the *button* will generate a random number between 0 and 127, the full range of MIDI pitches. The random number will be treated as the pitch in a MIDI message and grouped with a default velocity value, which we have supplied as 100. The note will last for 500 milliseconds and then the *makenote* object will output a velocity value of 0 for that pitch turning the note off.

Look at the *number* box connected to *makenote*'s last outlet as you click the *button*. It outputs the velocity value of 100 for a half-second and then sends the *note off* message: velocity 0. The *makenote* object keeps track of what numbers it receives and ensures that all notes are given a *note off*/velocity 0 message after the duration value, in this case, 500 milliseconds.

Now, let's actually hear what this sounds like by adding the object *noteout*, so that *makenote* can communicate with our soundcard.

55. Create a new object called *noteout*

With the patch unlocked, if you hold your mouse over the two outlets of the *makenote* object, you will see that it sends MIDI pitch numbers out of the left outlet and MIDI velocity numbers out of the right outlet. Similarly, the *noteout* object takes pitch numbers in its leftmost inlet and velocity numbers in its middle inlet.

56. Connect the outlets of the two *number* objects receiving from *makenote 100 500* to the first two inlets of *noteout*

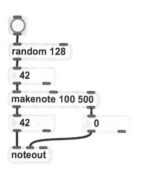

FIGURE 4.7

Sends a random number out.

The *noteout* object takes a number in its third inlet to specify a MIDI channel number. You can also specify a default argument for the MIDI channel by supplying a number in the object box after the word *noteout*. For now, we'll use the object's default MIDI channel, channel 1.

57. Lock your patch and click the *button* to generate a random number that will be synthesized as a MIDI pitch with a velocity of 100 and a duration of 500 milliseconds

Since the duration of each note lasts a half-second, it would be nice to have the patch automatically generate a new random note each half-second.

Adding Timing

The *metro* object functions like a metronome sending out bangs at a specified interval of time. The time, in milliseconds, is specified as an argument for *metro*. In the same patch, unlock your patch and:

58. Create a new object called *metro* and give it the argument 500.
59. Create a *button*.
60. Connect the outlet of *metro 500* to the inlet of *button*.

When the *metro* object is "on," it will cause the *button* to blink (send bangs) every 500 milliseconds. To turn the *metro* on, we will use the *toggle* object. The *toggle* object is an on/off switch for Max objects. Like a light switch, *toggle* has two states: on or off. The *toggle* is such a common object in Max that it has its own key command shortcut for putting the object in your patch by pressing the *t* key.

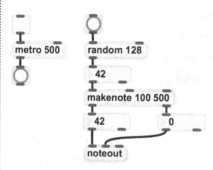

FIGURE 4.8

Sends a random number out.

61. Create a new object called *toggle*.
62. Connect the outlet of *toggle* to the first inlet of *metro 500*.
63. Lock the patch and click on the *toggle* to turn it on.

An *X* means the *toggle* is on and that the ***metro*** object will begin sending out bang messages to the *button* every 500 milliseconds.

64. Click on the *toggle* again to turn it off.

The *toggle* actually only outputs the numbers 0 and 1, where a 0 indicates that something is off and 1 indicates that something is on. We could have also sent the *metro* object a *message* box containing a 1 to turn it on, and another *message* box with a 0 in it to turn it off, but *toggle* provides a more graphical way of doing it.

Since our ***metro 500*** is outputting bangs, it seems we have an extra *button* in our patch. Unlock your patch and:

65. Delete the *button* connected to *metro 500*'s outlet by highlighting the *button* and pressing delete.
66. Connect the outlet of ***metro 500*** to the inlet of the *button* above the ***random 128*** object.
67. Move the *toggle* and *metro* objects above the *random* object—don't worry if they extend beyond the boundaries in the M4L patch.

With the *toggle* turned on, the *metro* will trigger a random number to become synthesized every 500 milliseconds.

68. Lock the patch and click on the *toggle* to turn it on.
69. Click on the *toggle* again to turn it off.

This patch creates what we will affectionately refer to as *Random Atonal Trash* (or *RAT patch*).

Now that we've made our first *RAT patch*, we will discuss some of the ways that you can control this patch. Currently, the patch has only one control: the *toggle* to turn the patch on and off, which generates random pitches. However, there are many variables within the patch that could conceivably have controls. For instance, if you want to change the speed of the *metro*, you can send a number, either as a *message* box or a *number* box, to *metro*'s right inlet to replace *metro*'s default argument of 500. Unlock your patch and:

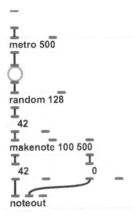

FIGURE 4.9

Creates random atonal trash.

70. Create a *number* box to the upper right of ***metro 500***.
71. Connect the first outlet of the *number* box to ***metro 500***'s second inlet.

67

If you change the number inside of the newly created *number* box by clicking in it (locked) and typing a new number,[1] the number of milliseconds *metro* will wait until it sends out another bang will change from every 500 milliseconds to whatever number you specify. This is how you replace arguments for objects. Arguments don't change visually within objects just internally, so even though the 500 remains in the object box, *metro*'s argument will change to whatever number you enter in the *number* box. Since we've "hard-coded" the number 500 as *metro*'s default argument, when you open the patch, the *metro* object's default time interval will be 500 milliseconds and, thus, will send out bangs every 500 milliseconds until a new number is supplied to *metro*'s second inlet.

Since *metro*'s speed and *makenote*'s duration are both 500 milliseconds, it makes sense that if we change the argument for one, we should change it for the other or else we'd have either overlapping or staccato notes. If you hold your mouse over *makenote*'s third inlet, you will see that it receives a duration value.

72. Create a new *number* box near **makenote 100 500**.
73. Connect the first outlet of this *number* box to the last inlet of **makenote 100 500**.

If you specify the same argument for both **metro** and **makenote**, you will ensure that generated notes are legato and not too staccato or overlapping.

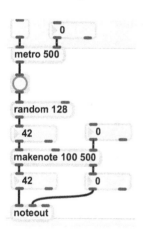

FIGURE 4.10

Control your RAT patch by changing the default arguments.

74. Lock the patch and click on the *toggle* to turn it on.
75. Change the arguments for **metro** and **makenote** by clicking in the newly created *number* boxes.
76. Turn the *toggle* off.

This patch functions fine as it is, but what would really be useful for those who will use this patch (your users) would be some sort of graphical object that allows you to control numbers more easily than the *number* boxes alone. One such object is the *live.slider* object. Unlock your patch and:

77. Create a new object called *live.slider*.

When you create a new object called *live.slider*, the object turns into a vertical control resembling a fader on a mixing board. By default, *live.slider* outputs the numbers 0–127 depending on where the horizontal knob in the *live.slider* is positioned. If you connect the *live.slider* to the two number boxes that con-

---

1. Note that the argument will actually change as soon as you click away from the object or press the *return/enter* key.

trol *metro* speed and *makenote* duration, you can control both numbers simultaneously with one control.

78. Connect the first outlet of *live.slider* to the inlet of the *number* boxes connected to the last inlet of *metro* and *makenote*.
79. Lock the patch and click on the *toggle* to turn it on.
80. Click on the *slider* and increase or decrease the horizontal knob to send the numbers 0–127 to the argument inlets of *metro* and *makenote*.
81. Turn the *toggle* off.

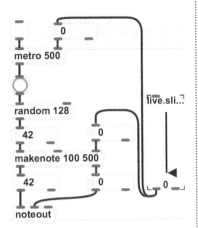

69

As mentioned earlier, by default, *live.slider* outputs numbers from 0–127. To increase or decrease the range of numbers *live.slider* outputs, open up *live.slider*'s *Inspector* menu. Unlock your patch and:

82. Open the *Inspector* menu for *live.slider* and change the *Range/ Enum* value of this *live.slider* from *0. 127.* to *20. 1000.*

On some slower computers, if the *metro* object tries to send out bangs at a rate faster than around 20 milliseconds, it isn't always stable. For this reason, we set the minimum *live.slider* range so that the max speed that *metro* will operate at is one bang every 20 milliseconds, and the slowest speed at one bang every 1,000 milliseconds (1 second).

83. Lock the patch and turn the toggle on.
84. Adjust the *live.slider* to adjust the speed of the *metro* and the duration of each note via the *makenote* object.
85. Turn off the *toggle*.

Tempo

As musicians, we tend to think about musical time in terms of tempo, beats per minute (bpm), and beats as opposed to milliseconds, the time measurement we're using with the *metro* object. For this reason, we will modify this patch by replacing the milliseconds value in the *metro* object with a beat value like *4n* for *quarter note* or *8n* for *eighth note*.

Max Version 5 introduced a new way of dealing with time by using the *transport* object. The *transport* object is like a master clock for handling time inside of Max by which other time-based objects can be synced. In the same way that many DAWs have a transport window for adjusting tempo and time signature, the *transport* object can allow a user to make changes to the tempo and time signature and have these changes reflected in all time-based objects synced to the *transport* object, such as the *metro* and *tempo* objects. Outside of working exclusively in Max, and when using the *transport* object in a Max for Live patch, the *transport* object slaves itself to Live's transport. This means that tempo adjustments in Live's transport will be reflected in the *transport* object. In short, adding the *transport* object to this patch will allow us to slave the *metro* object's clock to Live's tempo.

Unlock the patch and:

86. Create a new object called **transport**.
87. Change the **metro** argument from **500** to **4n**.
88. Change the **makenote** argument from **500** to **4n**.
89. Delete the *number* objects connected to *metro* and *makenote*.
90. Lock the patch and turn the *toggle* on.
91. Press the *play* button in Live to begin slaving the **transport** object to the tempo set in Live.
92. Adjust the tempo in Live's transport to hear changes in tempo reflected in the Max for Live patch.
93. Turn off the *toggle*.

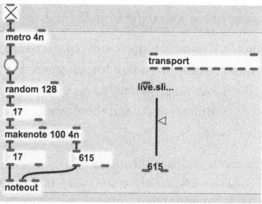

FIGURE 4.12

Metro object receives time info from Live's transport via the transport object.

At this point, the *live.slider* object is now useless; so let's connect it to the second inlet of *makenote* so that it can control velocity output. Unlock the patch and:

94. Connect the first outlet *live.slider* object to the second inlet of *makenote*.
95. Open the Inspector for *live.slider* and change the *Range/Enum* value of this *live.slider* back to **0. 127**. from **20. 1000**.
96. Lock the patch, turn on the *toggle*, and adjust the velocity of the patch by using the *live.slider* object.
97. Turn off the *toggle*.

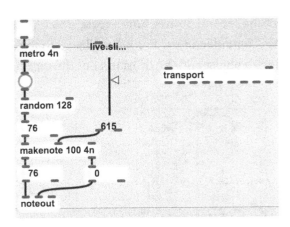

FIGURE 4.13

Patch velocity controlled by live.slider.

In order to change the beat from *4n*, a quarter note, to another value, we can simply create a *message* object that connects to *metro* and *makenote*. Unlock the patch and:

98. Create a new object called *message*.
99. Double-click inside the *message* object and enter **8n**, then press *enter*.
100. Connect the outlet of *message 8n* to the second inlet of *metro* and the third inlet of *makenote*.
101. Lock the patch and turn on the *toggle* to hear random quarter-notes.
102. Click the *8n* message to trigger eight notes instead of quarters.
103. Turn off the *toggle*.

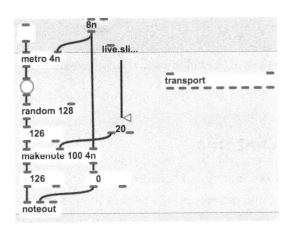

FIGURE 4.14

Message object 8n allows for a quick change of beat value.

Creating a bunch of *message* objects containing other beat values, like *1n* for whole note, *2n* for half note, and so on, would be easy at this point. Instead, let's create a menu containing a number of beat types. Unlock the patch and:

104. Create a new object called *live.menu*.
105. Open the *Inspector* for *live.menu* and change the *Range/Enum* value to *1n 2n 4n 8n 16n*.
106. In the patch, delete the *message 8n* object.

107. Connect the second outlet of *live.menu*, which outputs the messages contained in the *live.menu* object, to the second inlet of the *metro* object and the third inlet of the *makenote* object.

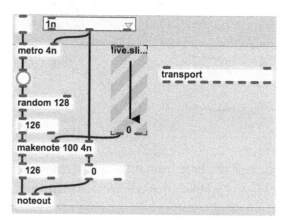

Other beat division values are possible, but let's start with these numbers.

108. Lock the patch and turn on the *toggle*.
109. Change the beat division by clicking the different messages contained in *live.menu*.
110. Turn off the *toggle*.
111. Highlight all contents of the patch and drag everything down so that the *toggle*, *live.menu*, and *live.slider* are visible within the boundaries of the patch in Live's *Detail View*. Note that we discussed using *Presentation View* for Max patches in chapter 3, which you can certainly apply in this instance to your liking or later on.
112. Click and save the patch so that it is accessible from Live's *Detail View*.

Making It Diatonic

At this point, the random atonal generator sounds more like Schoenberg than Eno, so let's map these random atonal pitches to ones from a key using a MIDI effect plug-in.

113. From the Browser in Live, select *MIDI Effects>Scale*.
114. Click the arrow on the left and find *C Major*.
115. Drag the device to the right of the Max MIDI Effect, but before the *Brushed Bell* device. Note that if your previously recorded pitch material is in a key other than C Major, you should select that key instead.

The interface for *Scale* shows the note input (x-axis) versus note output (y-axis) on a 12-by-12 grid. Each square represents a pitch class from C–B (MIDI pitches 0–11). In other words, with the C Major preset selected, the first two squares displayed horizontally represent the pitches C and C#. Since they are both set to the lowest vertical square, any MIDI Cs that are received will sound as C and any C#s received will also sound as C. If you turned the whole bottom row orange it would cause all MIDI pitches received to sound as C. The default C Major preset for *Scale* maps C# to C, D# to D, F# to F, G# to G, and A# to B as shown below.

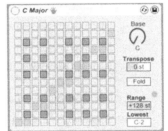

116. In the M4L device, turn on the *toggle* to play notes exclusively in the diatonic key C Major.
117. Turn off the *toggle*.

FIGURE 4.16

Scale device maps MIDI pitches to C Major scale.

Controls

With the instrument we've created, we have the potential to control the tempo of these random pitches by clicking the *slider*. We also have the option to turn the *toggle* on and off as desired. The possibilities for expansion include the inclusion of multiple random-pitch generators mapped to different instruments.

In Max for Live, there are numerous objects optimized for use with M4L. For example, the objects *live.toggle*, *live.slider*, and *live.menu* are M4L versions of objects that have existed in the Max programming language for years: *toggle*, *slider*, and *umenu*. Using these objects instead will allow you to easily assign MIDI devices to control these objects instead of having to use the mouse. A Max patch comparing the standard Max objects to these M4L objects is included in the chapter examples folder.

118. Click the edit button on the *Max MIDI Effect* device.
119. Create a new object called ***live.toggle***.
120. Delete the *toggle*.
121. Connect the outlet of ***live.toggle*** to the first inlet of *metro*.
122. Save and close the patch.
123. In Live, enter *MIDI Map Mode* or *Key Map Mode*.

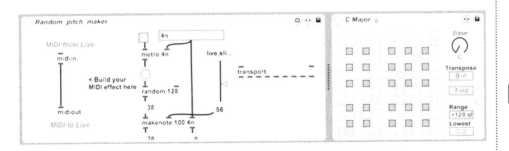

FIGURE 4.17

Random-pitch maker in Detail View.

You will now see that the *live.slider, live.toggle,* and *live.menu* objects can be assigned to MIDI device controls in the way discussed in previous chapters. Examples of other *note value abbreviations* include:

- 4n: quarter note
- 4nd: dotted quarter note
- 4nt: quarter note triplet
- 8nd: dotted eighth note
- 8n: eighth note
- 8nt: eighth note triplet
- 16nd: dotted sixteenth note
- 16n: sixteenth note
- 16nt: sixteenth note triplet

Other note values can be used with different numbers like we used for the beat divisions of *tempo*: 1 for whole note, 2 for half note, and so on.

On Your Own

Compose a new ambient piece in a style that contrasts with the one you just created employing different instruments and control devices. As you work, think about these questions as themes in your composition:

- In what context or audience will your work be experienced?
- What moods and tonal sonorities are meaningful to you given the performance context or audience for your piece?
- What control interface will be used for your piece, if any, and who will do the performing?
- Although there is not typically a set form in ambient music, what types of musical shapes and gestures will your piece possess?

For each of these questions, review this chapter and the ways we've discussed to manipulate these musical aspects using Live. As you become more familiar with the tools in Live, you should notice that the technical aspects of using the software become more transparent and accessible, allowing you to focus on the musical aspects in creating music in your preferred style.

In Live
Review the Live documentation on *Playing Software Instruments* from the *Help* menu.

In Max
Review the *Help* file for each new object discussed.

Pop and Rock Music

There are many ways that popular music ensembles can enhance their performances through interactive methods. These methods include triggering the playback of drum-machine patterns or studio-created sounds that can't be produced live, creating karaoke-style backing tracks, and using an array of effects to enhance live instruments and vocals.

In this chapter, we will begin with raw, unprocessed recorded files from a studio session and add effects to create a produced mix. Then, we will examine ways to implement those production techniques in a live setting. We will spend much of this chapter discussing the various, sometimes confusing ways of working with multiple audio outputs and the overall signal path of our session.

Enhancing the Recording with Effects

Let's look at a studio recording session by a band and discuss some ways to bring the "studio magic" into a live performance situation.

1. In the chapter examples folder, open the session *Thorns_Dry* in the *Thorns* folder.

Notice that the tracks in *Arrangement View* are grouped in a folder labeled *Dry_Tracks*.

2. Click the arrow next to the label to expand the folder.

Tracks that are not already grouped in folders can be organized in this way by highlighting them and using the key command +*G* (Mac) or ctrl+*G* (Windows).

3. Press the space bar to begin playing the tracks.

As you can probably hear, these tracks have very little or no processing on them: The vocals and acoustic guitars were recorded with microphones; the drums and string parts were synthesized; and the electric guitars and bass guitar were recorded by plugging the instruments directly into the soundcard without going through an amp or any effects processes. Recording in this way allows some flexibility in terms of creating the desired tone of the instrument through the use of amp simulation software.

Standalone hardware guitar processors and stompboxes typically convert an analog guitar input signal to digital, perform their tricks (distortion, chorus, flange, etc.), then send out the signal as an analog output where it is sent to another stompbox in a chain that repeats the process. With a software-based approach, you convert the guitar signal to digital once, use a MIDI foot controller to switch effects on and off, and then send the final digital mix from the output of your soundcard to a full-range PA. One downside is that the sound of your vintage amp head and 4 x 12 stack combination, with your favorite mic placed just off-axis, might take a while to simulate using an amp plug-in, if at all. There are, however, numerous upsides apart from the relief of never having to lug around that amp rig. Your recorded guitar tracks are clean and can be processed in a number of ways with multiple amps in different sound-placement configurations. The signal can even be reamped back out to an actual amplifier. In a live situation, you can bank on a consistent tone without having to wait for the tubes to warm up. After all, as good as your tube amp sounds onstage, does it actually sound like that through the PA once the sound tech plops a mic in front of it?

In an ideal scenario you'll always be working with the best-sounding equipment, whether the instruments are drums, guitars, or keyboards. Everyone will have an exceptional sense of tone, phrasing, feel, intonation, and tempo. However, in many actual situations, the guitarist hasn't changed his strings since he bought the guitar, and the drummer has no idea how to take the drum skins off. In our current scenario, for better or worse, these are the sounds we recorded and will be working with. Even though this dry recording lacks some life, we can do a number of things to make these tracks really shine. Assuming that we're happy with this recorded performance and don't want to make any edits, let's proceed to applying some processes to enhance the sounds we've recorded.

Let's begin by examining the effects on each track. Typically, it's a good idea to start mixing with the bass and drums, but for now let's isolate a track and apply some processes. We can listen to the full mix and make balance adjustments once we're satisfied with the way each track sounds in isolation.

1. Solo the *Acoustic Arpeggio* track by clicking the *S* on the *Mixer* section of the track.
2. Click on the *Acoustic Arpeggio* track as if we were adding effects to it.
3. Play the session.

For this track, let's add a *Simple Delay* to make those notes bounce around a bit:

4. From the Browser at the left, choose *Audio Effects* and then expand *Simple Delay* in the Browser by clicking the triangle at the left.
5. Drag the preset *Eighth Note* from the Browser and then drag it onto the track's device pane.

The delay devices in Live, like many of their other devices, have the option to *sync* automatically to the *Beats Per Minute,* or *BPM*, set by the track by enabling the device's *sync* buttons. Notice that the BPM for this session has been set to 125, the tempo at which this song was performed. For this device, the numbered buttons represent beat divisions for the delay time.

6. Highlight some region of the track that has audio content (not blank space) and press the key command +L (Mac) or *ctrl+L* (Windows) to loop that region.
7. Click at the start of that region and press the *play* button to play back that looped region.

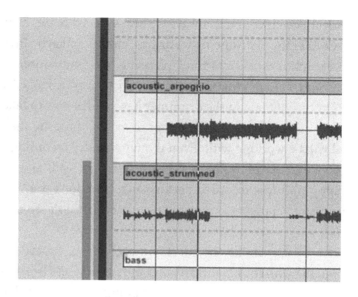

FIGURE 5.2

Region of acoustic track highlighted.

8. While the region loops, audition different settings using the *Simple Delay* effect.

9. Toggle the *Device Deactivator* for this effect to *A/B* test the effect on and off.

In essence, adding effects in this way is about using the technology to facilitate your creative idea. If you wanted this track to sound distorted, there are distortion effects you can apply to it, either using the Live device or third-party plug-ins. An understanding of what each and every known audio effect is beyond the scope of this book. At the end of this chapter, we've provided Andi Allan's helpful and humorous "Monkey FX Guide" that explains a number of audio processes in a practical manner. For our purposes in this chapter, let's assume you've selected all of the effects you like for each track.

10. Either (1) continue adding effects to each track as we did for the *Acoustic Arpeggio* track; or (2) open the *Thorns_Processed* session in the chapter examples folder.

The *Thorns_Processed* session is a final version of this session with effects applied to all tracks. Please note that some of the tracks in this session require *Amp*, a device available in Ableton Live Suite. If you receive an error that a device could not load, please take a few moments and download the trial of Ableton Live Suite or simply substitute this device for another one.

11. Click the arrow next to the *Processed Tracks* label to expand the folder.

12. Play the session.

Notice that the track sounds much different from before. On your own, you should consider soloing each track and examining the types of effects used. Again, consult the effect guide provided at the end of this chapter.

Artist Profile: Trent Reznor

Trent Reznor is an American composer and the leader of the band Nine Inch Nails (NIN). NIN was formed in the late 1980s and grew in popularity during the 1990s with songs that blended elements of alternative and industrial rock, such as distorted guitars and aggressively compressed vocals, with electronic elements, such as sequenced drum patterns and studio-processed sounds and timbres. A few of the many works exemplifying this merger include the songs "Head Like a Hole" (1990), "The Perfect Drug" (1997), and "Every Day Is Exactly the Same" (2006).

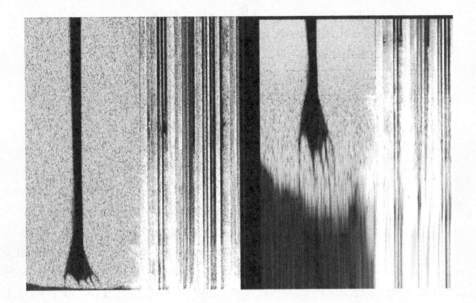

79

FIGURE 5.NIN

Spectroscope revealing that filtered white noise on NIN's "The Warning" resembles a hand reaching downward.

Automation

You can change the settings of your effect devices throughout the piece while the song is playing using *Automation*. Automation allows you to draw or record changes in the individual settings of device parameters. For example, at around the 3-minute mark in this song, the instruments all cut out except for the vocals and the acoustic guitar. In the *Thorns_Processed* session, reverb has been applied generously to the vocal track. During this quieter part, to create a different sense of space in the mix, we're going to use automation to quickly reduce the reverb until the whole band joins in again.

13. If your *Vox* track doesn't already contain a reverb track (the *Thorns_Processed* session has the *Vocal Hall* preset applied), add it now.

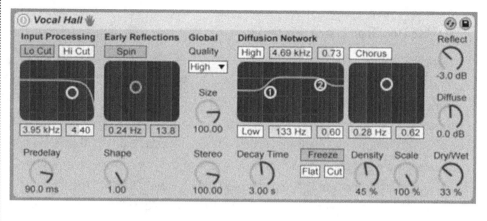

FIGURE 5.3

Reverb effect applied to Vox track.

14. Locate the *Dry/Wet* knob at the bottom right of the device. This is the knob that controls how much of the reverb effect is applied to the vocals.

15. Automate this knob by *ctrl+clicking* (Mac) or *right clicking* (Windows) the knob and selecting *Show Automation in New Lane*.

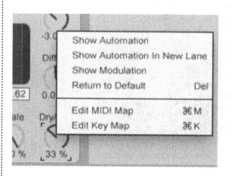

FIGURE 5.4

Effect parameter selected for Automation.

An automation lane for this effect parameter has been opened beneath the *Vox* track. The red line in this lane represents the current value of the selected parameter, in this case, the *Wet/Dry* knob for our reverb. You can click along the red line and add various points to the automation. As the track plays, the automation point is read by the effect and the *Wet/Dry* knob will change its value gradually as it moves from one point to another according to the position of each point.

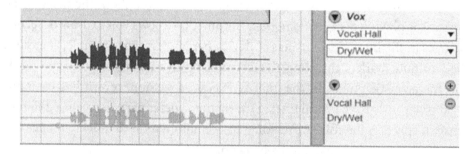

FIGURE 5.5

Automation lane shown for Dry/Wet parameter for effect on Vox track.

16. Click on the red automation line to add a point.

17. Adjust the automation point value by clicking the point and dragging it.

In Live, just about anything can be automated including device parameters, track volume, tempo settings on the master track, and more. Clicking multiple points can become tiresome if you require a lot of automation. Alternatively, we can press the *main record* button and adjust the parameters in real time to record automaton as the track plays.

18. Click the *Record* button from the main transport at the top of Live.
19. Press the *space* bar to begin playback.
20. As the track plays, adjust the level of the automated *Wet/Dry* knob for the reverb device.

Notice how multiple points appeared in the Automation Lane while you moved the knob. Now, you can fine-tune these points by clicking and adjusting them or simply by deleting them.

Automation is a powerful way to control your session. Keep in mind that most controls in Live can be automated and that most controls can be mapped to keys and external devices like MIDI controllers. For non-Live devices like third-party plug-ins, Live provides a mechanism to automate those parameters as well by clicking the *Configure* button then selecting the desired controls from within the third-party plug-in's interface.

Making It Performable in a Live Situation

Now that we've made some production choices about this session, let's figure out how to perform with it in a live situation. The most obvious consideration for this depends upon which instrument you play. For example, if you are a singer, you can simply delete the recorded vocal clip, set the track's input to come from your microphone, and sing along. Your live singing voice will still receive the same effects as if it were the recorded clip.

21. Delete the recorded vocal clip on the *Vox* track.
22. Set the *Vox* track's *Input Type* to *Ext. In* and select the input channel for your microphone.

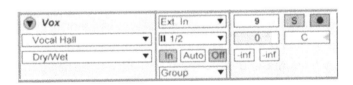

FIGURE 5.6

Vox track record-enabled (armed) with monitoring set to Auto.

Currently, the *Vox* track is set on *Auto* monitoring. As a reminder from a previous chapter, this means that microphone input will not go through to the output unless the track is armed for recording. Before you proceed to arm the track for recording, please take a moment to consider feedback. Particularly if you are using a computer with a built-in microphone, it's very easy for feedback to occur. In the same way that we use headphones to avoid the bleed of other instruments from reaching our microphone while recording, use headphones to prevent feedback.

Feedback occurs when a microphone is placed too close to a speaker. The speaker outputs the sound picked up by the microphone that is the sound of the speaker that is picked up by the microphone that is the sound of... *squeal!!!!* . . . angry audience.

23. When you are safely out of feedback's way by the use of headphones or by moving your microphone far enough away from your speakers, enable the *Record* button for this track.

Alternately, instead of enabling *Record* for this track, you can switch the monitoring mode from *Auto* to *In*. This is particularly useful if you want to receive microphone input simultaneously on multiple tracks but don't want to record—for example, if you want to delete the guitar clip and play guitar through the *Electric Guitar* track while singing on the *Vox* track.

24. Disable the *Record* button for the *Vox* track.
25. Switch the monitoring for the *Vox* track from *Auto* to *In*.
26. Sing, rap, scat, talk, or do other things into the *Vox* track.

At this point, if you play the track from the beginning and sing through the *Vox* track, you are getting the basic concept of playing along with a computer. Unlike musicians, computers are incredibly consistent performers who don't complain about long rehearsals and don't mind if they don't get paid. However, if you overwork them, they'll get hot and shut down on you. Going forward, there are a number of things that we can do to improve this performance experience from the point of view of you, the performer.

For example, it's a lot easier to keep time with a consistent clock source like a metronome.

27. Enable the metronome and play back the track.

The blue *Preview/Cue* volume on the master track, next to the master track volume, determines the metronome volume. It also controls the preview volume of things in the Browser. *Preview/Cue* is like a hidden track for auditioning sounds, the metronome, and other things intended to be heard by the performers and not the audience.

FIGURE 5.7

Preview/Cue volume on master track positioned to the right of the volume.

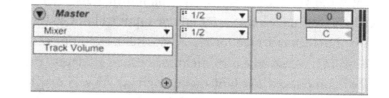

28. As the track plays, adjust the *Preview/Cue* volume to hear the metronome volume change.

Now, it would be really useless in most cases if what you heard through the *Preview/Cue* track came out through the main speakers during your performance. As a result, Live allows you to change the output channel of the *Preview/ Cue* track. As you can see on the *Master* track, there are two output options: the topmost one controls the output channel of *Preview/Cue*, and the other controls the output channel of the *Master* track. If you have a soundcard with multiple outputs, you can send the *Preview/Cue* output to your in-ear monitoring system and the left and right stereo *Master* outputs to the house PA. If you are using a soundcard with only left and right (stereo) outputs, you can send the *Preview/ Cue* out channel 1, the left speaker, and the *Master* out channel 2, the right speaker. In the latter scenario, it makes sense to replace the left speaker with a headphone monitoring system so only the performer can hear the metronome.

To demonstrate:

29. Set the *Preview/Cue* output to 1.
30. Set the *Master* output to 2.
31. Listen to the track with headphones.

If you hold the left headphone speaker to your ear, you will hear only the metronome click. If you hold only the right headphone speaker to your ear, you will hear the summation of all of the audio into just that mono channel. Obviously, you can see that one benefit of using a soundcard with multiple output channels is that you can route audio to various output destinations.

Look at the *Vox* track and notice that its output destination is set to *Group*. If we mute the group folder track, we will mute all of the tracks whose outputs are set to *Group*.

32. Mute and unmute the folder track to mute all tracks whose outputs are set to *Group*.

Notice that the group folder track also has a destination output, *Master*, that is, the channel configuration specified by the *Master* track. If the *Master* track is set to come out of channel 2, all tracks routed to *Master* would automatically be sent out of channel 2. Suppose that we wanted all of our tracks to come out of the *Master* output except for our vocal track; we want that to come out of another output channel. We would simply need to change the output setting on the vocal track from *Group* to *Ext. Out*.

33. Change the output channel on the *Vox* track from *Group* to *Ext. Out*.
34. Select *1* from the pulldown menu beneath *Ext. Out* to specify that the *Vox* track will come out of output *1*, the left headphone speaker output.

35. Turn off the metronome.

36. Play back the track noting that the entire ensemble will be coming out of the *Master* output channel (specified by the group folder track), which is set to output channel *2*, the right headphone speaker. The *Vox* track, as you sing or talk, will come out of the output channel *1*, the left headphone speaker.

In some ways, this "signal path" talk can be the most difficult part of electronic music, in particular, working with multiple sound sources in a somewhat complicated way. Sometimes, you just need to take a deep breath and think it through.

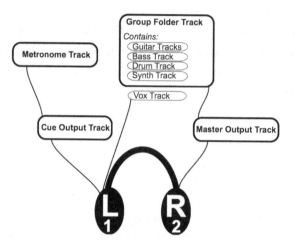

FIGURE 5.8

Signal flow diagram of tracks routing to Output tracks and, eventually, soundcard outputs.

Individual instrument tracks (except the *Vox* track) share the settings of the *Folder Group* track output. This folder track is routed to the *Master* track and the output of the *Master* track is set to output channel *2*. The *metronome*, though it's muted, is part of the *Preview/Cue* output>the *Preview/Cue* output is set to output channel *1*. The *Vox* track, though still in the group folder, has its output set directly to output channel *1*.

Tracks as Groups

Live is very flexible about where audio is routed. In fact, you may have noticed that you can set the output of tracks to many other places besides speaker outputs.

37. On the *Vox* track, click on the output destination currently set to *Ext. Out.* but don't change the setting.

Notice that you can even route this track to other tracks! Why would someone route tracks to other tracks? Suppose you need a microphone at your keyboard rig for when you sing and play keyboard at the same time, but you also need another microphone at the front of the stage for when you're not playing the keyboard (or for when you've switched to the keytar). You can make two copies of the *Vox* track and set different microphone input settings from your soundcard. However, you can also make two new tracks with different microphone settings and route them to the one *Vox* track. With the latter, you'll save computer resources by not making multiple copies of the effects.

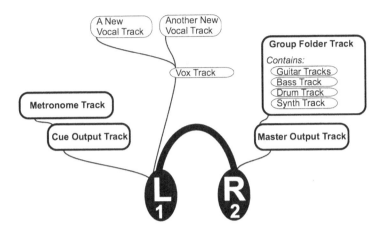

FIGURE 5.9

Signal flow where tracks are routed to Output tracks as well as other tracks.

This is just one example of the flexibility of Live in terms of routing audio. Some DAWs have separate *Busses* or *Aux* tracks to do this, but in Live, tracks can receive from other tracks and send to other tracks giving you lots of flexibility.

Send and Return Tracks

Another option for audio routing is to use *Send* and *Return* tracks. You may have noticed that this session has two *Return* tracks in it labeled *A Return* and *B Return* above the *Master* track.[1] You may have also noticed that there are two volume controls beneath the track volume for each track.

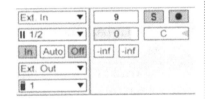

FIGURE 5.10

Two Send volumes positioned beneath the track volume.

If the level is increased for each of these *Send* volumes, the tracks signal will be sent through the main track output and also through the *Sends*.

38. Increase the first *Send* volume for the *Vox* track and the *Strings* track to about -6 or so.

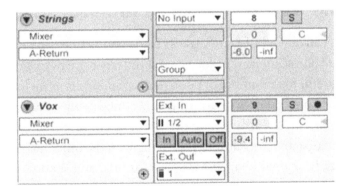

FIGURE 5.11

Send volumes and output destinations on the Strings and Vox tracks.

1. If you haven't done so already, select the small *R* in a circle at the bottom-right corner of the session to reveal the *Return* tracks.

We've now sent some of the signals from these tracks from our *Send* to our *Return* track. We can audition this by soloing the *Return* track.

39. Solo the *A Return* track.
40. Play the session.

As you can hear, the strings and the vocals come through the *A Return* track. If we add an effect device to this *Return* track, we will be able to apply the effect to any or all of the tracks in our session by simply increasing the value of the *Send* volume for that track.

41. Click the arrow to the left of the *A Return* track to reveal that the *Return*'s output is set to *Master*.

FIGURE 5.12

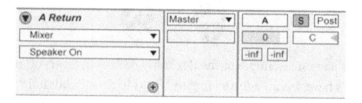

Return track's output set to Master track.

42. From the *Audio Effects* label in the Browser, expand the *Simple Delay* by clicking the triangle, and drag the *Eighth Note* preset onto the *A Return* track.
43. Play back the session.
44. Increase and decrease the *Send* volumes for the *Vox* and *Strings* tracks (or other tracks) to demonstrate the concept of using an effect on a *Return* track.

Adding the *Simple Delay* to the *A Return*, in this case, is only intended to prove the point that *Returns* can be a great way to share resources like *Devices* among several tracks.

45. Delete the *Simple Delay* from the *A Return* track.

Using the *Return* Tracks as Monitor Mixes

Another great advantage of *Return* tracks is the option of setting up submixes of the tracks in your session in order to send different mixes to several outputs. This can be useful for a number of performance applications including monitor mixes, multichannel compositions, surround sound setups, and more. Let's examine a performance-ready version of the *Thorns* session that has been set up to allow a guitarist and a vocalist to play along with the other instruments in the *Thorns* tracks, hear their own custom monitor mix, and send all the necessary audio to the house PA.

46. In the chapter examples folder, open the session *Thorns_Live* in the *Thorns Live Project* folder, but do not play it yet.
47. In the session, expand the folder *Live Instruments* to reveal the *Guitar Live* and *Vox Live* tracks.

The *Live Instruments* folder contains two tracks: one for our guitarist and one for our vocalist. As we previously discussed, having these musicians play into Live would be simple:

- Plug the guitar or the vocalist's mic into an input on your computer's soundcard.
- Set the input of the track to that same input number.
- Set the track to *In* (watch for feedback!).

Getting the audio back out to the house PA sound system would also be simple:

- Connect a cable from an output of your soundcard to the input of a mixer or powered speaker.
- Set the output of your track to that same output number.

In the *Thorns_Live* session, you will see that the inputs and outputs have all been defaulted to *1* and *2* so that it is compatible with the built-in number of inputs and outputs for most computers of those reading this book. If you have a multichannel soundcard, you can route the input and output channels accordingly. The *Guitar Live* track name, for example, is actually named *Guitar Live— Out 3 & 4* as a reminder for the performer to ensure that this track has its output set to those channels. As we play the session, imagine that an actual singer and guitarist are playing on these two channels along with the other tracks in the session.

48. In the session, close the *Live Instruments* folder track.
49. Expand the *Thorns* folder to reveal the tracks.

The tracks in the *Thorns* folder are similar to the ones we've been looking at except that they've been exported as audio files with all of the effects we applied, then reimported. The effects, as a result, are permanently applied to these tracks—there's no way, for example, to remove reverb from the strings.

Freezing Tracks

The tracks in the *Thorns* folder (Step 49) were rendered using the normal *File>Export Audio/Video* routine in order to create a new audio file with the audio effects permanently applied to the track. The benefit of this process is that you no longer require instances of the audio effects in your session—especially useful if you are trying to save CPU usage or intend to mix in another program or if you are working on a computer that doesn't have the same effects you have on yours. Once this is process is done, however, there is no way to undo the effects from the track—the effects are "burned in" or "hard-coded." In Live, there is a nondestructive approach to this called *Freeze Tracks* in which effects are applied to tracks and then disabled to save CPU resources. The process is fully reversible and can be executed as simply as *ctrl+clicking* (Mac) or *right clicking* (Windows) a clip and choosing *Freeze Track.*

Among the tracks in this folder is a track labeled *Click*. It is a rendered file of a single snare drum hit that has been looped and arranged in a pattern.

50. In the chapter examples folder, locate the audio file *vjmanzo_ click.aif* in the *Thorns Live Project* folder.

This click track will help us keep in time as we play along with the tracks. It's an improvement over using Live's built-in metronome because it will always remain in sync with the other tracks in the folder despite Live's global tempo setting. It's also an improvement because we can route its output to any number of places just as we can with any audio track. For example, we don't want the sound of the click track to come through the main house PA, but we do want the ability to send it to the monitor mixes of our performers, helping them to stay in sync as they play with the other tracks in the session.

In our session, notice that there are four return tracks named:

- *House PA Mix Out 1 & 2*—this will be a "Main Mix" that our audience hears through the main PA.
- *Basic Monitor Mix Out 5*—this will be a mix that our performers hear on stage. Since this mix contains a click track, it's preferred to use in-ear monitors or headphones as monitors as opposed to floor-wedge speakers.
- *Guitarist Mix Out 6*—this will be a custom mix sent to the guitarist's monitor mix that contains the *Basic Monitor* mix plus some other tracks at varying volumes.

- *Vocalist Monitor Mix Out 7*—this will be a custom mix sent to the vocalist's monitor mix that contains the *Basic Monitor* mix plus some other tracks at varying volumes.

Again, each of these *Return* track outputs will be sent from Live through the soundcard outputs to the house PA and monitor mixes. The concept is for the guitarist, for example, to create a balance of the tracks in the session that he feels comfortable playing to. He probably wants to hear his live playing louder than the rest of the tracks; he may not want to hear the singer at all; he may want to hear just himself and the *Click* track. However he prefers to create his monitor mix is his own business. Since it is a *Return* track that is sent to a monitor mix that only he can hear, his desired mix will not affect what the other performers hear. Same with the vocalist's track: she may prefer to hear herself a lot, hear the background instruments faintly, and not hear the *Click* track at all.

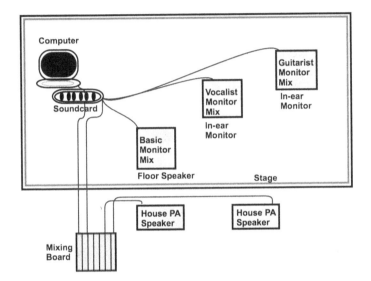

FIGURE 5.13

Stage setup with soundcard outputs run to monitors on stage, and a mixer on the floor.

To simulate the experience, let's solo each *Return* track and play back the session. Again, for the purpose of this chapter, the output channels for each return track are set to *1 & 2* so as to be compatible with the default speaker setup of most computers. Note, once again, that each *Return* track is named with a description of what the mix contains as well as the desired output channels from the computer's soundcard (*Out 1 & 2*, *Out 5*, etc.).

51. Solo *A Return* track *House PA Mix*.
52. Play the session, then stop.

Notice that the output for every track in the session is set to *Sends Only*. This means that the track signal will be sent only to the *Return* tracks at whatever volume is indicated in the *Send* volumes. The signal will not be sent out in parallel to the *Group* track or to the *Master* track. In fact, in this session, the *Master* track volume has been set to *–inf* dB, which means "no output." The

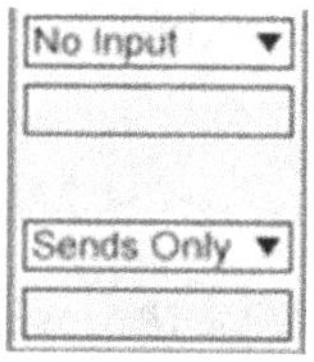

FIGURE 5.14

Track output sent to Sends Only.

volume of the *Master* track, of course, doesn't really matter because we're routing all of our signals to *Return* tracks and sending them where we want.

The *Click* track has its signal set to send on *B Send* and return on *B Return*.

53. As you continue to listen with *A Return* soloed, increase the volume of *A Send* for the *Click* track until you hear it.
54. Then set the volume of *A Send* for the *Click* track back to *–inf.*
55. Solo each *Return* track and compare the *Send* values of each track in both the *Thorns* folder and the *Live Instruments* folder.

Multiple Sessions in One Session

If you prepare a session for each of your compositions in the way we prepared this one, you can combine sessions to produce a continual sequence of works. To demonstrate this concept, let's append another premade session to the end of our *Thorns_Live* session. You will notice that *Locator* marks have been placed at the beginning of the session and at the point where the *Thorns_Live* tracks are ending. *Locators* are created by clicking the *Set* button at the right of the session above the *Track* names. These are called *Markers* in some other DAWs and are simply ways that we can mark positions.

Locators can be useful in a number of contexts. While recording, it can be useful to click the *Set* button to make *Locators* each time the talent you're recording does something noteworthy like make a mistake, play one section exceptionally well, sing the wrong lyric, and so on. *Locators* can also be placed at certain parts in *Arrangement View*, like loop sections, and mapped to keys and MIDI controls. For instance, you may be learning a new piece of music and decide to place *Locators* at the verse, chorus, and solo sections of the piece, so that you can quickly revisit them by clicking on the *Locator* marker. Rehearsing in this manner works well when used with *Loop Switch* and *Loop Points*.

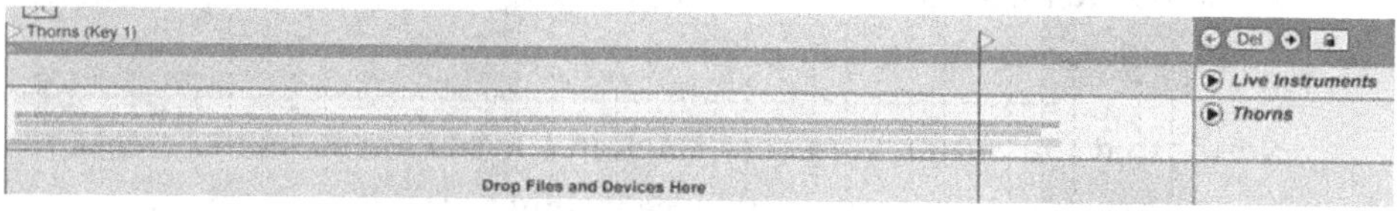

FIGURE 5.15

Grouped folder track for Thorns with two Locators.

We will append a second Live session to *Thorns_Live* tracks and align it to the second *Locator*.

56. In the *Browser Sidebar*, select the *Chapter Examples* folder in *Places* that we set up in an earlier chapter.
57. From within the Browser content pane, expand the *Chapter 5* folder.
58. Expand the *Air Project* folder to reveal the session *Air.als*, but do not click it.

As mentioned, the *Air.als* file is just another Live session similar to *Thorns*. Instead of opening it up and copying the tracks into our session, we're going to drag the session file into our current session. This will bring in all of the tracks from that session with their respective *Send/Return* track settings. Ensure that you can see the *Drop Files and Devices Here* message and both *Locators* in the session's arrangement timeline. If you cannot see this, zoom out on the session and fold up the *Thorns* folder track and the *Return* tracks to make more room on your screen. You should also close the *Detail View* panel at the bottom of the screen if it is open.

59. Zoom out on the session using the *Zooming Hotspot* at the top of the program screen.
60. Fold up the *Thorns* folder track.
61. Close the *Detail View* panel at the bottom of the screen by clicking the triangle on the bottom right of the program screen.
62. Drag the *Air.als* file beneath the *Thorns* folder track.
63. Zoom out on the session again.

Notice that the tracks are mapped to *Sends* and *Returns A* and *B* already—these were inherited from the settings in the *Air.als* session.

64. Fold up the *Air* folder trtack.

FIGURE 5.16

Two folder tracks overlap each other.

At this point, you will see that both folder tracks, *Thorns* and *Air*, overlap each other. The solution is an easy cut-and-paste operation.

65. Highlight the entire *Air* folder track region by clicking behind the tracks and dragging your mouse toward the beginning of the session.
66. Click *Cut* from the *Edit* menu or use the key commands +*X* (Mac) or *ctrl+X* (Windows) .

67. On the same *Air* folder track, click on the second *Locator* line.
68. Click *Paste* from the *Edit* menu or use the key commands +*V* (Mac) or *ctrl*+*V* (Windows) .
69. Zoom out on the session.

FIGURE 5.17

Grouped folder tracks positioned sequentially.

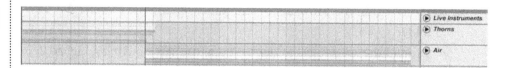

Now, as your session plays and the live musicians play along with the session tracks, the *Thorns* piece will transition naturally into the second piece in your concert, *Air*. If you have other pieces to drag into this concert, you can repeat the steps we used to append *Air* to *Thorns*.

As a final touch, the two *Locators* in this session have already been mapped to the computer keys *1* and *2*. As the session plays, you can quickly jump from one song to another by pressing the number keys *1* and *2*. This can be helpful while rehearsing so that you don't have to use the mouse to click when you want to play the piece again. The final version of this session has been saved as *Complete Concert* in the *Thorns_Live Project* folder.

Multichannel Concepts

Imagine that you want to set up a walking tour of some sort at a museum exhibit or a gallery where people walk along a path and see various works of art hanging on the walls or on easels. Next to each work of art is a speaker. As you begin the tour, you hear some music coming out of the speaker placed at the entrance. As you walk along the path, the music continues to play from the speaker next to the first work of art you approach. As you stand near the work of art, you continue to hear the music coming from the speaker nearest that work, but you also hear a spoken narrative about the artwork coming through the speaker. As you move to the next work of art, you continue to hear the same music, as if the music is continually following you as you move from artwork to artwork, but as you approach the next work you hear another voiceover narrative regarding the piece you're now standing in front of.

Think about the technical aspects of implementing such a design:

- A single computer with a multi-output soundcard.
- Looping audio tracks of music and narrative in a Live session.
  - Music track is sent to the main outputs *1* and *2*.
    - Cables from the soundcard's main outputs *1* and *2* are sent to two powered speakers near the tour's entrance.
  - Music and the first narrative voice track are mixed and then sent to a *Return* track that has its outputs set to the soundcard's output *3*.

□ Cables from the soundcard's output *3* are connected to a powered speaker placed near the first artwork.

- Music and the second narrative voice track are mixed and sent to a second *Return* track that has its outputs set to the soundcard's output *4*.

□ Cables from the soundcard's output *4* are connected to a powered speaker placed near the first artwork.

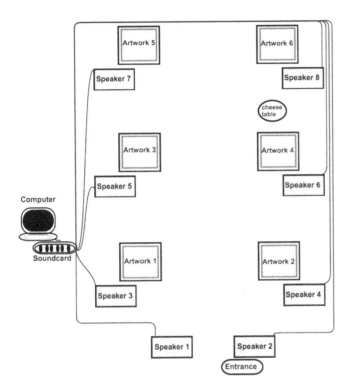

93

FIGURE 5.18

Signal flow: bird's-eye view of the conceptual exhibit layout with speakers.

Now think about the implications of this type of setup for your own creative works. Perhaps you want to have performances in which, instead of looking at a work of art, attendees look or even interact with a musical instrument or a controller. Perhaps you want to make a walk-through tour of synthesizers through the years where a single piece of music is composed using every synth in the gallery, but as you near each instrument, the other instruments seem to lower in volume and the instrument you're standing in front of comes to audible prominence. Perhaps you set up your DJ rig or band on a stage at one side of the room, but you also place speakers at the other side of the room exactly parallel to the position of your band's setup or in some other arrangement. You then set up a bunch of *Return* tracks and route audio from your Live session to each speaker. You also set up a screen that displays an animated version of each band member or instrument that plays in your session. With an understanding of how to route audio, you are limited only by your creativity.

Live for Practicing

Have you ever had to learn a fast solo from a recording and had difficulty determining what notes the musician was actually playing? One strategy we can take in Live is to import the song and slow down the tempo of the track without dropping the pitch; this is called *Warping* in Live.

> 70. In the *Chapter Examples* folder, open the session *uncertainty* in the *uncertainty Project* folder.

Notice that this track has a few markers set up at the solo. If you were to learn this solo by ear, you may find it helpful to slow down the tempo so as to better determine each note being played. If you tried to slow down your record player to achieve the same assistance, you would soon learn that the pitch drops as a result of the turntable playing back at a slower speed. Most modern DAWs have some way to deal with "Time Stretching" (or the opposite, "Time Compression") in order to change the speed of playback without changing the pitch. To do this in Live:

> 71. Double-click the *uncertainty* clip title bar to open *Detail View*.
> 72. Click the *Warp* button.

With a track set to *Warp*, you can adjust the tempo of the track from the main transport (or *Detail View*) while retaining the original pitch of the clip. Several warp modes are available for use. The differences between them involve varying degrees of CPU power consumption in exchange for a more transparent process. For example, the *Complex* or *Complex Pro* effects allow you to change the tempo of the clip to a great extent without producing strange doubling sounds in the file known as *artifacts*. Less CPU-intensive warping algorithms will produce more or different artifacts. Live suggests that some settings are ideal for certain instrument settings. For this example, we'll use *Complex Pro* because we are only using a single clip; we're not performing in front of anyone; and we want the clip to sound natural, without artifacts, and slower.

> 73. From the pulldown menu, select *Complex Pro*.

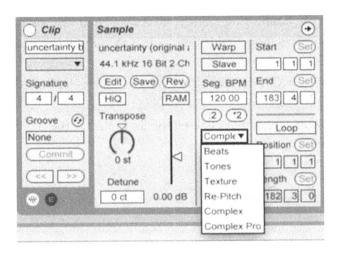

FIGURE 5.19

Warp mode enabled for clip.

74. Play the clip.
75. Click on one of the markers to jump to a section of the solo.
76. As the song plays, decrease the tempo from the main transport.

At a slower tempo, it's much easier to hear the notes. Use this method to learn to play along with fast songs and to determine complicated parts. Don't forget that you can also cut up sections of the piece in *Arrangement View* and loop them. This can be useful for learning different sections of a fast solo over the course of time.

On Your Own

Understanding the path that your audio signal flows can be difficult depending on the number of "links" in the chain (effects, speaker outputs, etc.). Considering the final illustration of the museum exhibit and the implications for your own creative work, devise an "installation" that allows you to perform in a popular music style with some creative way of using multiple channels of audio. If a soundcard with multiple output channels is unavailable to you and you are limited to stereo outputs, devise a creative way to take advantage of the resources you have. Perhaps you can do something interesting with delay effects between speakers that are placed at opposite ends of the room. You may find it helpful to draw flowcharts that represent the path the audio travels in and out of your system.

Remember:

- Group tracks into folders using the key command +*G* (Mac) or *ctrl+G* (Windows).
- Automation allows you to draw or record changes in the individual settings of device parameters.
- In the same way that we use headphones to avoid bleed of other instruments from reaching our microphone while recording, use headphones to prevent feedback.

- Switch the monitoring mode from *Auto* to *In* if you want to receive microphone input simultaneously on multiple tracks without recording.
- The *Preview/Cue* volume on the master track determines the metronome volume.
- *Locators* are created by clicking the *Set* button at the right of the session above the *Track* names.

Monkey FX Guide

The Monkey FX guides were created by Andi Allan (http://www.monkeyfx.co.uk/fxguide.html) and are used here with permission.

Envelope Filter

Envelope filter is a bit like an automatic wah (not to be confused with auto-wah). Imagine that you have a wah pedal and a well-trained monkey.

When you hit the strings hard, the monkey pushes the rocker pedal forwards. As the volume decreases the monkey pulls the rocker pedal back. So the volume envelope of the guitar signal determines the position of the pedal, via the monkey. Now imagine that the monkey is a tiny monkey hidden in a pedal, and that the rocker pedal is a rocker pedal hidden inside your stompbox. Then it's a simple step to imagine that there's actually no monkey or rocker pedal, and that it's all done in electronics.

So basically, if you hit the strings hard you get a treble boost, and as the signal from the strings dies away the boost fades. If you regulate how hard you play, you can get a similar sound to how many people use wah, emphasizing the upper frequencies as you hit the strings.

Harmoniser

A harmoniser is a specialized pitch shifter. I'll break out the monkeys again for an analogy-rich description, if I may.

Imagine that there is a well-trained monkey. This monkey has a pair of headphones on, through which he can hear what you're playing. He also has a guitar that sounds just like yours. There's a dial on the front of the box where you choose what key you're playing in, and another that lets you choose what interval you want (e.g., a fifth, a major third or whatever else). The monkey looks at what you've chosen on the two dials, hears what you're playing and plays a note at that interval in the scale you've chosen. His signal and yours are mixed together and fed back out.

As in previous analogies, imagine that the monkey is inside the pedal/rack unit, and is tiny, with a tiny guitar and a tiny pair of headphones. Then simply imagine that there isn't really a monkey, and that it's all done with some very clever electronics. Ta da!

Analog Delay

Imagine a line of laid back, hippy monkeys, each with a guitar just like yours. They're sitting on little stools in a cunning arrangement such that each monkey can only hear the monkey seated before him. The first monkey hears what you played, turns to the next monkey and plays it back to him. He then turns, and plays to the next monkey. At each stage, little mistakes are introduced due to the hippy monkeys' inherent laid-back-ness. At the end, the last monkey plays, and his guitar is connected to the output.

The monkeys are in a big, big circle, and the first monkey, as well as hearing what you're playing, can also hear the last monkey—but not very well. There's a baffle between them, which cuts down how much he can hear. The first monkey plays both what you're playing and what he can hear of what the last monkey is playing, and this is passed on as before.

Now imagine the monkeys are tiny, as before, with tiny guitars and tiny stools and a tiny baffle. They're in a box. A knob labeled "feedback" controls the baffle. Then, kapoosh! The monkeys disappear and are replaced by a Bucket Brigade chip, and off we go.

Digital Delay

Exactly the same as analog delay, but there are many more monkeys, and they're all actuaries and very precise. Some people miss the laid-back-ness of the hippy monkeys, but many like knowing that little actuary monkeys are taking very good care of what they're playing. Some of the monkeys know special tricks, like making what they play come out of the output even though they're not the last monkey.

Chorus

Thousands of monkeys are seated on stools in a large hall. Each has a guitar like yours (getting repetitive yet?). They are all seated at different distances from you, and hence hear what you're playing at different times. As soon as you start to play, they all copy what you're playing. In an analog chorus, laid-back hippy monkeys (see analog delay) are used; in a digital delay straight-laced actuary monkeys are used. Because they are all playing just slightly out of sync with you, it gives a much richer, fuller sound. In most types of chorus, the monkeys are actually sitting on an old-style fairground carousel, and therefore each gets nearer and further away from you, hence playing with a different delay as the carousel turns and giving a warbled sound.

Yada yada tiny tiny monkeys yada yada. Nice knob controls how fast the carousel spins. Ta da!

Phaser

Similar, overall, to chorus, but there are only, typically, 2, 4, 8, or maybe 12 monkeys in total. Phaser gives a sucked, whooshing noise.

Flanger

Two monkeys. One has a guitar just like yours, but with a tremolo bridge (if yours doesn't have one). He plays the same notes as you, but the other monkey is quite mischievous and is constantly wobbling the tremolo arm up and down. When the sound of the first monkey's guitar is mixed with yours, the subtle pitch differences create a whooshing, almost jet-like sound. Some flangers use several teams of monkey guitarists and tremolo wobblers.

Compression

Picture the scene. Sicily, 1947. A monkey. With a volume pedal. He has tinnitus, so he doesn't like loud noises, but needs things to be a certain volume level in order to hear them, poor little mite. He is wearing headphones. When you play, if it's too loud, he turns the volume down a little. If it's too quiet, he turns it up. He can do this quite quickly if he wants, but there's a big dial in front of him, telling him how fast he's allowed to turn the volume control. There's another control that determines how loud his headphones are compared to your guitar.

Pop the little chap in a box and paint it (traditionally) blue and off you go. Oh, it might be a good idea to replace him with some sort of electronics gubbins, to save his poor hearing.

Some compressors allow you to have a little effect loop in between your guitar and his headphones, so that you could (for instance) have him only listen to the bass part of your guitar sound, but work the volume control according to that.

Solid State Overdrive

Take an infinite number of monkeys, each with a guitar. The first is a third the size you are, and plays notes at 3 times the pitch of yours. The second is 1/5th the size of you and plays at five times your pitch, and the third is 1/7th the size of you and plays at seven times your pitch, and so on for the rest. The smaller monkeys are quieter than the larger ones, as you'd expect. They all play along with you, and the sound from each guitar is added into your signal. This gives quite a harsh fuzzy sound.

Tube Overdrive

As above, but now the monkeys are different sizes. The first monkey and guitar are half the size of yours, and therefore play an octave higher than you. The next is a quarter the size of you, and plays two octaves higher, the next 1/6th the size of you and plays at 6 times your pitch and so on. Again, this gives a fuzzier sound, but one that's much smoother and easier on the ears than the SS over-drives.

Fuzz

Essentially the same as solid-state overdrive, but the monkeys play louder, with the end result that the sound coming out is very very messy indeed. The monkeys particularly like this, because they get to play good and loud and generally make a racket. Fuzz monkeys are generally fed the most bananas.

Boutique FX

Boutique FX function in basically the same way as non-boutique FX, with the following differences:

1. They only use free-range monkeys, who are very well fed and trained and love their work.
2. They are almost exclusively made with analog, hippy monkeys.
3. The monkeys, instead of having stools, have comfy designer chairs to sit on. Lay-z-boys are particularly popular. The boxes they live in are also brightly decorated, which the monkeys love.

These factors combine to make many people think that boutique FX produce better sound, due to the happier monkeys. However, these monkeys are very expensive to raise, and so the boutique FX tend to cost many more bananas to buy. There is much debate as to whether it's worth it.

Univibe

Again, a monkey sitting on a stool. He plays the same thing as you, but there's another monkey spinning the first monkey's stool rapidly. This makes the first monkey dizzy, and the sound his guitar makes is therefore rather warbly. It's like a combination of flanger and chorus. Univibe is seen as rather cruel to the monkey on the stool, and therefore many guitarists prefer the sound of a Leslie speaker cabinet, in which a speaker (or two speakers) is/are rotated by a motor. Many say that the Leslie is much superior in sound as well, but they're bigger, heavier and more expensive than even a boutique monkey based univibe.

99

Electroacoustic Music

lectroacoustic music is used colloquially to refer to compositions where a live performer interacts with an electronic performer to create music. Examples of electroacoustic works include Mario Davidovsky's *Synchronisms* in which an acoustic instrumentalist, such as a guitarist, performs with a recording of sounds that were created in a studio. The term *electroacoustic* has also been applied to other works in which live performance was not a requisite, such as works for fixed media created in a studio but intended to be played from a computer or multichannel system. In the latter case, and sometimes in both cases, the term *algorithmic composition* is also used to describe this type of music. *Algorithmic* in this case suggests computer processes using the compositional process, as distinct from non-computer algorithms or processes that traditional composers use to create music, such as avoiding parallel fifths and writing within a certain range of notes.

Rowe (1993) has identified and defined three methods of algorithmic composition: generative, sequenced, and transformative. Generative methods use sets of rules to produce musical output from the stored fundamental material. Sequenced techniques use prerecorded music fragments in response to real-time input. Aspects of these fragments may be varied in performance, such as tempo playback, dynamic shape, slight rhythmic variations, and so forth. Transformative methods apply transformation to existing musical material to produce variants, which may or may not be recognizably related to the original material. For transformative algorithms, the source material is complete musical input.

In this chapter, we will discuss approaches to electroacoustic composition in which a performer plays music that has been noted while simultaneously interacting with computer processes. We have already discussed a number of approaches to generating pitches algorithmically using Max for Live as well as approaches to using various effect devices inside of Live. Our focus here will address how to make the compositional process easier for composers and the performance process easier for performers.

Artist Profile: Mario Davidovsky

Mario Davidovsky (b. 1934) is an Argentine-born composer best known for his collection of electroacoustic compositions *Synchronisms*. He was a pupil of Aaron Copland and Milton Babbit. Davidovsky's *Synchronisms* feature innovative and idiomatic writing for acoustic instrumentalists who play along with tape recordings of electronic sounds produced in a studio. Davidovsky's *Synchronisms No. 10*, for example, was written for classical guitar and tape. During this 9 1/2 minute piece, a guitarist performs from a notated score and remains unaccompanied for almost 4 1/2 minutes, at which time the studio-created sound portion of the composition begins playing from a tape or other sound source. As can be heard in recordings of this and other *Synchronisms* by Davidovsky, a great deal of effort has been placed on ensuring that the tape portion works to complement the acoustic playing and vice versa. Often this process involves recording performances of the acoustic instrument and manipulating them in the studio. In a live context, the performer would play along with the tape as if it was another performer on the stage. In the case of *Synchronisms No. 10*, portions of the guitarist's score are marked to show places where the electronic sounds would enter or make some noteworthy musical gesture.

Preparing the Canvas

Composing art music for acoustic instruments is time-consuming. It's a much easier process to set up a few looping drum and bass patterns and improvise a solo around them. Considering that an electroacoustic piece, or at least the type we'll be working on in this chapter, involves writing well for an acoustic instrument as well as for electronics, there are even more variables to consider. The assumption in this chapter is that we will build a skeleton for an electroacoustic composition that you can refine later.

Let's begin by considering some ideas for what our piece will look like when we're done:

- An instrumentalist will be on a stage playing some piece of music you've composed.
- At times during the piece, the sound of the instrumentalist will be processed in a number of ways with effects.
- Also at times during the piece, the computer will play generated sounds as the instrumentalist plays, which may include, for example, clips of sounds or some sort of process that creates sounds (such as a Max for Live patch).

Now that we've considered several technical concepts, let's consider some musical ones:

- The piece will be of some length (measured in bars or minutes).
- The texture of the piece will involve the instrumentalist, the processed sounds for that instrument, and other generated sounds, yet they do not have to all play at the same time.
- The form of the piece (the piece's division into sections of music similar to *intro, verse, chorus,* etc.) will probably dictate the length of the piece and the texture of each section.
- Each section of the form related to the computer parts will have to be triggered in some way, for example, according to time; pitch tracking/score following; or a controller event such as the performer, the composer, or someone else pressing a button.
- The instrumentalist will play independently from a notated score. The processed sounds for that instrument will depend upon the instrumentalist executing their job properly when triggered, and the generated sounds will play independently when triggered.
- While we can conceivably make any sound with a computer using millions of effects, it is probably best to utilize a few effects well. This is analogous to the idea that a composer could compose a piece for every instrument in existence all on one stage, but the novelty of such a compositional design doesn't mean that the writing, motivic development, balance, and formal structure will be interesting.

Of course, these are just some guidelines we'll be using to make our composition in this chapter. Let's begin by selecting an acoustic instrument that will be the human part of this piece. Any instrument will do. When in doubt, I always tell my composition students to think about the audience that they want to reach (their parents, friends, teachers, etc.), then think about writing the type of piece that might reach them (something "pretty-sounding," something virtuosic, something funny, etc.). Perhaps your piece involves a singer reading some text you wrote to your significant other, or maybe you have a friend who is a hotshot clarinetist and you want to really show off his or her skills.

1. Select some acoustic instrument or hybrid (electric guitar, violin with a pickup, etc.) in your mind to be the *main instrument* in this composition

Now that we've decided on an instrument timbre, let's pick a palette of effects that we can use for the processes that will be applied to this instrument. At the risk of getting too technical, keep in mind that most effects are all related to some degree. For example, we can say that there are many effects related to volume: *compressors* make the highs low and the lows high, distortions make everything really *compressed*, EQs raise the volume of certain frequency bands, and so on. We can also say that there are many effects related to delays: *simple delays* make a copy of the input at some point in time after the event, *reverb* is just a bunch of delays, *chorus* is a delay with a slight variation in pitch, and *flange* is a delay with a moving delay time. Let's say that this piece will explore aspects of delay to some extent, and also add a bunch of effects to an audio track. This is analogous to an artist who chooses a bunch of paint colors to put on his palette; we are choosing a bunch of effect devices to put on our audio track.

2. Create a new Live session.
3. Ensure that you are in *Session View*.
4. From the *Browser Sidebar* at the left, select *Audio Effects>Simple Delay>Eighth Note* and drag it onto the *1 Audio* track.
5. Select *Audio Effects>Reverb>Hall>Concert Hall* and drag it onto the *1 Audio* track to the right of *Simple Delay*.

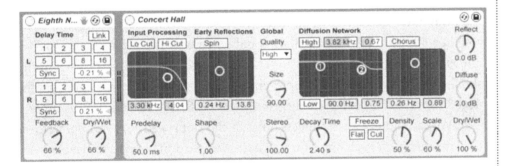

FIGURE 6.1

Delay and reverb effects added to a track.

For now, we'll limit our piece to just these two effects. Of course, you can always add more effects or change them later on (or even now). The point of starting with these two devices is that we can have one effect, the delay, to play with *time*; and the second, the reverb, to play with *space*. In particular, we are going to use these effects to accomplish things that acoustic instrumentalists can't easily do on their own. For example, a musician could conceivably perform in a hall large enough so that the notes they play echo at a predictable tempo and the performer can harmonize with the echo. But only using a delay effect allows us to adjust the tempo of the delays, the number of delays, and the volume of the delays. Regarding the reverb effect, we can say that reverb on our track will be used to create the impression that the instrument is in a hall, but it's much more than that. By adjusting the *Dry/Wet* amount of reverb on the instrument, we can create the illusion that the instrument is, at times, far away and, at other times, very near. These are just two creative ideas that electro-acoustic compositions can employ that traditional compositions really cannot.

Preparing the Form

Let's discuss the structure of the piece and how the live performer will interact with the computer. In the chapter on rock and pop music, we discussed ways to interact with the computer in *Arrangement View*. In many cases, that same approach would work here:

- Line up your generated sounds along the timeline on one track.
- Add effects to another track that the performer plays through.
  - Automate the effects over time.
- Mark sections in the timeline that refer to places in your score.
- Press the *space bar* and play as the playback head moves along.

That approach will definitely work. However, we can also set this piece up so that it takes advantage of *Clip View*. It will be a similar approach.

6. Rename your *1 Audio* track to *Instrument Track*.

Our goal here will be to think of each clip slot on the *Instrument Track* as a different section of music in the composition. The first clip slot, clip slot 0, for example, can represent the first eight bars of music and whatever the states of the delay and reverb effects are during those eight measures (e.g., the effect could be off during these bars, they could be on only slightly, or their *Dry/Wet* knobs could be gradually increasing). The second clip slot (directly beneath clip slot 0 on the next *Scene*) will represent the next section of music, perhaps the next 32 bars, and all of the changes in the effects that occur during this time.

We can't automate the effects on each clip slot because, at this point, there isn't any audio on each clip slot. Furthermore, we don't intend to have our instrumentalist record into each clip slot, stop playing and automate the effects for each section, and then resume playing! We want to have the performer play and step through each *Scene* with different automation settings mapped to each clip slot. One solution will be to drag a blank audio clip onto each clip slot and apply automation to the blank audio clip.

7. In the chapter examples folder for chapter 6, locate the file *blank.mp3*.
8. Drag the *blank.mp3* audio clip onto clip slot 0.

If prompted to choose an analysis type from *Harmony*, *Melody*, or *Drums*, choose *Drums*. For our purposes, this analysis method doesn't matter much.

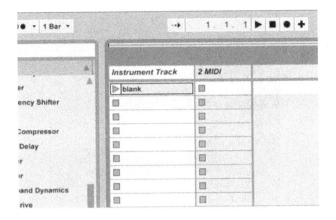

FIGURE 6.2

A blank.mp3 clip added
to clip slot 0.

9. Double-click the *blank* clip slot.

As you can see in the *Clip View* window, this *blank.mp3* clip has no sound in it. We'll use this blank clip to map out the structure of our piece.

10. Click the small circled *E* at the bottom left of the *Clip View* window to reveal the *Envelope* window.

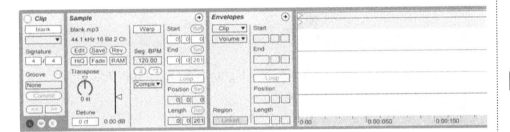

FIGURE 6.3

Envelope window
enabled in Clip View.

The *Envelope* window allows us to draw automation lines for each clip slot. However, we'll first need to enable *Warp* on this clip.

11. Click the *Warp* button in the *Sample* window.

The clip is now *Warped*, which means that changes to the tempo of the track will be applied to the duration of this clip. Since this clip has no sound, *Warp Mode* doesn't really matter in terms of the quality of playback for this clip. In fact, you can even uncheck the *HiQ* button to save a little CPU energy. Instead, we intend to stretch this blank clip to the duration, in bars and beats, so as to delineate a section of our composition.

Notice that the *Start* section in the *Sample* window shows the clip's start time at *1 1 1* and *End* at *1 1 3*, where each of the three numbers refers to *bars, beats,* and *sixteenth-note divisions,* respectively, and in which the latter two numbers have a maximum value of *4* if the *Clip* time signature is set to *4 / 4*. We decided earlier that this first section would be *eight bars* in duration so let's set the *End* value to *9 1 1*, a full eight bars ending at the first beat of the ninth bar.

12. Set the *Start* value to *1 1 1*.
13. Set the *End* value to *9 1 1*.

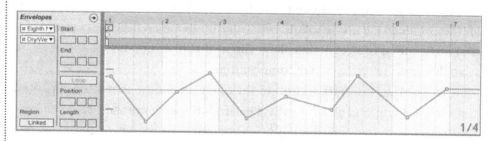

FIGURE 6.4

Clip length set to eight full bars.

14. Hold your mouse on the numbered portion of the *Sample Display/Note Editor* window in *Clip View* until your mouse turns into a magnifying glass, then zoom out to see that the *blank* clip has had its duration stretched to eight full bars.

FIGURE 6.5

Clip View with zoomed-out Sample Display/Note Editor window.

15. In the *Envelope* window, select *Eighth Note* from the *Device Chooser* pulldown menu.
16. Beneath the *Device Chooser* menu, select *Dry/Wet* from the *Control Chooser* pulldown menu.

Notice that the red automation line appears in the *Sample Display/Note Editor* window. This allows you to draw an automation line for the *Dry/Wet* parameter of the delay effect.

17. Draw an automation line for the eight-bar duration in the *Sample Display/Note Editor* window.

FIGURE 6.6

Automation drawn for an effect parameter.

Let's test what we have so far.

18. Double-click on the track title bar *Instrument Track*.
19. Set the *Dry/Wet* of the *Reverb* device to 0 so that we can hear just the delay effect.

20. Put on your headphones and arm the *Instrument Track* for recording or set its monitoring type to *In* (again—be cautious of feedback!).
21. Test that your voice is coming through the microphone into the *Instrument Track*.
22. Click the *play* button on the clip slot containing the clip *blank. mp3* while singing, speaking, rapping, playing, clapping, squeaking, or making some other form of sound.

Notice that the delay effect automated the *Dry/Wet* parameter as we suspected it would. Let's apply this same technique to the next section of music in our composition. We'll make this next section of the composition 32 bars in duration.

23. Highlight and copy the *blank* clip.
24. Paste the clip into the slot directly beneath it on the *Instrument Track* (slot 1).
25. Double-click this slot (slot 1) to open *Clip View*.
26. Set the *Start* value to *1 1 1*.
27. Set the *End* value to *33 1 1*.
28. Zoom out on the *Sample Display/Note Editor* window to see all 32 bars.

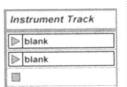

FIGURE 6.7

Two blank.mp3 clips in slots 0 and 1 used to delineate formal sections of the composition.

107

Since we copied this clip, it has retained its *Warp* status and all of the automation we previously drew.

29. Select a few device parameters for both the delay and reverb effects and automate them throughout the 32 bars.
30. Copy the *blank* clip into clip slot 2 and repeat steps 25–29.

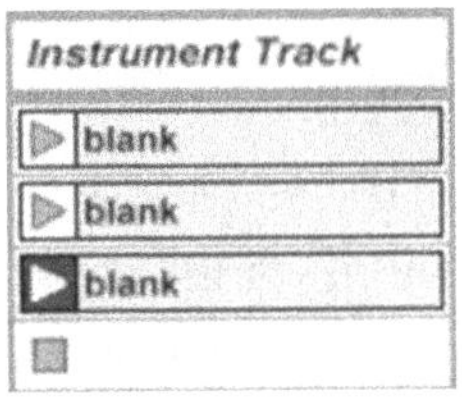

FIGURE 6.8

Three blank.mp3 clips.

At this point, we have defined three different sections of the composition that refer to the measures of a written score that the performer will read from. From here, creating effect settings for the remaining sections of the composition should be clear. We have not yet addressed two important parts of this composition:

- Computer-generated sounds.
- Moving the computer parts through each of the formal sections of the composition.

Preparing Computer-Generated Sounds

The approaches for preparing the computer-generated parts of this composition have no limits. You can approach it from any direction: using synthesizers to make interesting sounds, creating a Max for Live patch to randomly play pitches, recording sounds from the hall where the piece is to be performed—anything can work. For our purposes, let's take a recorded clip of the acoustic instrument for our piece and use it as the basis to create a number of interesting sounds. The treatments we perform on this clip will be processes that we wouldn't necessarily want to do in real-time, like slowing it down, chopping it up, dropping the pitch, combining it with other sounds, and so on. The result is that the acoustic performer has a score to read from, the computer is going to apply automated effects to that performer's sound, and the computer is also going to play back some interesting sounds that we are about to make. (Note that the word "interesting" in the preceding sentence is completely subjective.)

31. Switch to *Arrangement View*.
32. If possible, record or obtain a recording of the acoustic instrument you've chosen for this piece onto a new track, preferably playing in the same key or tonal center of your composition. If this is not possible, from the chapter examples folder for this chapter, drag the *gravity.mp3* clip onto a new track.
33. In *Arrangement View*, play the clip.

The *gravity.mp3* clip is an excerpt of recorded electric guitar, so the main instrument chosen for this book example is obviously the electric guitar. Ultimately, the clip you use for your composition will be different. We can perform a number of processes on this recorded clip or others like it; in fact, many of the effect devices in Live are designed to do such things. While the novelty of some effects is interesting at first encounter, what is really needed is for artistic decisions to be made about their implementation. It's one thing to throw a bunch of interesting sounds together or lots of effects on a clip, but it's an entirely different approach to strategically place a delay on a particular sound at a particular point in the composition, or to create an interesting volume envelope for a bizarre effect.

34. Double-click the *gravity* clip to open *Clip View*.

Before adding any effect devices, there are a number of novel ways to manipulate the clip as it exists. In particular, we can slow it down, drop the pitch, and reverse it. Let's do all three:

35. Click the *Warp* button to map this clip to the tempo defined in Live. Note that this will change only the playback tempo of the

clip but not the pitch. If prompted, click *Yes* to insert *Warp markers* into the clip.

As you know, there are several warp modes available for use, and less CPU-intensive warping algorithms will produce more or different artifacts. Understand that the presence of these artifacts in your composition may even be desirable to you, so you should consider auditioning them all and selecting one based on your creative objective.

36. Select *Complex Pro* as the *Warp Mode* to change the tempo of the piece while retaining the pitch.
37. Click the **2* button once to halve the original tempo of the clip.
38. Play the clip.

Let's disguise the musical figure recorded by reversing it. This will cause the clip to play backward and will produce a uniquely strange envelope as the clip plays.

39. Click the *Rev* button.
40. Play the clip.

Notice how the clip is already starting to take on a voice of its own that is different than what we began with. Since the main instrument for this piece will likely occupy the same sonic range of pitches that this clip involves, let's drop the pitch of this clip one octave.

41. Click and drag the *Transpose* knob to the left to *-12*. That is, we are transposing this clip down 12 semitones, which is the equivalent of one octave.
42. Play the clip.

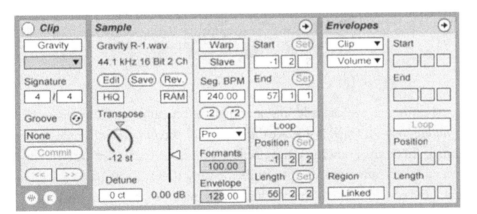

FIGURE 6.9

Gravity guitar clip warped and pitch-shifted down an octave.

Let's chop this clip up into sections or sounds and use them as individual clips in our clip slots. To do this, identify some section of the clip that you find interesting. This could be a short section where the sound fades in dramatically as a result of the *Reverse* function we applied.

43. Chop up the clip into several sections. Note that it may be easier to do this by disabling *Snap to Grid* from the *Options* menu.

While cutting up the clip, we can move a few related sections together and rejoin them into a single clip by *consolidating* them. To do this:

44. Move a few edited sections of the clip together.

45. Highlight all sections; then using *ctrl+clicking* (Mac) or *right-clicking* (Windows), select *Consolidate* from the contextual menu.

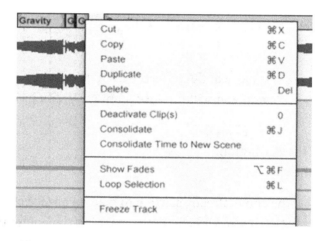

FIGURE 6.10

Contextual menu allowing highlighted clips to be consolidated into one clip.

46. Drag the consolidated clip and all other sliced clips you've made to various clip slots within *Session View*.

47. In *Session View*, rename the track to *Computer Sounds*.

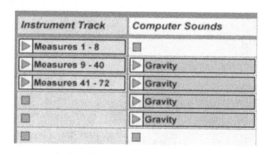

FIGURE 6.11

Processed sound clips dragged from Arrangement View to empty clips in Session View.

From here, we can add and automate effects and other processes to the *Computer Sounds* track just as we did earlier for the *Instrument Track*. As mentioned, there are numerous, novel effect processes that exist; largely what is needed is a creative approach to implementing these effects in your composition. Let's add an effect to this track and automate one of the parameters.

48. From the *Browser Sidebar* at the left, select *Audio Effects>Frequency Shifter* and drag the *Ring* preset onto the *Computer Sounds* track.

49. In *Session View*, play back one of the clips while clicking on and adjusting the *Amount* parameter.

Perhaps one idea for this clip with this effect is to sweep the *Amount* parameter from 0 Hz to 400 Hz over some period of time. We have already discussed how to draw automation curves for this effect, so let's look at an approach to *record* the automation.

50. Arm the *Computer Sounds* track for recording.
51. Highlight the clip for which you want to record automation.
52. Click the *Session Record Button* to begin recording.
53. Adjust the *Amount* parameter accordingly while recording.

FIGURE 6.12

Session Record Button used here to record automation.

54. Play back the clip to ensure that the automation operates in the way you'd like. Remember that you can fine-tune the automation by drawing in points.

Preparing the Session for Performance

111

One larger consideration is how to make this session performable. There are numerous approaches, and the approach you take largely depends on how many people you'd like to be involved in the performance process. For example, you can easily set up a microphone on stage for your performer, then have another person backstage follow the score as the performer plays and triggers the various scenes. If you enter *Key Map* or *MIDI Map*, you will see two hidden controls with an *arrow up* and an *arrow down*. These controls can be easily mapped to a MIDI foot pedal or switch that allows the performer to "step" through each of the scenes.

If you'll recall, the approach we took in the pop and rock chapter was to require only that the performer start playing back the piece from *Arrangement View* while following along with a click-track. Another option in *Session View* is to set *Follow Actions* for each of our clips. Since we have each of our clips set to a specific number of bars and beats, *Follow Actions* allow us to specify what to do at the end of those bars and beats, such as "play the next clip," "play a previous clip," and "play a random clip." Let's set each scene in our session to play in succession.

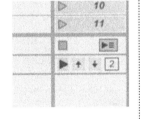

FIGURE 6.13

Two "hidden" controls allow you to step through scenes when mapped to keys or MIDI.

55. Double-click on the first clip in the *Instrument Track* to open *Clip View*.
56. In *Clip View*, click on the circled *L* to reveal the *Launch* window.

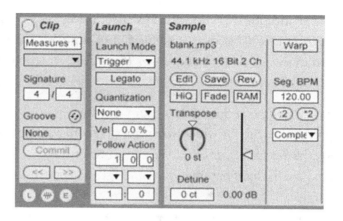

FIGURE 6.14

Launch window revealed in Clip View.

The features we're going to concern ourselves with here are the *Quantization* settings and the *Follow Actions*. The *Quantization* setting in our example is set to *Global*, meaning that this clip will infer its own setting according to what is defined at the top of the program next to the metronome. In our example, this is set to *None* because we want each clip in our track to play immediately after one other.

Here's the slightly confusing part: the end of our first clip is 9 1 1 in bars and beats, for a total of 8 full bars. Because of this, we want to set the *Follow Action* to occur *after* 8 bars. To do this, we set the *Follow Action Time* value to 8 0 0.

57. Set the *Follow Action Time* value to 8 0 0.

The next part is easy: What action do you want to take once the clip has played for 8 full bars? View the options from the first pulldown menu:

58. Click on the pulldown menu beneath the *Follow Action Time*.
59. Select *Next* so that the next clip will play following this one.
60. Click the *play* button on this clip and notice that as the *blank. mp3* clip finishes the eighth bar, it immediately jumps to the next clip slot in the track and plays it as a result of *Follow Action*.

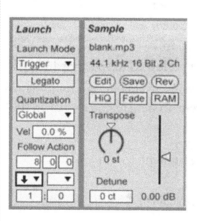

FIGURE 6.15

Follow Action set to trigger Next clip after 8 bars have played.

You may be asking yourself, "How do I set the *Follow Action* settings so that the entire *Scene* has a *Follow Action*, not just a clip?" The answer is to simply *Group* the tracks and repeat the *Follow Action* process outlined above on the *Group* folder track.

61. Highlight the tracks *Instrument Track* and *Computer Sounds*.
62. *Group* the tracks command +*G*, (Mac) or *ctrl*+*G* (Windows).

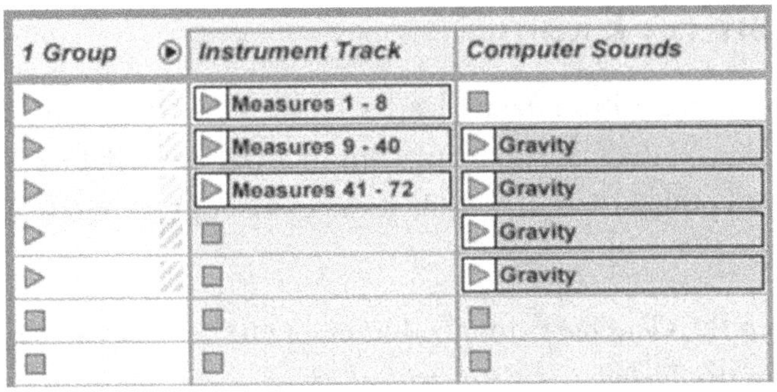

FIGURE 6.16

Tracks grouped into a Folder track.

Technically, we're just going to apply *Follow Actions* in bulk to all of the clips in the *Group*. To this extent, we should first drag the *blank* clip to any clip slots in the session that are empty. For instance, in the first 8 measures, if the *Instrument Track* has a clip, the *Computer Sounds* track should as well.

63. Drag the *blank.mp3* clip from the *Chapter Examples* folder onto any empty clip slots in this session.

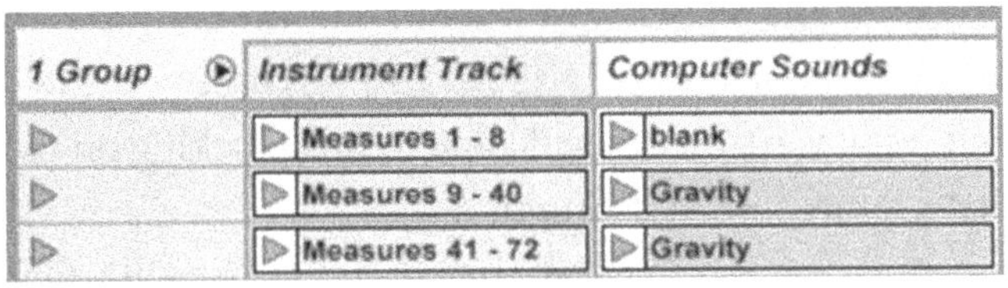

113

FIGURE 6.17

Blank.mp3 clip added to all empty slots in the composition.

Now, we can apply the *Follow Actions* to all clips in the *Group* folder track.

64. Double-click the first clip slot for the *Group* folder track.
65. Set the *Follow Action Time* to 8 0 0 and the *Follow Action* to *Next*.
66. Double-click the second clip slot for the *Group* folder track.
67. Set the *Follow Action Time* to 32 0 0 and the *Follow Action* to *Next*.
68. Click the play button on the first *Scene* on the *Master* track.

Notice that each of the first two *Scenes* plays and continues directly into the next *Scene*. The necessary steps for completing this piece are, essentially, to fill in the blanks where the *main instrument* needs some notes and the *effect automation* for both tracks needs some attention.

69. *Save* and *Close* this session. (Note that this has been included in the *Chapter Examples* folder as *Basic Piece*.)

Composition Examples

Two working composition examples have also been included in the *Chapter Examples* folder. Both deal with firing clips in novel ways. Before we begin looking at the first composition, let's look at the basic approach to firing clips using Max for Live.

> 70. From the *Chapter Examples* folder, open the session *Firing_Clips* from the *Firing_Clips Project* folder.

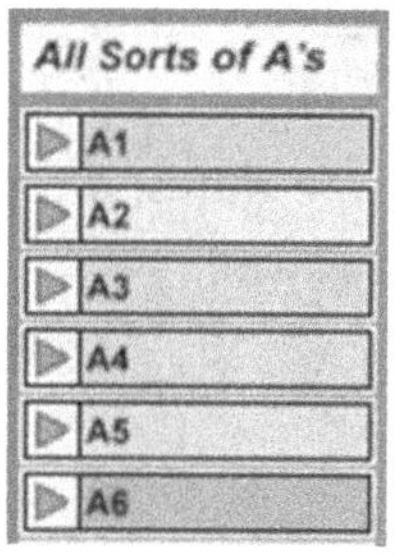

All Sorts of A's
- A1
- A2
- A3
- A4
- A5
- A6

FIGURE 6.18

The pitch A at multiple octaves in the first six clip slots of a track.

In this very simple session, we see six clips in one track. On this track is a Max for Live patch that shows the evolution of how one might fire a clip with a Max patch.

In short, even though it may look complicated, it's simple. The first segment of the Max patch, near the circled number 1, shows *live.object* receiving a *message* object with the command *call fire*. Here's the explanation: the actions you want to take on Live itself from a Max for Live patch are carried out via the *live.object*. In this case, we're telling live to *fire* something, but we haven't yet defined what to fire. Clicking on the *call fire* message in the first segment won't do anything.

In the second segment, at the circled 2, the *live.path* object receives a somewhat longer and mysterious message from a *message* box. The *message* simply reports some information about the track and clip referenced in the message: *visible_tracks 0 clip_slots 0*. This refers to the first clip (Clip 0) on the first track (Track 0). If the *message* box contained *visible_tracks 1 clip_slots 2*, it would play the third clip on the second track, but obviously this session has only one track. The information received from *live.path* informs the *live.object* of where to perform its calls.

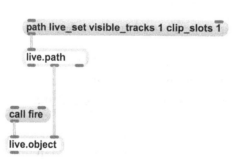

FIGURE 6.19

Basic objects for selecting a clip and firing it in Max for Live.

> 71. In *segment 2* of the M4L patch, near the circled *2*, click the *message* box **path live_set visible_tracks 0 clip_slots 0** to focus the *live.object* on *Clip 0* on *Track 0*.
>
> 72. Near the circled 3, click the *message* box *call fire* to fire this clip.

Okay, right there: that's the concept. Everything else is an accessibility improvement on this basic concept. For example, in the next segment, the *Clip* number *0* has been replaced with a *$1*, which serves a placeholder for incoming numbers. When a number is entered into the *number* object, the *message* box will use that number instead of the *$1*.

73. In segment 3, by circled number 4, click on the *number* object and enter a number between *0* and *5*.
74. Then click the *message* box **call fire** near circled number *5* to fire that numbered clip.

Simple, actually! The fourth segment dresses the patch one step further so that when you enter a number into the *number* box, it then sends a bang to the *call fire message* box via the *button* object.

75. In segment 4, by circled number *6*, click on the *number* object and enter a number between *0* and *5*.

The final segment shows one of the many user interface (UI) objects available in Max.

76. In segment 5, by circled number *7*, click on the *number graphic* to fire clips.
77. Close this session.
78. In the *Chapter Examples Folder*, open the file *Bug Music* inside of the *Bug Music Project* folder.

The *Bug Music* session is an algorithm that models some of the ways that insects are attracted to the chirping sounds of other insects. In this session, clicking the *First Chirp* button begins a pattern of *call-and-response clip firing* to simulate the chirping patterns of insects. Insects gradually synchronize their chirps to the other insects until they are in chirping in sync.

79. Click the *First Chirp* button on the *Control* track to begin this gradual quantization algorithm.

Notice that this piece really does the same process as described above: it fires clips using a Max for Live patch. This particular piece just has a more elaborate scheme for firing the clips, but the mechanics are the same.

80. Close the *Bug Music* session.

Installation for Foghorn

Let's examine an installation piece, *Installation for Foghorn*, by composer Frederick Bianchi for multiple foghorns as part of a large spatial sound design. The installation consists of 30 distributed computer-controlled foghorns, and it was designed for implementation on five islands off the coast of Mount Desert Island in Bar Harbor, Maine.

Conceptually, the installation is a large wind chime covering five miles of ground space that is achieved in Live through these processes:

- An M4L patch is used to detect the pitch and volume of acoustic wind chimes through a microphone.

- The pitches trigger the playback of clips containing just-automated envelope curves on six tracks.
  - The track that plays is determined by the pitch detected from the chime.
  - The clip that plays is determined by the volume of that pitch detected from the chime.
- The envelope curves in the clips are sent from Live using an M4L patch to an Arduino microcontroller connected to the computer. The Arduino board controls the amount of air sent to the fog-horns via servo motor valves.
- Since the chimes operate on wind, the installation is sustainable and will vary based on the amount of wind coming from Maine's coast.

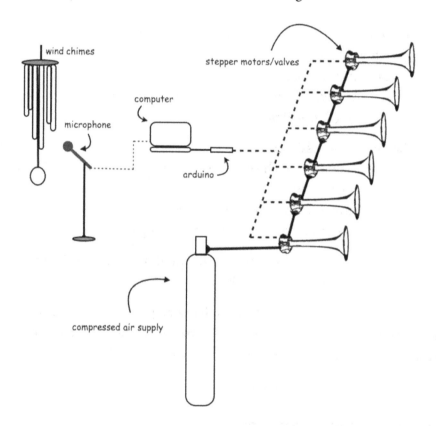

FIGURE 6.20

Concept for Bianchi's Installation for Foghorn.

81. Open the *foghorn* session in the *Foghorn Project* folder in the *Chapter Examples* folder for this chapter.

In this composition, the first track picks up the audio signal from the chimes through a microphone. An M4L patch on the track runs the signal through a narrow audio filter to detect certain pitches, and the volume that they are sounded from, for each of the chimes. It then uses the level of each chime's volume to trigger one of several clips on a track associated with that chime. Each of the tracks contains a second M4L patch that communicates with the custom Arduino microcontroller. The clips for each track control the envelope of air that is allowed to enter an airhorn placed on one of the islands. As the wind moves the chimes, the envelopes are triggered and the airhorns sound. Since you probably don't have chimes, airhorns, or Arduino-controlled motors handy, let's simulate this activity within the session.

82. Double-click the *Chimes Input* track.
83. Click the *Simulate* toggle in the M4L patch loaded in *Detail View*.

You won't hear any sound, but you should see clips firing in a pseudo-random pattern so as to simulate the tracking of pitches from the chimes through the microphone.

84. When a clip is fired, double-click on that clip to see the automated envelope for that clip.
85. Double-click on one of the *Chime* tracks to reveal the M4L that sends MIDI controller data on *MIDI Control Change message 7* from Live that is interpreted by a custom Arduino controller.

If you unlock the *Chimes Input* M4L patch, you will see the same segment of Max code as described in the two previous examples—it's the same technical approach, but an entirely different artistic implementation.

Nil for Guitar and Computer

Let's now examine a piece called *nil* for guitar and computer.

86. Open the *nil Project* folder in the *Chapter Examples* folder for this chapter.
87. Open the PDF score called *nil (2010).pdf*.

This session is structured similarly to the composition we just made:

- A guitarist plays live through a microphone coming on the *Instrument Dry* track.[1]
- The *Instrument FX* track receives the signal and applies the effect automation.
- The *Computer Parts* track contains interesting sounds made from processing a guitar recording in various ways.

In this session, a MIDI rendering of the actual guitar part has been placed into each of the *Instrument Dry* clip slots to simulate what the live performance would be like. The *Follow Actions* portion of this session has been varied to some extent: instead of *playing the next Scene* when the previous bars and beats are reached, a Max for Live patch has been created to trigger the next scene when the clip reaches its end according to minutes and seconds instead of bars

---

1. The live instrument signal is routed to its own output channel currently with volume set at *-inf*) and a separate track with effects. This allows you to add more of the dry live instrument signal if needed in the performance hall.

and beats. Instead of setting the *Follow Action* to *next* after a certain bar is reached, this M4L patch jumps to the next scene on "clip end." For many users, this is a trivial enhancement, but for some users, it's gold.

88. Open the Live session *nil*.
89. Double-click on the *Instrument Dry* track to reveal the *vj.FollowOnClipEnd* Max for Live patch.

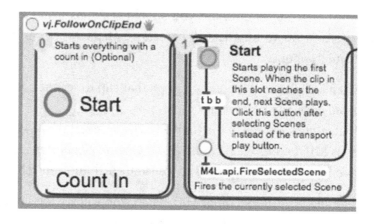

FIGURE 6.21

M4L patch allows piece to count in at tempo before firing clips.

90. Instead of clicking on the *Play* button in Live's transport, click the yellow *Start* button at the far left of this patch. Ensure that the first clip (*Clip 0*) on the *Instrument Dry* track is selected before clicking the *Start* button.

The patch will tell the performer to "wait" for 4 seconds, then it will count them in at the tempo of the piece (100 BPM). In short, the Max patch does some small tasks worth pointing out: it gets the duration in milliseconds of the clip in the currently selected slot, and after that amount of time has been played, it switches to the next scene. Simple! The actual steps have been outlined and explained in the patch itself, but here's the breakdown by section numbers 0–5:

• Section 0: Starts the M4L patch with a timed delay to give the performer time to sit down if they are the one starting the piece.
• Section 1: Gets the duration of the currently selected clip and fires the scene that it's in.
• Section 2: The clip number of the clip that is now playing is sent to the next section.
• Section 3: The start and end times of this clip (in seconds) are defined and the total duration of the clip (in seconds) is determined.
• Section 4: The seconds value is converted to milliseconds, and the next scene will be selected in that number of milliseconds—at that time, the process will restart.

- Section 5: Continually looks to see if Live is playing and, if the *Stop* button has been pressed, the previous section will not be allowed to jump to the next scene.

Though this is a little advanced for users new to Max, the data flow is clearly defined for each of the patch's sections. It's okay if you don't understand everything going on in the patch at this time. As you continue to work with Live and M4L, things will become much clearer.

As the piece plays, you can follow along with the score. Keep in mind that if you intend to start a different section of the piece, you should click the *Start* button in the patch with the intended clip on the *Instrument Dry* track highlighted.

91. Close this session.

On Your Own

Create or finish an electroacoustic piece similar to the one we began composing at the beginning of this chapter. Consider aspects about the composition itself including form, tempo, tonality, mood, and more. Make considerations for texture, dynamics, and instrumentation for both the acoustic instruments and the digitally controlled elements of your composition.

Remember:
- While *Warping* clips, strange sounds known as *artifacts* may appear while using less-CPU-intensive algorithms.
- Click the *Session Record Button* to begin recording.
- *Follow Actions* allow us to specify what actions to do at specific bars and beats.
- Set the *Follow Action Time* to the number of bars you want to play your clip.

7

Modern Hip-Hop and Trap Music

Hip-hop has humble roots in the remix—the appropriation of a loop from a preexisting song to use as the basis of a new (usually simpler) backing track for a rapper. As hip-hop evolved through various trends and production techniques, sampling slowly gave way to original beatmaking and production. Sampling as a production method was highly popularized and refined by West Coast producers such as Dr. Dre in the 1990s and 2000s, and it was perfected by East Coast producers such as Kanye West in the 2000s and beyond. However, in some circles the utilization of resampled material became problematic due to either high royalty fees and occasional lawsuits or the fact that many of the catchiest tracks had already been used in other productions. The hip-hop scene was in need of some originality; enter the trap producers.

The term *trap music* originates from the release of rapper T.I.'s 2003 album *Trap Muzik*. The label was meant to describe the socioeconomic "trap" of modern street culture, featuring songs about drugs, thug life, and living under the assumption that one could never escape the trap. The album musically featured many of the emerging tropes of "dirty South" production, including dry-crack snares, fast rolling hi-hats, and generally minimal production, especially on verse sections. Unlike the concurrent "hyphy" rap movement from the West Coast, the tempos in dirty South production are generally slower and leave more room for the complexity that will eventually follow.

Trap-style production, an evolution of the dirty South style, was continued mostly by producers of rappers such as Rick Ross. It eschewed samples in favor of melodic hooks that used orchestral (or cheaply synthesized orchestral) sounds that might have been imagined as the soundtrack to an unreleased action movie. These synths were then combined with aggressive beats, using very loud sub kicks and an absurdly busy style of high-frequency cymbal patterns.

In the early 2010s, underground trap producers began performing original instrumentals without rappers, instead substituting either sampled/distorted vocals or "one shot" shouts and repeating catchphrases. Also, these producers (performing mainly at clubs used to hosting live house and dubstep DJs) began to integrate elements of other electronic dance styles into their songs, such as harsh synthesizers and buildup/drop sections. In our example, we will recreate a typical trap-style instrumental, with a bit of a buildup and plenty of the common tropes found in these producers' works.

Suggested Listening

Search for instrumentals if you prefer not to hear lots of profanity:

Rick Ross (produced by Lex Luger): "MC Hammer"
Rick Ross (produced by J.U.S.T.I.C.E. League): "I'm Not A Star"
Waka Flocka Flame: "Hard in Da Paint"
Just Blaze x Baauer: "Higher"
Nero: "Won't You (Be There) (Baauer Remix)"
Major Lazer: "Original Don (Flosstradamus Remix)"
Dillon Francis: "Bootleg Fireworks (The Rebirth)"

Artist Profile: Just Blaze

Justin Smith, a.k.a. Just Blaze, has been producing mainstream hip-hop albums since 1999 for the likes of Jay-Z, Eminem, and Rick Ross. His production technique involves creating a large number of stems (premade standalone tracks that play for a full song duration), running them through an Ableton Live *Session View*, and then putting them back into Pro Tools for mastering.

Like many hip-hop producers, he began producing beats on an Akai MPC sampler but then moved to standalone computer software to produce beats. Interestingly, he does almost all of his drum work freehand, that is, without quantization. His discography is unique as it spans the trend from mostly sampled hip-hop production to the more modern, mostly synthesized production style shown in this tutorial.

Drum Patterns

For drums we will begin with a simple 808-inspired rack, but modify it to do pitched snare rolls. We will also be exploring the influence of traditional afro-cuban rhythms on modern day hip-hop.

1. In the extreme upper left of the Live window, set the song tempo to 75 BPM.
2. From your Browser, choose *Drums*, and search for *Kit-Core 808*. Drag this *Drum Rack* into your set.
3. In the upper right of the Live window, click the *pencil* icon to change to *draw mode*.
4. Double-click a blank clip slot to create a new MIDI clip. Set the length to 2.0.0.
5. Right-click in the *MIDI editing panel* and select *1/4* under *Fixed Grid*.
6. Draw in *claps* on beats 2 and 4 of both measures.
7. The kick drum should have a pattern similar to a 3–2 clave pattern often found in bossa nova and other Latin styles of music. Feel free to modify the pattern for optimum groove potential.
8. Draw Hi-Hat notes in a general sixteenth note pattern, but add lots of rolls. The idea is the fill up the empty space between the kicks and claps. (Switch to the thirty-second note grid) and fast triplets (switch to triplet grid at various note lengths).
9. Draw syncopated accent notes on the *Snare line*. Do not create a traditional snare pattern—try to avoid beats 2/4 and try to stay out of the way of the big beats. Feel free to switch to *Triplet grid*, but do not write anything faster than sixteenth notes on the snare part.

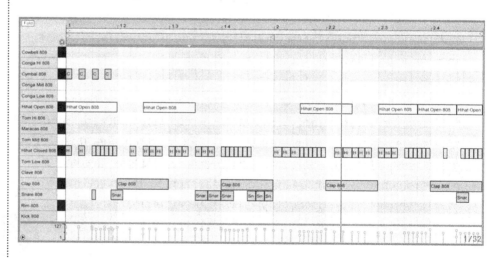

FIGURE 7.1

Trap-style beat on stock 808-based kit—note how the snare acts as ornamentation with the Clap providing backbeats and frequent use of Triplet grid.

Now that we have a simple drum pattern, we will create the pitch-bending snare part often found in modern hip-hop and trap music using the *Clip Automation panel*.

10. Double-click the drum clip.
11. Click the small *E* icon in the lower left of the clip panel to reveal *Clip Automation* parameters.
12. Under *Envelopes* choose the snare sound from the *Drum Rack*. Set the upper box to *Kit-Core 808*. Set the lower box to *Pitch*.
13. Using the *pencil tool*, draw in variations to the pitch of the snare part. You can make a clear pattern, such as rising pitch, or simply draw a random curve and listen to the results. Since the snare is not the primary backbeat, this part is effective in its unstable sound.

Now we will do some quick variations before moving on to other parts.

14. Copy and paste the *drum pattern* a few times on the *Drum Rack* track.
15. Make different versions of the part by subtracting parts. For instance, make one with no kick drum, or one with an extra open hi-hat part. As we make the rest of the song, feel free to make more variations of the drum pattern as is appropriate for your track.
16. Make at least one variation that uses the kick rhythms on the *Snare line* and has no kick part.
17. Apply a *Compressor* to the *Drum Rack* track. Set the ratio as *inf:1* and the *Threshold* at -14.5 dB.
18. Apply a *Limiter* to the *Drum Rack* track.
19. Set the *A Send* knob on the *Drum Rack* to about 60% to apply reverb.

FIGURE 7.2

Variation clips on main drum track—all are based on the original "full" clip made at the beginning of the chapter.

Sub Kicks and Bass Lines

The sub kick is very important in trap music, and it mirrors the kick drum part while adding a bit of tonal information to the song.

20. In your Browser, click *Instruments*, then *Operator*.
21. Search for *Sub2*. You should see the result *Sub2 Sine Bass.adv*.
22. Drag this instrument into your set.
23. Copy the clip you made on the *Drum Rack*.
24. Paste the clip on the *Sub2* track.
25. Double-click the clip you just pasted to view it in the *MIDI editing panel*.

26. Erase every note except for those on the *C1 line*. This will leave only the rhythm from the kick drum we made in steps 1–19.

27. Select the remaining notes and click the *Legato* button. This will ensure the long sine wave plays at full duration.

28. Click the *Dupl. Loop* button. Now the clip length is 4.0.0, which leaves more room to create a logical bass line that will not be too repetitive.

29. Change the pitch of some notes on the bass line. For most hip-hop bass lines, perfect fifths and minor thirds work well, as do minor seconds. Leave all beat 1 notes on *C1*.

30. Erase some notes. The sub bass should not simply ride atop the kick drum, but should support it as an embellishment. Since the sub usually does not play alone, it does not have to have all the rhythmic information as the drum part. Leaving space also has the benefit of not overpowering the listener with hard sine bass for 100% of the loop. Try playing both parts together and hearing which beats sound better silent. The example leaves an entire measure empty and does not sound lacking in bass.

31. Holding your *shift* key, select both the *Drum Rack* and *Sub2* tracks.

32. Right-click the title of one track and select *Group*.

33. Rename the new group to *Drums*.

34. In your Browser, change to *Audio Effects*.

35. Apply an *EQ Eight* to the new *Drums* group.

36. In *EQ Eight*, change the filter type above *filter #6* (simply labeled 6) to the *high shelf* setting.

37. Lower the frequency, and boost the highs by about 5 dB.

38. Apply a *Glue Compressor* to the *Drums* group, placed after *EQ Eight*.

39. Set the *Threshold* to -11.0 dB and the *Makeup* to 6.00 dB.

40. Turn on the *Soft* button by the *Clip* label. This applies a gentle limiter to the group.

FIGURE 7.3

The Sub2 Sine track clip playing a reduction of the kick drum pattern, placed on a few strategic scale degrees for this song.

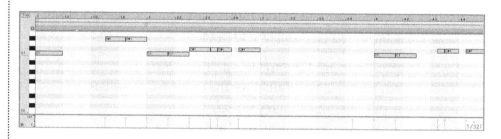

Buildup Patterns

We will make a sound unique to trap music, as well as a typical accelerating drum pattern to accompany it. This particular sound type is often attributed to the producer Lex Luger and is found in almost all of his productions. First, we need to find a sample of either a long turntable scratch or the related winding-down sound that can be made on reel-to-reel tape machines. For the purposes of this tutorial, the sample is provided in the example set.

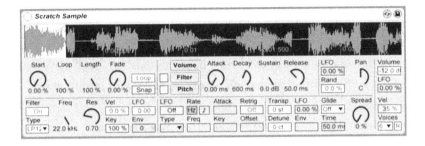

FIGURE 7.4

Sample of record scratching loaded into Simpler.

41. In your Browser, click *Instruments* and locate *Simpler*.
42. Drag *Simpler* into a blank area of your set.
43. Drag the scratch sample into the *Simpler* region marked *Drop Sample Here*.
44. Adjust the end-point marker on the *waveform* to before the -0:00:500 mark—this is a bit before the first silent gap in the waveform.
45. Click the *Loop* button.
46. Click the *On* button under *Filter*.
47. Double-click a blank clip slot on the *Scratch Sample* track.
48. Set the clip length to 2.0.0.
49. In the *MIDI editing* box, draw a *C3* note at full velocity that lasts the duration of the clip.
50. Click the small *E* to reveal clip automation parameters.
51. Under the *Envelopes* label, set the first box to *Scratch Sample*.
52. Set the second box to *Transpose*.
53. On the pink line overlaid on the *MIDI clip*, double-click to make dots at the beginning and end of the clip.
54. Drag the first dot to *-12*.
55. Drag the second dot to *+12*.
56. Change the second box to *Filter Freq*.
57. Double-click to make *dots* at the beginning and end of the pink line on the clip.
58. Drag the first dot all the way down to 30 Hz. Leave the second dot alone.

125

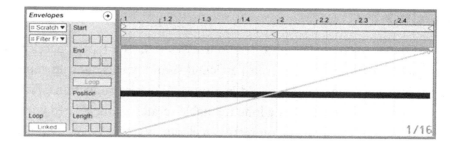

FIGURE 7.5

Long note clip on Simpler combined with automation of Simpler's Filter Frequency to create a filter sweep, appropriate for a buildup scene.

We now have an appropriate buildup sound effect. Now we will make an accompanying drum part. This does not need to be very elaborate, but rather a supplement to the sampled scratch track.

59. On the *Drum Rack* track, duplicate an existing "full" clip, that is, a clip with all groove elements present (kick, snare, hats, etc.).
60. Delete the notes on the *snare drum* and *clap* rows.
61. Highlight all notes on the *kick drum row*.
62. Using the *arrow* key, move them up to the *snare drum row*.
63. On the *clap row*, draw eighth notes for the first half of the clip and sixteenth notes for the second half of the clip.

Chord Sequences

We will need to build some internal consistency to the track's tonal language. To this end we will use MIDI plug-ins to manage the chords we program on the new melodic tracks. We will also be choosing a background supportive part to establish an underlying simple chord structure for each scene. Feel free to choose a different pad-style synth instrument when following this section.

64. In your Browser, click *Instruments*.
65. Click the *disclosure triangle* next to *Instrument Rack*.
66. Type *sucker* in the search bar. Drag the highlighted *Sucker Delay* instrument into your set.
67. Click *MIDI Effects*.
68. Choose *Chord* and drag it onto your *Sucker Delays* track.
69. Set the following *Shift*s in the *Chord* effect: *Shift 1* = +3 st, *Shift 2* = +7 st, *Shift 3* = +12 st.
70. From *MIDI effects,* drag *Arpeggiator* into the device chain between *Chord* and *Sucker Delays*.
71. Set the *Rate* knob on *Arpeggiator* to 1/32.
72. Set the *Steps* knob to 2.
73. Set the *Style* to *Chord Trigger*.

74. Click a circle next to any clip slot on *Sucker Lead*. Record yourself hitting a C4 randomly. Hit stop after about two measures.

75. Set the *A Send* dial to about 75% to add reverb.

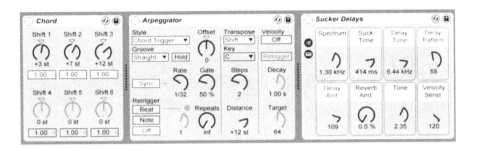

FIGURE 7.6

Device chain combining a major chord with Arpeggiator for quick "filler" treble synth track.

This clip can play throughout the track now, acting either as a soft pad background or tonal support for the stabs we will write in the next step.

Stabs

One possible element to add to trap production is the use of sampled orchestral instruments. Often the desired effect is to impart a cinematic feel to the music, and in our case we will be using sampled trombones and strings. Unlike actual cinematic music, these instruments play patterns similar to drum parts—very simple melodies with syncopated patterns using almost the same rhythms from the kick drum and sub bass parts.

76. In the Browser, click *Instruments*.

77. Disclose the *Instrument Rack* category.

78. Disclose the *Strings* category inside *Instrument Rack*.

79. Find *Strings Ensemble Staccato*. Drag this instrument into a blank area of your set.

80. In the Browser, change to *MIDI effects*.

81. Find *Chord*. Drag it onto the *Strings Ensemble* track.

82. Set the Shifts on *Chord* accordingly: *Shift 1= +3 st, Shift 2 = +7 st, Shift 3 = +12 st, Shift 4 =-12 st, Shift 5 = -5 st, Shift 6 = -9 st.* Note that this creates a seven-note minor chord when played.

83. Copy one of the full clips from *Drum Rack* and paste it onto the *Strings Ensemble* track.

84. Delete all notes in this clip except for the *C1 row*.

85. Select all notes on the *C1 row*.

86. Using the *arrow* keys, move them up to the *C4 row*.

87. Change a few of the notes to *C#4* (or another note of your choosing—keep it simple and in key).

127

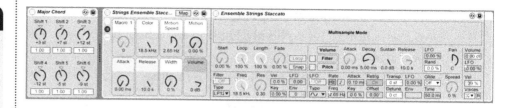

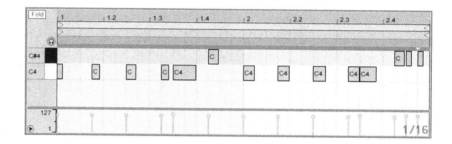

This part can now be used wherever you would like. Now we will make a similar option using a trombone instrument.

88. In the Browser, click *Instruments*.
89. Disclose the *Instrument Rack* category.
90. Disclose the *Brass* category inside *Instrument Rack*.
91. Find *Trombone Section Staccato*. Drag this instrument into a blank area of your set.
92. Copy a clip from the *Sub2 Sine* track and paste it onto the *Trombone* track.
93. Add notes on the existing note rows to complete rhythms throughout the clip—it should sound similar, but more complete than the actual *Sub2* clips.
94. Set the *A Send* dial to about 50% to add reverb.

Lasers

Of course we need lasers. The iconic *Harlem Shake*, a popular Internet fad from 2012, made the use of dry "zapping" sounds prevalent in many examples of trap and modern hip-hop. These can give a hip-hop track a futuristic feel, and they are easy to make as well.

95. In your Browser, click *Instruments* and find *Operator* (*Operator* appears to be a folder, but can also be dragged into the set as a default "blank" instrument).
96. Drag *Operator* into a blank area of your set.
97. Set the *Wave* type to *Saw D* to make a basic sawtooth wave.
98. Click the box next to the *Pitch Env* dial.
99. Set the *Pitch Env* dial to -22%.

100. Set the *Decay* to 800 ms.
101. Double-click in a blank clip slot on the *Operator* track to create a blank MIDI clip.
102. Using a *C3* and *C4*, record a syncopated pattern different from those found in the *Kick* and *Sub2* parts.
103. After recording, click in the *MIDI editing* box; hit *cmd-A* to select all and *cmd-U* to quantize the recording.
104. Click the *pencil* icon in the top right of the Live window.
105. Right-click in the *MIDI editing* box—set the *Adaptive Grid* to *Narrowest.*
106. Draw in short pickup notes before some of the longer notes you recorded to give your recording a stuttering sound.
107. Feel free to move a few notes to other lanes, but again keep the melody very simple.

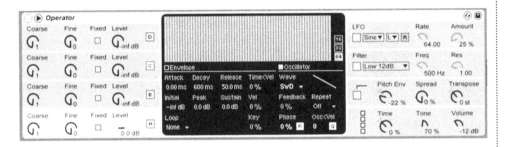

FIGURE 7.9

Operator set to produce "laser" sounds by combining a sawtooth wave with a pitch-bending envelope (on right under Pitch Env).

129

Now we have all the instrumental ingredients for a trap tune. Next we will distort some vocal shouts to finish off the track setup.

Chipmunk Vocals and Shouts

This section requires some vocal material, either sampled from another song or self-recorded. For this tutorial, you can use the samples provided in the example. When choosing your own vocal samples, try to avoid whole lyrics and instead prefer either single phrases or simple *hype tracks* (Waka Flocka Flame does many hype tracks that work very well for sampling, many of which consist of him saying the word "pow" continuously for several minutes).

108. Drag a vocal sample onto a blank area in your set.
109. Using the *Transpose* control, adjust the pitch of the clip—if the clip was already out of tune with the song, use this opportunity to also put it in tune using your ears.
110. Click *Audio Effects* in the Browser.
111. Click the *triangle* next to *Vocoder* to reveal its presets.
112. Find *Formant -5* and *Formant +5.*
113. Try one of these two on your voice track—depending on the sample, it may sound good or not.

114. Try taking a lowered sample and adding the *+5 formant*, or vice versa.
115. Trigger or loop the vocal samples as needed throughout your track.

If you decide you would like to be able to trigger a sample manually without quantizing or looping, do the following:

116. Double-click the clip.
117. Click the small *L* in the lower left of the device panel.
118. Under the *Launch* parameters, set *Quantization* to *None*.
119. Turn *Warp* off.

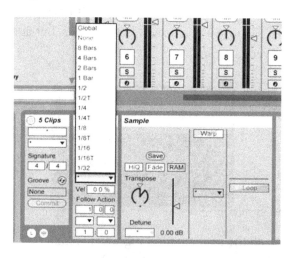

With multiple clips selected, setting trigger quantization to None will allow free, arrhythmic triggering of the vocal shouts.

130

It can be desirable to create a space in your *Session View* for many shouts and sound effects and use an external piece of hardware like a Novation Launchpad or Push to trigger these un-quantized samples. You can also assign them to MIDI notes or Keystrokes as well using the programming modes in the upper right of the window.

Keystrokes assigned to trigger different audio clips.

120. Click the *MIDI* or *KEY* button in the upper right of the Live window—everything will turn blue (or orange for *KEY* mode).
121. Click the clip you want to trigger.
122. Play the *note* or *drum pad* (or typing keys) on your MIDI device you want to use.
123. A numbered indicator should appear on the clip (if it doesn't, look in your *Preferences* and be sure that the *Remote* setting is turned on for your MIDI device).
124. Click the *MIDI* or *KEY* button to exit assignment mode.

Many trap-style productions have meme-like phrases used as shouts that reappear in many tracks, sometimes for the purpose of identifying the producer. Many Lex Luger songs begin with a vocal shout of a woman saying his name. Likewise many Rick Ross tunes begin with an oft-reused sample of a woman saying "Maybach Music." In independent trap circles, a common shout is a radio DJ saying, "Damn son, where'd ya find this?" It is not necessary to use these exact samples, but being aware of their use is an inherent part of trap culture.

Composition Examples

In the example set the scenes are structured like this:

Scene 1:	Intro	No kick drum, strings with backing synth
Scene 2:	Short build	Scratch sample, accelerating drums, strings, and chipmunk shout
Scene 3:	Drop 1	Add kicks, sub bass, and trombone
Scene 4:		Add shout and strings, remove trombones
Scene 5:	Break	Just trombones, synth, and shouts
Scene 6:	Strings	Strings, no kick or sub, shouts
Scene 7:		Add trombone
Scene 8:	Build	Scratch sample, accelerating drums, strings, and "Woo"
Scene 9:	Drop 2	Full drums, sub bass, lasers, "Damn son"

Drums	2 Kit-Core	3 Sub2 Sine	Not Drums	5 Scratch Sa	6 Trombone	7 Sucker Del	LASER	9 Strings En	Shouts		Master
						2 7-Sucker	○	1 9-Strings			Intro
	No Kick						○	1 9-Strings	Sophie Lyric 05		Build
	Snare build			▶			○				Drop 1
	Full dry	▶			1 5-Trombo		○				2
	Full dry						○	Full dry	Shana Improv 0		Break
					1 5-Trombo	2 7-Sucker	○				Strings
	No kick dry				1 5-Trombo	2 7-Sucker	○	1 9-Strings	Tyson Improv 1		3
	No kick dry				1 5-Trombo	2 7-Sucker	○	1 9-Strings	Tyson Lyric 13		Build
	Snare build			▶		2 7-Sucker	○	1 9-Strings			Drop 2
	Full dry	▶					1 8-Operato				4
							1 8-Operato				5
							○		DAMN SON! WH		6
							○				7
							○				8

FIGURE 7.12

Full Session View and track groupings, showing the three major stems (drums, non-drums and vocals).

When recording to Arrangement View, it is important to remember where the builds fit into typical four-bar phrases. Since they are two-bar scenes, they need to be triggered during measure 2 of a four-bar phrase (or measure 6 of an eight-bar phrase).

131

On Your Own

Listen to various hip-hop styles made by producers old and new. Try creating tunes in those styles. As you create, ask:

- Which producers seems to use synths more than samples?
- How loud should the kick and sub bass be? Try playing your tracks in various settings, such as live PA systems or hip-hop headphones—does it still sound appropriate?
- How could a hip-hop track be performed live using Session View? Try using your arrangement, selecting a portion, and using the right-click option *Consolidate time to new scene* to create performable segments.
- If possible, find an actual rapper to perform original material over your beats. Feedback from a vocalist may be helpful in determining the right groove.

Notice the workflow we have established here; starting in Session View, recording to Arrangement View, and possibly bouncing back to Session View for performance. You will notice most of the examples in this book are developed in this manner.

In Live

Review the Live documentation on *Creating Beats* from the *Help* menu.

House Music

House music is an essential loop-based dance music style. While it has been present in underground circles since the 1980s, its influence today is decidedly mainstream.

In this chapter we will construct the essential elements of house music, starting with typical drum patterns associated with the genre. We'll then go on to produce a number of options for pad and bass sounds. We will also learn about the signature ducking sound achieved in house music through the use of sidechain compression.

Suggested Listening

Moby: "Go"
Paul Oakenfold: "Ready, Steady, Go"
Benny Benassi: "Satisfaction"
Dada Life: "Happy Violence"
Swedish House Mafia: "Antidote"
Daft Punk: "One More Time"

Artist Profile: Daft Punk

Guy-Manuel de Homem-Christo and Thomas Bangalter are the two notoriously secretive producers behind the robot masks of their stage act, Daft Punk. Though initially just a blip on the French house scene, the two developed an extremely unique stage show involving a gigantic pyramid, and they are rarely seen publicly without their signature robot masks. They are considered one of the first truly marketable mainstream electronic music acts.

Their production method has evolved quite a bit over the years, and Ableton is used heavily in their preproduction process. They will typically improvise on analog synths in their studio, using Live's *Session View* and looped recording ability to lay down grooves. They will then bounce these tracks between various DAWs and hardware-effect units to nail down the sound they are trying to create.

Kick Drum and Essential Elements

There are two key elements of any song deserving of the "house music" label: a tempo of 120–140 BPM and a constant kick drum rhythm. In fact, the kick drum element is arguably the most essential element of house music. The reason behind this may lie in the origins of house—DJs accustomed to playing hip-hop or pop records experimented with synchronizing a drum machine to their vinyl loops. The drum machine provided a constant beat, allowing easier hearing of the tempo as well as a more forgiving situation if the vinyl on the live platters was out of sync for a bit. It is unclear if the constant kick trope grew out of how it could energize a crowded dance floor or simply give DJs a stronger pulse with which to beatmatch, but the sound is idiomatic of house and is unmistakable.

1. In your Library, click *Drums*.
2. In the *search* box, type *909*.
3. Drag *Kit-Core 909.adg* into a blank area of your set.
4. Click the *X* in the *search* box.
5. At the top of the list, select the blank *Drum Rack* device and also drag it into a blank area of your set.
6. In your Library, click *All Results*.
7. In the *search* box, type *HB Kick*.
8. Choose *HB_Kick_01.aif* and drag it onto the *C1* box of your blank *Drum Rack*.
9. Holding the *shift* key, select both tracks by clicking their titles.
10. Right-click one of the titles and choose *Group Tracks*.

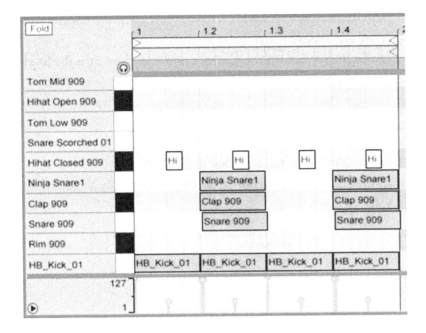

Typical house drum pattern; note the subtle offset to "fatten" the snare sound.

We now have two Drum Racks—one based on the Roland TR-909 drum machine (a house music production staple for decades) and a heavier kick drum with more low-end. The layering of these two will give our track more power, and a separate kick track will make sidechain ducking easier in later steps.

Electro-Bass Synth

Now we will create a typical electro-house synth instrument. To save some time and processing power, we will make this synth effectively double its sound on multiple oscillators even though the instrument resides on one track. We will accomplish this by exploring the routing options within *Operator*. *Operator* is a powerful FM and additive synthesizer that uses a unique system to establish routes between four oscillators. Any of the four oscillators within *Operator* can exist as its own separate sound generator or as an effect to another oscillator.

Now we are ready to make our instrument:

11. In your Library, click *Instruments*.
12. Choose *Operator* and drag it into a blank area of your *set* (outside the *drums group*) .
13. Click the routing icon in *Operator* (four vertical boxes located to the left of the *Time* knob in the lower right of *Operator*—it looks somewhat like a piece from Tetris).
14. You will see a panel with several shapes made of four squares each. These are signal routes. Choose the route on the far right—four horizontal boxes.
15. On *Oscillator A*, turn the *Coarse* knob to *0.5* (this will play an octave below any note you play).

135

16. Change *Oscillator A's Wave* to *SwD* (Sawtooth wave with unfiltered overtones).

17. On *Oscillator B*, turn the *Coarse* knob to *3*, then turn the level all the way up to *0.0 dB*.

18. Change *Oscillator B's Wave* to *Sw64* (Sawtooth wave with lots of overtones, but not all).

19. Turn on the box next to the *Pitch Env* knob.

20. Set the *Pitch Env* dial up to about 50%.

21. In the black center part of *Operator*, locate *Decay* and change its value to *600 ms*.

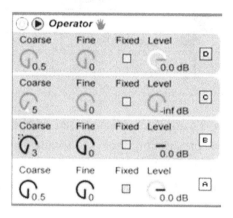

FIGURE 8.2

Operator settings for house-bass instrument.

136

The instrument now exists and is playable. We will now supply some note matter to the track to allow us to write a bass line. Instead of playing a melody on this, we will cause a melody to emerge by automating *Operator's Coarse* dials (thus changing the pitch).

22. Double-click in the first clip slot on your *Operator* track to make a new clip.

23. Set the clip length to *2.0.0* (two measures).

24. Draw a full-clip-length *C1 note* at full velocity (from the beginning of the clip through the end).

25. Click the *E* in the lower-left-hand corner of the clip detail pane to reveal automations.

26. Under *Envelopes* locate two pulldown boxes.

27. Change the top box to *Operator*.

28. Change the lower box to *Osc-B Coarse Frequency*.
29. Using either the pencil tool, or by double-clicking, add some points to the automation line for the *Osc-B Coarse Frequency* parameter.
30. Holding the *option* key, drag some of the ramps on the automation line to create curved sections—in playback these will sound like pitch bends.
31. Play back the clip, and continually adjust this breakpoint view until you hear a pattern you like.

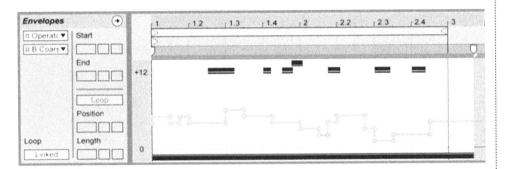

FIGURE 8.3

Clip Automation for the A-Coarse Frequency, creating a rhythmic sequence effect.

In the included example, there is also a synth pad track next to the bass line. Feel free to improvise a short synth pattern, or simply record a single chord pattern loop when making the MIDI loop for this part.

32. In your Browser, click *Instrument* and locate *Instrument Rack*.
33. Click the disclosure triangle to open the *Instrument Rack* presets.
34. Locate *Synth Lead* and open this folder.
35. Select *10 Saws Lead* and drag it into a blank area of your track.
36. In your Browser, click *MIDI Effects* and locate *Chord*.
37. Open *Chord* and choose *Major Chord*, then drag it onto the *10 Saws Lead* track.
38. Double-click a blank clip slot on the *10 Saws Lead* track.
39. Change the length of the new clip to *4.0.0* (four measures).
40. Record a simple 2–3 note line using the nondiatonic chords this instrument now produces.
41. Add more *Saw*-based tracks or pads as needed.

137

Setting Up Mix Groups and Sidechain Ducking

Now we will start to make our mix sound very active by adding a sidechain ducking effect.

42. Right-click the *Operator* track, and select *Group Tracks*.
43. Select the new group, press *command-R*, and name it *Synths*.
44. In your Browser, click *Audio Effects* and locate *Compressor*.
45. Drag *Compressor* onto the *Synths* group.
46. In *Compressor*, locate the *triangle* button in the upper left of the device and press it to reveal *sidechain controls*.
47. Click the *Sidechain* button.
48. In the box located under *Audio From*, select *Drum Rack*.
49. In the box under that select *Kit 909 Classic | HB Kick 01 – Post Mixer*.
50. Set the *Gain* to around 10 dB.
51. Set the *Ratio* to inf :1.
52. Set the *Threshold* to around -16 dB.
53. Listen to a drum loop and your synth loop play simultaneously—the synths should duck in volume every time the kick drum hits.

FIGURE 8.4

Compressor on synths group set to Sidechain from the Kick Drum located on the Drum Rack. Note the increased gain on the left and the low Threshold to ensure ducking on every kick.

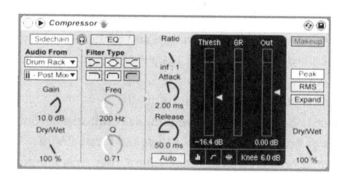

House Subgenres around the World

At this point we have made the elements of a modern house tune. Since house can be broadly defined as any music at around 130 BPM with a constant kick pattern, what constitutes the different subgenres of house? Here is a handy geographic guide to house music subgenres by region:

Subgenre	Region	Traits	Artist Example
Dutch house	Netherlands	Snare forms a loose soca pattern, heavy bass synths	Afrojack
Electro-house	United States	Aggressive synths, form elements from progressive house and drum and bass	Dada Life
French house	France	Continuous, lacking a strong form, heavy use of filters to distinguish sections	Daft Punk
Moombahton	United States	Dutch house slowed to reggae tempo (100 BPM), accidentally invented by Dave Nada when assigned to DJ the wrong party	Diplo
Deep house	United Kingdom	Continuous sequences, downtempo, chromatic sequenced chords (think patterns made up of all major chords, rather than diatonic)	Mark Farina
Progressive house	United Kingdom/ Sweden	Stricter buildup to drop form elements, like stretched-out trance, sometimes without snare drum	Swedish House Mafia
Acid house	United Kingdom/ United States	House with lots of TB-303 squelchy bass lines	808 State
Trance	Germany	Faster, with longer loops and strong, emotional melodic lines, trance-gates, supersaw synths	Paul Oakenfold
Techno	United States	Faster than house, with less strict kick patterns	Cybotron

Form and Arrangement

House music does not have an inherent form specific to the genre, mainly due to the broad definition of house music. That being said, many house tracks have two or more different groove sections, that is, pairings of synths, drum and bass parts, and most tracks have some internal consistency with energy-level control. For example, a track may start with a general energy-level groove, with most tracks playing, then cut a large amount of instruments such as drums for a time, gradually bringing them back in to increase the energy level. Sometimes this takes the form of a buildup section, other times it simply allows the track to change directions without an extreme dynamic change.

In our example, we move between two higher energy sections with a long drumless build section, composed of six scenes. Using more scenes to accomplish a build takes more time, but it allows many changes over time and sounds more dynamic than a static 8-bar buildup.

54. Organize your clips into logical scenes, with different sections for your song.
55. When your scenes make sense, hit the *global record* button, and record your song into *Arrangement View*.

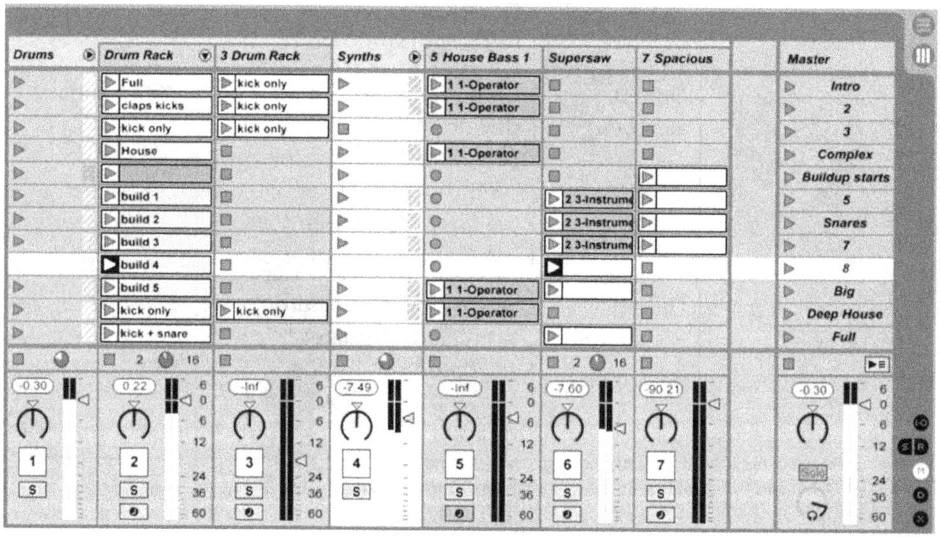

FIGURE 8.5

Scenes and track groups organized and ready for recording to Arrangement View.

On Your Own

House is sometimes used as an umbrella term for dozens of subgenres from various geographic regions and eras.

- Try to recreate the house style of a specific artist by analyzing how he/she made the staple devices of the genre.
- How might a visual display typical of a live house performance be achieved? How would it synchronize to the music, especially if the music is being triggered in Session View?
- How can the house tropes explored here be exploited in a way that no one has done before?
- How might vocals be incorporated into a house track?
- For the EDM enthusiasts: What makes house different from trance or techno? Is there an inherent difference?

Realize that anytime the correct tempo and kick drum pattern is used, a house influence is present. Try using this in tracks as a way to add energy and groove. You can also try using the sidechaining technique in genres outside of house music as a general purpose ducking technique.

In Live

Review the Live documentation on *Creating Beats* from the *Help* menu.

141

Breakbeat/Drum and Bass

B reakbeat, at its heart, relies on the ability to easily sample, deconstruct, and reorganize a drum beat. The technology to play back audio in this creative way did not exist until the 1980s. With the advent of the Akai S-series hardware sampler, musicians were able to record or import an audio loop such as a drum beat. Using standard keyboards or MIDI drum pads, they were then able to play back the audio loop in interesting ways. The tempo and pitch could be changed quickly and at will, and the waveform could be shuffled and scrambled in any way the performer chose.

DJs accustomed to looping drum beats by playing loops from two record platters (with little flexibility outside of slight speed and pitch adjustments and, of course, scratching) soon learned to use samplers to produce more interesting drum loops. The name of this subgenre, breakbeat, comes from the "break" solos played by drummers in the Funk and Motown eras.

Suggested Listening

Goldie: "Inner City Life"

Roni Size/Reprazent: "Brown Paper Bag"

LTJ Bukem: "Horizons"

Andy C.: "Roll On"

Renegade (Kevin Saunderson): "Terrorist" (an early example of the Reese Bass)

142

Artist Profile: Goldie (part one)

Clifford Price, better known by his stage name Goldie, began his artistic career as a graffiti artist in the United Kingdom. In the early 90s, he began creating breakbeat music using the Akai samplers of the day combined with live record loops and samples. His song "Inner City Life" appeared on the UK Singles chart in 1995, marking the first mainstream exposure to drum and bass, while "Timeless," a 21-minute opus of the genre, provided the first "serious" drum and bass track.

His production method typically involves hardware samplers playing into computer recording software, including Ableton Live, although he insists the method it uses to warp samples is "too f*** easy."[1]

Creating a Sampled Loop

To sample breakbeat in Live, we need to first procure a Funk track with a clean break. We'll pretend ours is from a well-known song by a cape-wearing, religious father-figure for the music in question.

1. In the chapter examples folder, open the file *Creating a Loop* within the chapter 9 folder.
2. Ensure that the session is in *Arrangement View*.
3. Locate the spike in the song's waveform that represents *Beat 1* of the drum loop at 4:22 seconds in.

It's okay if the downbeat of the loop contains overlapping release notes from other instruments on the recording; we can get rid of that later.

We will need to adjust the timeline so that the beginning of the clip starts on the downbeat we identified in the previous step. To do so, we will place a warp marker on this downbeat.

4. Double-click directly above the waveform, but below the timeline numbers to add a warp marker for that transient.
5. Right-click the warp marker and, from the long list of options that pop up, choose *Set 1.1.1 Here*.

Musical material before this beat will still exist, but it will be marked by negative numbers on the timeline since they occur before the warp marker 1.1.1.

1. Scarth, G. *Goldie*. Attack Magazine. April 17, 2013. *http://attackmagazine.com/features/interview/goldie*. Retrieved on August 23, 2014.

To turn this clip into a loop, we'll need to determine the tempo of the original sample and set Live to that tempo. By turning on the metronome at the top left, we will be able to double-check that the clip is looping properly in time.

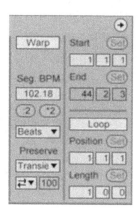

6. Enable the metronome.
7. In the *Clip* detail area, click *Loop*. Set the Position to 1.1.1. Keep the Length at 1.0.0 for now, though the first number can be adjusted as necessary.
8. Play back the clip to compare the tempo of the clip to Live's tempo.

Thanks to the sophistication of Live's warp algorithms, the clip will play back perfectly in sync with the metronome most times. In the event that it doesn't, there are several strategies to try. One is to manually mark known beats with warp markers, then drag them to the correct spots on the timeline (this is easiest to do with beats 2 and 4, which usually have loud snare-drum hits). Another option is to "roll the dice": right-click the 1.1.1 warp marker, then click *Warp from here*. This will cause Live to reanalyze the song and reposition all warp markers after this point. Sometimes this helps with situations where your song's tempo is way off from the clip's original speed.

Now that the clip loops in sync with Live's metronome, we can fine-tune the loop position. For instance, if beat 1 has a vocal or horn release, we can drag the loop bracket until we find a clean measure to use. Notice that when the loop bracket is moved the start point of the loop remains on beat 1, allowing subtle differences in repeats to be heard without altering the rhythmic feel of the clip.

9. Reposition the loop bracket as necessary to ensure you have selected a clean looping pattern without bleed from other instruments.

At this point, we can add some creative flavor to our loop. Transposing the clip up a few half-steps can create a lighter, speedier-sounding beat.

10. Transpose the clip as desired.

Another idea is to adjust the beat warp-gate amount. This control is located beneath the *Beats* warp method pull-down box.

11. Change the *two arrows* icon in the pull-down menu to the *forward arrow only* icon.
12. In the number box next to that icon, lower the value to 70.

This will produce a gate effect in which the sound cuts out faster after each note. This is especially useful for drying up cymbal-heavy breakbeats.

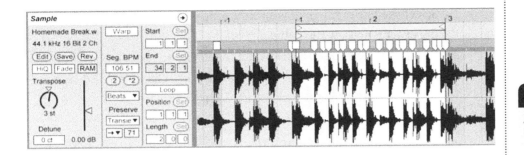

FIGURE 9.2

A properly warped drum break.

Sampled Drums

In breakbeat and drum and bass music, the foundation is the drum pattern known as the *breakbeat*. Breakbeats originated in the Funk music of the late 1960s and 1970s. A drum break can be found at some point in many Funk songs from the 1970s, either at the very beginning or about three-quarters of the way through the song. Even though there are many instrumental breaks in the song, the drum break is unique in that it is usually a four to eight bar passage where only the drums play. Such "clean" samples without other instruments playing are very useful in breakbeat, and are widely sampled material in pop, hip-hop and electronic dance music.

Advanced Drum Looping

Right now, we have a sampled drum beat with all of the hits in the same exact order they were originally played. What we will do now is scramble them to create a more interesting backdrop for the MIDI drums we will be adding later starting at step 23.

13. Copy the drum loop.
14. Switch to *Arrangement View*.
15. Double-click the stop button to reset the counter position to 1.1.1.
16. Create a new audio track.
17. Paste the clip on the new audio track.

Thanks to Live's adaptive grip, we can now select parts of this beat and drag them around using the colored stripe above the waveform. Try moving around various lengths, such as eighth notes, sixteenth notes, or even whole beats. Also try taking any part of the loop, copying it, and pasting it somewhere else. Allow an even number of bars to work—say two to four.

After reviewing your scrambled beat:

18. Adjust the start and end points to exactly fit between two odd numbers on the timeline (e.g., measure 1 and measure 3).

19. Select the entire range of your new loop—but be careful to select the exact length of the pattern.
20. Right-click and select *Consolidate time to new scene*.
21. If you like, the material in *Arrangement View* can be deleted, as a copy has just been made in *Session View*.
22. Switch back to *Session View*.

On your audio track there should now be a new clip consisting of the consolidated loop of the scrambled beat you made in *Arrangement View*.

Adding MIDI Drums

To really make our new drum pattern pop, we need to add clarity with a separate, more powerful drum track.

23. In the Browser, select *Drums*, then drag a blank *Drum Rack* into your set creating a new MIDI track.
24. In the Browser, select *Clips*.

For this example, we will need a very powerful, modern-sounding kick and snare. To quickly find options for these sounds, type "kick" or "snare" into the search box above the Browser. Audition several clips until one stands out to you—it is important that the samples sound like much heavier and more "produced" studio recordings than the breakbeat drums.

Once you find the kick and snare samples that you want to use:

25. Drag each sample you've identified into the slots of the blank *Drum Rack*. The traditional location is to place the *Kick* on *C1* and the *Snare* on *D1*, but this is not crucial to the outcome of our project.

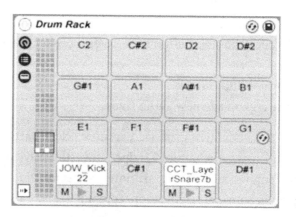

FIGURE 9.3

Drum Rack with kick and snare samples.

Breakbeat and, to a greater extent, drum and bass music rely on predictable drum patterns to propel the form of the music through a predictable course. We will program these patterns by double-clicking in a blank clip slot on the *Drum Rack* track and entering MIDI note values.

146

26. Double-click a blank clip slot on the *Drum Rack* track.

Since this drum rack contains samples, the clip view is automatically folded to show only the samples loaded into *Drum Rack*.

27. Draw MIDI notes on one of the two available lines in the *MIDI Note Editor*. Each line will represent a downbeat to trigger the two samples in the drum rack.

Remember, the breakbeats we sampled earlier will fill in all the rhythmic gaps (see figures 9.4 and 9.5 showing two common breakbeat kick/snare patterns).

28. Draw MIDI notes on one of the two available lines in the *MIDI Note Editor*. Each line will represent a downbeat to trigger the two samples in the *Drum Rack*.

As we finish our drum tracks, we need to mix the breakbeats so they can be heard evenly between the more powerful hits of the *Drum Rack*. To do this, we will employ a compressor to squeeze the dynamic range of the grouped drum tracks.

29. Select both drum tracks by holding *shift* and clicking the title bars of both tracks.
30. Right-click on either track and select *Group Tracks*. A third group track control will appear over the two drum tracks.
31. In the Browser, select *Audio Effects*.
32. Drag a *Compressor* device onto the newly created group track.
33. In the *Detail View* settings for the *Compressor* device, adjust the compressor setting to a ratio of 4:1.
34. Play the breakbeat and *Drum Rack* clips simultaneously.
35. On *Compressor*, adjust the *threshold* slider down until the breakbeat sounds like it fills in at a similar level to the *Drum Rack* clip.

147

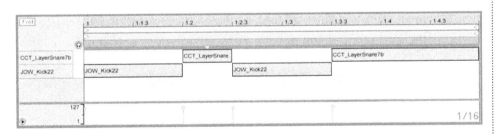

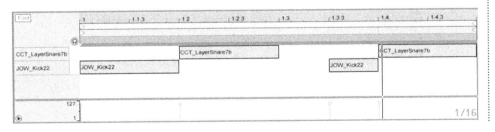

FIGURES 9.4–9.5

Two common breakbeat kick/snare patterns.

Artist Profile: Goldie (part two)

In the mid-1990s, artists such as Kevin Saunderson (Reese Project), L T J Bukem, and Photek had nailed down the overall sound of underground breakbeat music, but they neglected most elements of musical form in favor of longer continuous sets. Goldie broke this mold by releasing mainstream-friendly mixes that often included vocals. The vocal song form allowed the breakbeat music to flow between verse and chorus, thus providing regular structure to the song. A verse could provide a high-pass version of the beats while a chorus would drop into the lower frequencies and become heavier. Goldie's popularity paved the way for later artists such as Andy C to further develop these sections into the aggressive builds and drops common in today's drum and bass music.

Reese Bass

The Reese bass (named for Kevin Saunderson's Reese Project, an early 90s producer of breakbeat/drum and bass music) is often used as a complement to a standard subwoofer-range bass instrument. It is characterized by its smooth, somewhat unstable sound.

36. In the Browser, select *Instruments*.
37. Drag *Operator* into your set.

By default, *Operator* produces a simple sine wave. There are actually four oscillators found in *Operator*, labeled A, B, C, and D. On the lower right of the *Operator* device, there is a pattern of four squares that symbolically shows the routing between the four synthesizers.

38. Click the *Operator* pattern icon.
39. Change the *connection* icon to the flat horizontal-line arrangement. This will allow all four oscillators to connect directly to the speakers and will not allow any modulations between them.

FIGURE 9.6

Connection diagrams in Operator, with the rightmost pattern (indicating four oscillators and no modulators) selected.

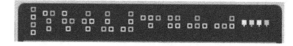

40. Click the *A* tab to select the first oscillator.
41. Change the *Wave* to *Saw D*. This indicates a mathematically produced Sawtooth wave with the highest possible resolution.
42. Change the wave types in *B*, *C*, and *D* to also be *Saw D* waves, and turn up the *Level* knobs on all four oscillators to match *A*. Watch your ears!

We will add instability by putting the four sounds slightly out of tune with one another.

43. Change the *Fine* adjustment on *B, C,* and *D* to something other than 0, but not more than 20 or 30. We still want to be able to hear the pitch center.

Unfortunately, *Operator* only allows upward adjustments of pitch, so be aware that pushing the intonation up will ultimately make the note a bit sharp.

If you find the sharpness issue bothersome, go ahead and set *Fine* to 500 on all four, and use that as the center. It will transpose your playing up a perfect fifth, which can be compensated for adding the Pitch MIDI effect set to -7 St. This is slightly inconvenient but does provide a more accurate pitch center.

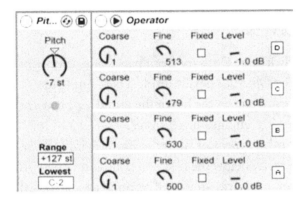

FIGURE 9.7

Operator's four oscillators, detuned and shifted 500Hz up, compensated for by a Pitch device set to -7 semitones, allowing for a centered pitch.

149

Figure 9.7 shows Operator's four oscillators, fine-tuned up a half-octave (to 500), and then adjusted out of tune, either sharp or flat, to maintain a pitch center. Note the Pitch plug-in in front of Operator compensating for the +500 adjustment by lowering the incoming MIDI note to -7 semitones. For example, an incoming MIDI note C4 will be adjusted down to F3, and then Operator will sound back at C4. Recorded MIDI patches will show F3, even though they will sound at C4.

We will do several things to make the Reese Bass more idiomatic now:

44. Click the *Filter* tick box, and lower the frequency to around 400–500 Hz. This evens out the sound and will allow a lower note to sound like a bass note.

We will now make the instrument monophonic with a nice Glide.

45. Click the *boxes* icon (lower-right-hand tab), and change *Voices* to *1*. Now only one note can be played at a time.
46. Click the *Pitch* settings tab (second to bottom right) and click the tiny *G* in a box under Glide. This allows notes to slide up or down to the next note when a legato pattern is played.

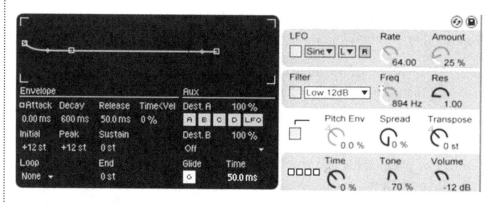

FIGURE 9.8

Reese Bass showing the Glide indicator and the Filter, set to low pass.

Sub Bass and Advanced Reese

Our Reese Bass sounds passable now, but it lacks some characteristic grit and is also missing some low frequency content. To add this, we are going to create a grouped instrument rack.

47. Right-click your *Operator* from part 5 and select *Group*. This places the *Operator* device inside a containing device. By clicking the *list* icon (on the left of the group), we can see that this device only contains our *Operator*.

48. Drag another *Operator* from the Browser into the *Instrument Rack*, directly below the first one. This allows two instruments to reside on one track—they will respond as one to MIDI note input, and output as a combined sound to the master track.

49. Click the new *Operator* to select it. Since this will be our *Sub Bass*, we will leave the waveform at *Sine wave*. Set the *Coarse* adjustment to 0.5. This will make our second *Operator* play an octave lower than the first.

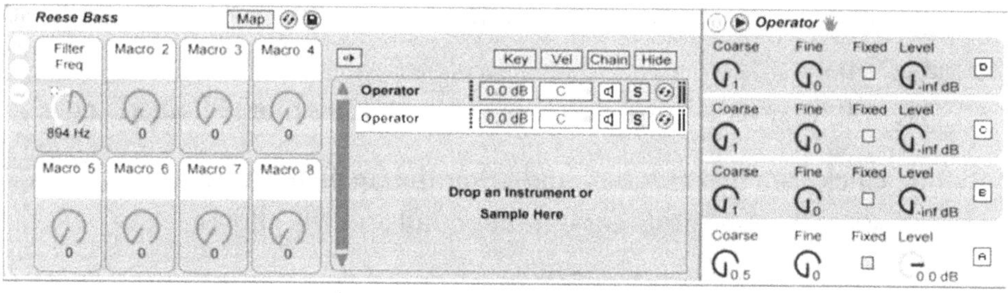

FIGURE 9.9

Grouped Operators: The second Operator is set to Coarse = 0.5, placing it down an octave from the first Operator. No Pitch plug-in necessary in this chain. Also of note—mapped Filter Freq macro knob (it is mapped to the first Operator).

50. Click on *Audio Effects* in the browser, and drag a *Saturator* effect to the end of the track's device chain. The *Saturator* is like a very simple amp simulator, and it simulates analog distortion similar to what would be found in an amp head. It also features a limiter to keep the drive from clipping when turned up.

51. As a finishing touch, click the top-left device button (the one that looks like a tiny Ableton knob) to reveal the Instrument Rack's *Macro* controls. From here, any control on any device

inside the rack can be controlled using a simple 8-knob interface. Many of the instruments supplied with Live use these to control complex parameters inside the instrument.

52. Click the square *Map* button above the Macro controls.

53. Click a control that might be handy to easily access (for instance, Operator's *Filter Frequency*, or Saturator's *Drive* knob) .

54. Click the *Map* bubble below the button you want to use for that control.

55. For simplicity, hide the rest of the device, and only leave the top *Rack* control lit—now your complex *Reese/Sub Bass* has a very simple set of controls you can access while writing your breakbeat tune.

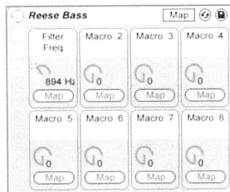

FIGURE 9.10

Macro Knob mapping. Click the top Map button, then select a control, then click the Map button beneath the desired knob.

Sampled Sirens and Other Instruments

Aside from the typical sampled drums and Reese Bass patterns, other sound effects and treble synths are needed. Since breakbeat was first developed in a culture of hardware keyboard and drum samplers, we will make our synth pads and effects from a single recorded source.

56. Find a sample with strong pitch content. In this example, we will use a recorded air raid siren, not an uncommon sound to find in explosive dance hall music.

57. In the Browser, click on *Instruments* and drag *Simpler* into a blank area of your session.

58. Drag your audio file into the *Simpler* device panel marked *Drop Sample Here*.

Simpler is a simple sampler. Thus, it really only takes an original sound clip and maps it to middle C on the piano, allowing easy pitch shifts on a keyboard. It does not try to analyze the sound to match the pitch, nor does it automatically trim the sound to an obvious starting point.

59. Adjust the left trim arrow in *Simpler* to make your sample play at the right moment in the clip. When a key on the piano is pressed, a small timer-line will pass over the sample to show

151

what point in the waveform is currently playing. A good technique would be to place this arrow right on the attack of your waveform (of course, listening to the sample is the best way to know if this is a good position). Another idea might be to start the sample from a more "settled" point in the waveform. In the included example, there are two tracks based off the same sample: one starts at the beginning of the waveform (with a sharp pitch bend as the siren starts) and the other starts in the middle of the sound where the pitch is already settled. Both work well in different contexts.

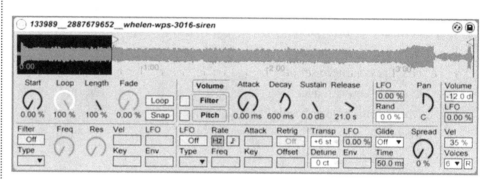

FIGURE 9.11

Simpler with siren sample loaded. Playback starts from the left arrow, and ends when the waveform hits the right arrow. Higher pitches play through the waveform faster.

60. The example in this book is a very long sample, which allows us to avoid some problems associated with having to loop samples. We tackle this problem more in depth in chapter 12 when we are looping vocal samples. For right now, make sure your sample is long enough to hold out for a couple seconds or so.

61. Now we need to tune the sample. *Simpler* includes transposition and "detune" settings, which allow half-step and cents adjustments, respectively. The main problem is that playing a C on the keyboard does not sound a C. This can create many problems if we try to combine this instrument with any others from the browser. If you are a well-ear-trained musician, you may be able to figure out the correct pitch without any software aids.

62. If you are having trouble finding the right pitch, here is a simple and futuristic way to solve the problem. In the Browser, click *Audio Effects*, then open the disclosure triangle next to *Spectrum*. Now drag the *Pitch* preset onto your *Simpler* track.

63. The device will now show on a graph what pitches are playing in the sample. Depending on the sample you chose, many peaks may be showing. The lowest peak is called the "Fundamental" pitch; higher peaks are called "Overtones." Together, these make up the overall timbre of your sampled instrument.

64. Play a middle C on the keyboard. Adjust the *Transp* setting in *Simpler* until the lowest peak in your sample lines up with C3 in the *Pitch* window. C3 is the designation for middle C in Ableton.

65. If you are skeptical of this technique, or just want to fine-tune your sample by ear, try adding an *Operator* track to your set. Hold the *command* key while clicking the *Arm* button on both tracks to play them simultaneously. If your sample is in tune, it will sound at the same pitch as *Operator*.

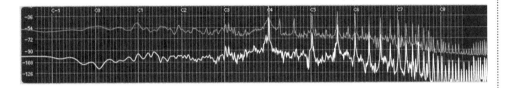

FIGURE 9.12

Spectrum in "pitch" mode. Note that C4 is the lowest peak, with many subsequent peaks also on Cs.

Buildup Scene

Drum and bass established a continuing tradition in electronic dance music—the build and drop. Although similar sections have existed in other styles of music (see "Twist & Shout" by the Beatles for a rock and roll example of a buildup), the relative isolation of parts and the ability to exaggerate sonic phenomena in postproduction have made buildup in EDM something of an art unto itself. Let's look at a very basic way to produce two parts of a buildup—first, a filtered noise sound effect, and then an accompanying drum pattern.

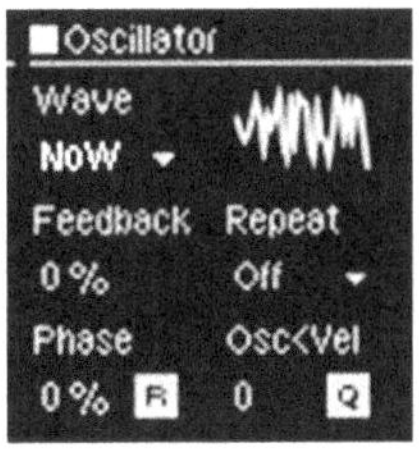

66. Add a new *Operator* track to your set.
67. Under *Wave* set it to *Noise White*. This will generate pitchless white noise, no matter what key is pressed.

153

FIGURE 9.13

Operator's waveform set to white noise.

> *White noise* is what plays when a random number is assigned to every sample in an audio waveform. It is pitchless because it is 100% random, covering all frequencies available.

68. Double-click in a clip slot on the *Noise* track we just made. Set the length of the clip to 16.0.0 (sixteen measures), and either program or record a note lasting through the entire duration of the clip.

69. In the Browser, click *Audio Effects*, then drag *Auto Filter* onto your noise track. We will not actually be using any of the automatic features of this effect, but it is a convenient way to add a low-pass filter.

70. Double-click the clip to show *Clip Detail* on the bottom panel. In the very bottom left of this panel are three buttons, the rightmost being a letter *E*. Click the *E* to show automation parameters for the clip.

71. We want an exponential curve for this noise, starting from a very low frequency and only letting higher sounds pass near the very end of the clip. To do this, we first need to select *Auto Filter* in the top parameter box, then *Frequency* in the lower parameter box. This will show the automation line for the knob that controls where the cutoff frequency for our filter is.

72. Double-click on the line near the beginning of the clip, and again near the end of the clip. The first dot should be dragged all the way down, and the second should be dragged all the way up. This creates a linear ramp of the filter frequency when played.

73. To make a nice exponential curve, place your mouse near the line where you want the knee of the curve to be. Holding the *Option* key, drag the line down to make the desired curve. We want this noise effect to increase most of the way during the last two measures of the clip. Now we have an interesting sweep effect that is really only loud during the end of the clip, but somewhat present throughout the buildup.

FIGURE 9.14

White noise MIDI clip with Auto Filter automation. Note the parameter selection boxes on the top left of the image. These determine what the pink line over the clip will do.

154

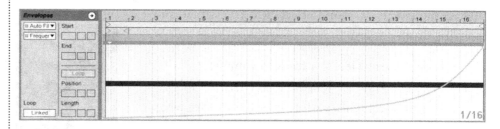

Now we will make an accelerating drum pattern to accompany this effect:

74. Change to your *Drum Rack* track.

75. Double-click in a blank clip slot on this track to make a new blank clip, and set its length to 16.0.0 (matching the noise we just made).

76. There are plenty of methods to making an accelerating drum pattern, and many readers probably have a couple ideas in mind at this point already. We will do a very simple method that accelerates by powers of 2.

77. Right click in your MIDI roll, and set the grid to *1 Bar*. Double-click in the first eight boxes on both *Snare* and *Kick* lanes. Make sure your velocity is all the way up when releasing your click.

78. Right-click again and set the grid size to half notes. Draw the next eight boxes in both lanes.

79. Right-click again and set the grid size to quarter notes. Draw the next eight boxes in both lanes.
80. Zoom in a bit by dragging down on the *timeline*.
81. Right-click again and set the grid size to eighth notes. Draw the next eight boxes in both lanes.
82. Right-click again and set the grid size to sixteenth notes. Draw the next eight boxes in both lanes.
83. Decide how you want the buildup to end. Should there be a short rest at the end? Should it continue in smaller notes ad infinitum? This is for you to decide. I simply stopped at sixteenth notes and left about two beats of rest at the end of the pattern. This will allow the track to "take a breath" before dropping into the powerful Reese parts.

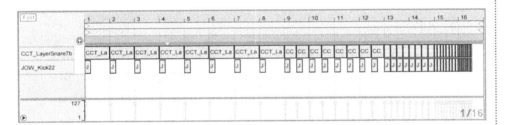

FIGURE 9.15

16-bar accelerating Drum Rack pattern, for the build scene.

Mixing

In breakbeat music, the key ingredient is the sampled break loop. It is important to ensure this pattern is audible when playing, and well balanced with the Drum Rack patterns. We will be doing the following steps all out of the *Audio Effects* section of the Browser.

84. Ensure you followed the mixing-related steps on your drum tracks from step 4. The drums should be grouped and compressed together.
85. As a safety measure, place a Limiter on the master track to ensure there is no clipping. If you notice during playback that the *GR* meter on this device is flashing often or all of the time, turn all of your tracks down. Generally, this Limiter should only be showing a slight bit of Gain Reduction. If it is constantly working, your music will sound flat, lifeless, and overly loud.
86. Now we need to group together all of the tracks that are not drum-related. This includes both sampled sirens, the Reese bass, and the white noise track. Hold your *shift* key and highlight the titles of these tracks.
87. Right-click on any of the highlighted titles and choose *Group Tracks*.
88. Rename the grouped track *Not Drums* (optional).

155

FIGURE 9.16

Grouped non-drum tracks, preparation for grouped sidechain compression. Effects applied to the leftmost Group track will be applied to the summed mix of the four tracks in the group.

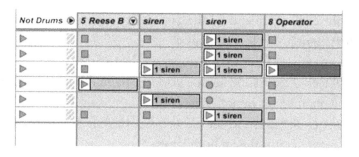

89. Click *Audio Effects* in the Browser. Drag a *Compressor* onto the *Not Drums* Group track. Keep in mind, this is being applied to the summed mix of the four non-drum tracks.

In the next few steps we will be making the non-drum tracks "duck," or lower in volume, when the Kick drum is played. This is an effective way to ensure the drums cut through the mix as well as add some rhythmic complexity to the synth parts.

90. Click the small triangle in the top right of *Compressor* to show the *Sidechain* controls. These allow *Compressor* to accept input from sources other than the track on which the device is placed. In this example, we will make the device reduce the volume every time the kick drum hits.

91. Click the *Sidechain* button. Now *Compressor* is listening to the source specified below the *Sidechain* button.

92. Change *Audio From* to *Drum Rack*, and the second box to *Kick Drum—Post FX* (your titles may vary).

93. Turn up the input *Gain* knob below the *Sidechain* button.

94. Turn *Ratio* all the way up to *inf:1*. This produces a reliable gain reduction whenever the threshold is crossed.

95. Lower the *Thresh slider* to about halfway.

96. Play a clip from the *Drum Rack*. You should see the *GR* meter pulling down in orange every time the kick drum plays. If you also play any track inside the non-drums group you should also hear the volume ducking down significantly whenever the kick drum hits.

156

FIGURE 9.17

Sidechain Compressor. Ratio = infinite, Threshold is low, and the input volume from the Kick Drum is increased. These settings work together to quickly lower the volume of the melodic group whenever the kick drum is actively playing.

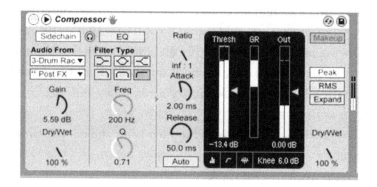

Form Considerations

Breakbeat styles, especially the drum and bass subgenre, have well-established form sections squarely aimed at exciting a large, packed-in crowd. In our example, there are three basic sections outlined in *Session View* scenes: an introductory section that features the sampled beat and slowly introduces the siren-based synths and drum rack, a "build" that features the accelerating drum pattern and white noise sweep, and the "drop" that features the Reese Bass and the drums. There is also a short "outro" which simply has a synth pattern playing by itself as a nice way to wind down the tune.

The scenes are set up as such in our example:

Scene 1:   Intro   Sampled break with treble siren pattern.
Scene 2:   "   Plus Drum Rack pattern. Audible ducking.
Scene 3:   Build   Accelerating Drum Rack pattern, treble siren,
                     midrange siren, white noise sweep. Very obvious
                     ducking.
Scene 4:   Drop   Both drum patterns, Reese Bass. Some audible
                     ducking.
Scene 5:   "   Midrange sirens, Reese Bass, only sampled drums.
Scene 6:   Outro   Treble siren pattern only.

Drums ▼	Not Drums ▶	5 Reese B ▼	siren	siren	8 Operator	Master	
▷	▷	☐	☐	▷ 1 siren	☐	▷	intro
▷	▷	☐	☐	▷ 1 siren	☐	▷	
▨		☐	▶ 1 siren	▷ 1 siren	▶	▷	build
▷	▷	▷	☐	○	☐	▷	drop
▷	▷	☐	▷ 1 siren	○	☐	▷	
☐	▷	☐	☐	▷ 1 siren	☐	▷	outro

FIGURE 9.18

Session View organized into major form sections. The Scene triggers on the right-hand side are set up to allow performance of this song using only this column.

157

When the parts are organized in this way we can easily transfer this to a linear song format for export or further production. We can also play these scenes in any order we choose. For instance, in this example we will double back on the intro after we hit scene four, so the song has a binary format. Drum and bass often uses the "Intro—Build—Drop times two" format, and we will continue that tradition here.

The way we set up our scenes allows us to easily go through this pattern twice while recording using only scene triggers. Of course, if you feel inspired to trigger an individual clip outside of its scene or simply to trigger a la carte, you can do this too—just try to follow the general format of reserving the louder drums and bass material for sections after the buildup scene.

To record your song into *Arrangement View*:

97. Double-click the stop button to reset the song timer to 1.1.1.

98. Click the black circular record button.

99. Start triggering scenes and/or clips.

An obvious suggestion that bears mention: do not loop the "build" section unless you really want to mess with your listeners.

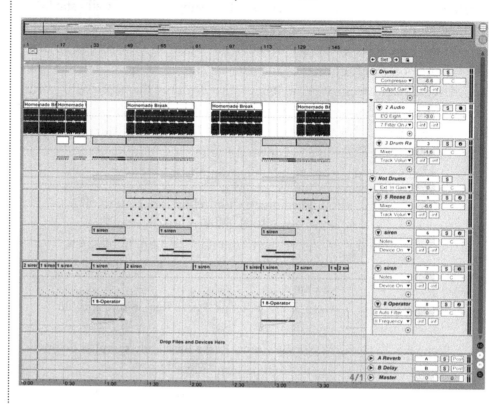

FIGURE 9.19

Song after recording to Arrangement View. Further editing can be done here, or it can be exported to a standard audio file.

On Your Own

Drum and bass is an active subgenre of EDM, but the use of breakbeats as a production technique occurs across the map of electronic-influenced pop music. Producers often use breakbeats when they want to achieve a naturalistic drum sound but still have total control over the groove and patterns. Try these ideas to keep you going:

- Try recording your own breakbeats. Have a drummer play some basic rock/funk beats while you record them. Take the recording into Live and use your original recording to make beat slices and loops.
- Add breakbeats to an existing song in another style; use them to "fill in" emptier or sparse-sounding drum patterns.
- Explore how different *Operator* routings change the Reese sound into other interesting synthesized instruments.

In Live
- Review the Live documentation on *Operator* in the Live manual (section 24.6).
- Review the Live documentation on *Simpler* in the Live manual (section 24.8).

Chiptune

n studying chiptune music, it is important to try to separate the technology used to create the music from the genres covered within chiptune. In practice, chiptune music is not a genre as much as it is an interpretation of many genres. Thus, one can produce a chiptune version of any other genre; the timbre and instrument choice is what makes it a chiptune song, not the other stylistic elements.

The first experimental computer music, such as that coming out of Bell Labs and IRCAM (Institute de Recherche et Coordination Acoustique/Musique) in the 1960s, inspired the next generation of computer engineers to include solid-state pitch synthesis chips on consumer PCs and video game consoles. Many of the first video games featured sound effects and interactive audio, but the first to feature a soundtrack composed using these chip elements was the 1980 game Rally-X. Programming tunes on these chips was quite difficult and required a mastery of high-level and assembly computer programming. Composing pleasing music was also problematic, since chips in the 1980s were only capable of producing simple periodic waveforms, such as square and sawtooth waves.

The evolution of the chiptune aesthetic is another part of the story. Many of the famous video game melodies of the 1980s were inspired recreations of Japanese synthpop music, specifically that of the Yellow Magic Orchestra (YMO). The YMO, while influenced by Isao Tomita and Kraftwerk's earlier work, also composed much of their music using rudimentary chips combined with live performance synthesizers and a mixture of live and programmed drumtracks. The YMO styles were mimicked by many early chiptune composers who worked for companies like Sega, Namco, and Nintendo. Songs in the YMO style had a strong melodic presence, fast tempo, and simplistic format.

Since this band was a three-piece outfit, many songs also mimic the minimal instrumentation of a lead synth, a bass/chord synth, and drums. During the 1970s, this music felt like a whimsical, parodic take on disco that seemed perfectly in place (and was achievable with current technology) when used as background music in video games.

In conclusion, a chiptune-style song must use simple periodic waveforms as synths and not grossly exceed the audio quality standards of 1980s computers. It should also try to have strong melodic hooks and a simplistic strong structure and generally be in a fast tempo.

Suggested Listening

Yellow Magic Orchestra: "Rydeen"
Koji Kondo: "Main Theme" from Super Mario Bros. (NES[1] game)
Yoshihiro Sakaguchi: "The Moon Theme" from Duck Tales
    (NES game) –
David Wise: "Wookie Hole" from Battletoads (NES game)
Minae Fujii: "Intro" from Mega Man 4 (NES game)
Brian LeBarton/Beck Hansen: "Threshold (8 Bit)" from Scott
    Pilgrim vs. the World
Crystal Castles: "Courtship Dating"

Artist Profile: Yellow Magic Orchestra

The most influential band you probably haven't heard of, YMO was a three-piece Japanese group formed as somewhat of a response to "serious" electronic acts such as Kraftwerk. Since their main active period was the late 1970s and early 1980s, there were no DAWs or laptops on stage. Their programmed sequences were set up during shows by an offstage technician, and the show was dependent on a great deal of live engineering and manual tinkering—a feat even by today's standards.

Their music was a mix of experimental electronic synths and poppy disco rock sounds, and was extremely popular in Japan. Similar-minded individuals would go on to become the sound programmers for Nintendo, Sega, and Capcom, shamelessly mimicking their signature grooves and melodic writing for use in the 8-bit video games that shaped an entire generation's childhood worldwide.

1. Nintendo Entertainment System.

Designing a Custom Chip Instrument

First we will explore how to more accurately imitate chip sounds despite having modern audio hardware, and in the process gain an appreciation for the circuitry behind these devices. Designing a monophonic chiptune-style synth in Max for Live can yield results more similar to the original genre, thanks to the highly direct nature of Max for Live. Since Max makes no assumptions about desired audio quality or resolution, we can achieve a very raw-sounding result here:

1. In your Browser, click *Max for Live*, then drag *Max Instrument* onto a blank track.
2. Click the *Edit* button on the top right of the *Max Instrument device* to open the patch in a *Max editor window*.

Before we get too far, we will clean up the patch a bit.

3. In Max, click *View* and select *Patcher Inspector*.
4. Click the *All* tab at the top of the *Patcher Inspector* window.
5. Under *View*, check the box next to *Open in Presentation*. This will eventually allow us to design a nice UI for our instrument.

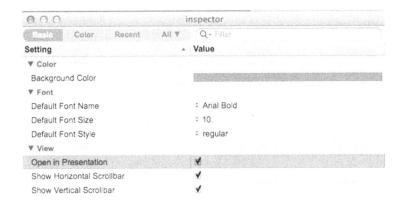

FIGURE 10.1

Default Max instrument device with Edit button highlighted in upper right.

FIGURE 10.2

"Open in Presentation" box checked in Patcher Inspector.

6. Drag a *selection* box around everything in the *Max Instrument* window (or simply use the select *all command*) and press *delete*. We will be starting from scratch.
7. Make the *Max Instrument* window bigger—we will need some room to work.
8. Now that we have done some housekeeping, let's review some Max keyboard shortcuts that will be used extensively in this section:

N = make a new object

M = new message

I = new integer number

F = new floating point number

C = new comment (feel free to add comments as you make the patch).

9. Type *N* to make an object. Name it ***notein***. ***Notein*** receives *MIDI notes* from Live.

10. Make another object. Name it ***ddg.mono***. ***Ddg.mono*** interprets the MIDI notes in a way that behaves as many mono synths are expected.

11. Connect the first outlet of ***notein*** to the first inlet of ***ddg.mono***.

12. Connect the second outlet of ***notein*** to the second inlet of ***ddg.mono***.

13. Type *N*. Name the object ***mtof***. Connect the left outlet of ***ddg.mono*** to the inlet of ***mtof***. *M-to-F*, or *MIDI to Frequency*, takes the incoming MIDI note number and converts it to a scientific Hertz frequency for that note.

14. MIDI is now coming into the patch.

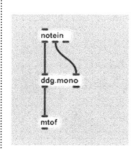

FIGURE 10.3

MIDI notes enter, are interpreted with ddg.mono, and finally MIDI note number is converted to frequency.

162

Now we will start building our *Oscillator bank*. Some common waveforms used in chiptune music include square waves, pulse waves, and sawtooth waves. We will design our patch to process all of these sounds, and allow the user to select which ones they want to use. The reason we are using a subpatch for this feature is that every oscillator will use the same exact inputs for frequency and will also share a common output path.

1. Type *N*. Name the object ***p oscillators***. The *p object* is a sub-patcher, and it is a patch within your patch. Hitting *enter* will cause the *subpatch* to open.

Inside the subpatch, do the following:

2. Type *N*. Name the object ***inlet***. The object will change to a graphical inlet numbered 1 after you hit *enter*.

3. Type *N*. Name the object ***rect~***. Connect *Inlet 1* to the left inlet of ***rect~***.

4. Type *N*. Name the object ***outlet***. Connect the outlet of ***rect~*** to the inlet of *outlet 1*.

5. Close the *subpatch*.

6. Connect *mtof* to the inlet of **p oscillators**.

7. Type *N*. Name the object **adsr~ 0 0 1 0**. ADSR generates a gain envelope for incoming sounds. By presetting *A=0, D=0, S=1, and R=0*, we are telling it to have instant attack time, zero decay effect, 100% volume during the sustain, and zero release time. We will make these items adjustable later.

8. Type *N*. Name the object **/ 127.** (note the period after *127*). Connect the right outlet of **ddg.mono** to the left inlet of **/ 127.**, which will take the incoming *Velocity value* (how hard you hit the keys) and divide it by its maximum value, making it into a fractional percentage, appropriate for use with ADSR.

9. Connect the outlet of **/ 127.** to the left inlet of **adsr~**.

10. Type *N*. Name the object ***~** and place it below **p oscillators**.

11. Connect the outlet of **p oscillators** to the left inlet of "***~**".

12. Connect the left outlet of **adsr~** to the right inlet of "***~**".

13. Type *N*. Name the object **plugout~**. Place it near the bottom of the patch.

14. Connect the outlet of ***~** to both inlets of **plugout~**.

Now we have a working, velocity-sensitive square wave synth with no frills. Try it out, will you? Now we will make the type of wave selectable.

15. Hold the *command* key and double-click to open **p oscillators**. Hit the *Lock* button in the lower left to unlock the patch if necessary.

16. Disconnect the outlet of **rect~** from the subpatch outlet by clicking the *signal line* and hitting *delete*.

17. Type *N*. Name the object **rect~ 440 .25**. Place it next to the first **rect~** object.

18. Type *N*. Name the object **rect~ 440 .10**. Place it next to the second **rect~** object.

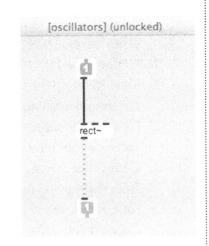

FIGURE 10.4

Inside the p oscillators subpatch.

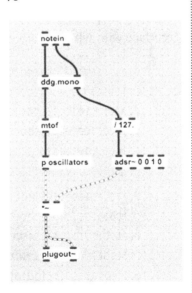

FIGURE 10.5

Working, velocity-sensitive square wave synth.

163

19. Type *N*. Name the object **saw~**. Place it next to the right of the other objects.
20. Connect the *Inlet* to the first inlet of these three new objects.
21. Type *N*. Name the object **selector~ 4**. Place it between the line of wave objects and the subpatch's outlet.
22. Connect the *subpatch* inlet to the leftmost inlet of the three **rect~** objects and the **saw~** object.
23. Connect each wave object's outlet to an input in Selector. Start from the right: connect **saw~** to the rightmost inlet, and continue leftward.
24. Check that the first inlet of **selector~** is empty.
25. Connect the outlet of **selector~** to the *subpatch* outlet.
26. Type *N*. Name the object **inlet**, and place it near the top right of the patch. It should read *2* after enter is pressed.
27. Connect inlet *2* to the leftmost inlet of **selector~**.
28. Close the subpatch.

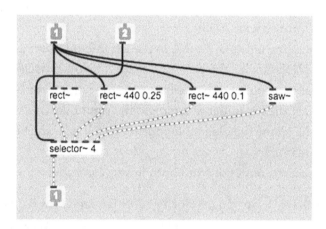

FIGURE 10.6

The p oscillators subpatch with four waveform options.

The subpatch is set up with some multiple oscillators now, but we need an interface with which to select the wave types.

1. Click the *Presentation Mode* icon on the bottom of the main patcher window.
2. Don't worry—your patch is still there. This is simply the interface that is presented to the user when your patch is loaded. We have not yet made an interface so this space is empty.
3. Type *N*. Name the object **live.tab**.
4. Right-click the *one two three* boxes. Choose *Inspector* from the list.
5. In the *Inspector*, scroll to the *Parameter list*. Double-click to the right of *Range/Enum* to change the button labels.
6. Type this (including quotes): **square "25% pulse" "10% pulse" sawtooth**

FIGURE 10.7

Range/Enum values for
live.tab.

7. Hit *enter* and close the *Inspector*.
8. Drag the bottom resize handle on your tab and pull downward until the labels you typed are all visible. Position the box somewhere above the black line that looks aesthetically pleasing.
9. Click the *Presentation Mode* icon again to switch back the patcher.
10. You should see the *live.tab* (possibly resized) with an orange border, signifying its presence in the user interface.
11. Type *N*. Name the object **+ 1**.
12. Connect the left outlet of *live.tab* to the left inlet of **+ 1**.
13. Connect the outlet of **+ 1** to the right inlet of ***p oscillators***.
14. Save the patch and close. Try switching waveforms while playing notes.

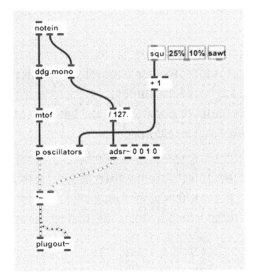

165

FIGURE 10.8

The live.tab is routed to
p oscillators. The orange
box around live.tab
denotes its use in
Presentation Mode.

FIGURE 10.9

Presentation Mode for the
same patch in Fig. 10.8.

Still here? Okay, now we will add some nice touches that are actually difficult to find in other synths, namely controllable *Glide* and *Vibrato*.

It is important that we process *Glide* before *Vibrato*, and since *Glide* is a pitch-to-pitch calculation, we do not want *Vibrato* to be cancelled out in the process of adding *Glide*.

1. Switch to Presentation Mode.
2. Type *N*. Name the object *live.dial*.
3. Right-click the *live.dial* and choose *Inspector*.
4. In the *Inspector*, scroll to the *Parameter list*. Change the Long Name and Short Name values to **Glide**.
5. Change the Unit Style value to **Time**.
6. Change the Range/Enum value to **0. 1000.** (zero seconds to one second, or 1,000 ms).
7. Close the *Inspector*.
8. Place the *live.dial* in an aesthetically pleasing spot above the black line.
9. Exit *Presentation Mode*.
10. Disconnect *mtof* from *p oscillators*.
11. Type *N*. Name the object *pack 0 0*. This takes two inputs and creates a list from them.
12. Connect the outlet of *mtof* to the left inlet of *pack 0 0*.
13. Connect the left outlet of the *Glide* dial to the right inlet of *pack 0 0*.
14. Type *N*. Name the object *line~*. The *line~* object takes incoming numbers and "slides" to change numbers, similar to a portamento on a keyboard instrument.
15. Connect the outlet of *pack 0 0* to the left inlet of *line~*.
16. Connect *line~* to *p oscillators*.
17. Save and close the patch. Adjust the *Glide* setting and play a bit—notice that interrupting a currently sounding note with another key press will activate *Glide*, and it will take the same length of time specified by the *Glide* dial to change notes.

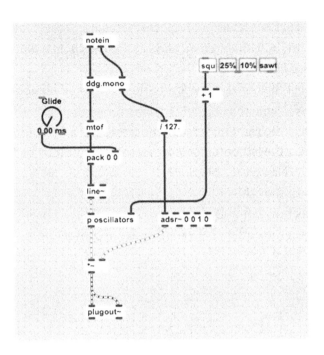

FIGURE 10.10

Glide causing linear ramps between note changes. Notice the adjustment in frequency is made before any sound is generated.

Now we will add Vibrato, which will make our synth sound very accurate. Scientifically speaking, Vibrato is simply a cycle of pitch variation up and down from a central pitch. We will design ours so one knob controls both speed and intensity, since they are somewhat related when a live performer employs acoustic vibrato.

1. Switch to *Presentation Mode*.
2. Type *N*. Name the object *live.dial*.
3. Right-click *live.dial* and choose *Inspector*.
4. In the *Inspector*, scroll to the *Parameter list*. Change the Long Name and Short Name values to *Vibrato*.
5. Change the Unit Style value to *Float*.
6. Change the Range/Enum value to *0. 10*.
7. Close the *Inspector*.
8. Place the *Vibrato* dial in an aesthetically pleasing location above the black line.
9. Exit *Presentation Mode*.
10. Place the *Vibrato* dial near the top of the patch.
11. Disconnect *line~* from *p oscillators* by selecting the patch cord and pressing *delete*.
12. Type *N*. Name the object *cycle~ 1*. This generates the signal of a sine wave, but we will never hear the actual sine wave. This will function as an LFO to our synth's pitch.
13. Connect the left outlet of the Vibrato dial to the left inlet of *cycle~*.
14. Type *N*. Name the object *number~*. This is like a number box that uses audio signals instead of control signals as its method.

167

15. Right-click *number~* and select *Inspector*.
16. Scroll to the *Value section*, and change the *Update Interval in Millesec Option* to **20**.
17. Connect the outlet of *cycle~* to the left inlet of *number~*.
18. Type *N*. Name the object * **1.**; don't forget the . after the 1.
19. Connect the right outlet of *number~* to the left inlet of * **1**.
20. Connect the left outlet of *live.dial* to the right inlet of * **1**.
21. Type *N*. Name the object +~.
22. Connect the outlet of * **1.** to the left inlet of +~.
23. Connect the left outlet of *line~* to the right inlet of +~.
24. Connect the outlet of +~ to the inlet of *p oscillators*.

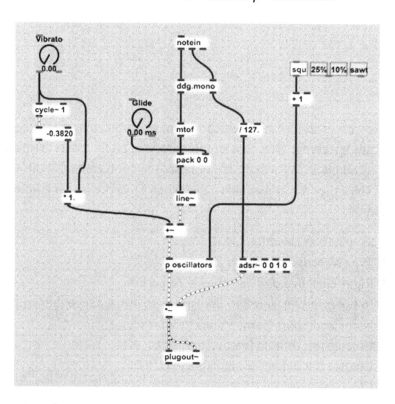

FIGURE 10.11

Synth patch with working Vibrato and Glide.

Boom—we have working Vibrato and Glide!

Let's add some finishing touches. To really make this synth great, we need to add Attack/Release controls. We will also add a scope to let us see the actual waveforms we are making.

25. Switch to *Presentation Mode*.
26. Type *N*. Name the object *live.dial*.
27. Right click *live.dial* and select *Inspector*.
28. Scroll to the *Parameter section*, and change the *Long name* and *Short names* to **Attack**.
29. Change the *Unit Style* to **Time**.
30. Change the Range/Enum value to "**0. 1000.**"
31. Close the *Inspector*.

32. Repeat steps 2–7, but name the second dial *Release.*
33. Type *N.* Name this object *scope~.*
34. Right-click *scope~* and choose *Inspector.*
35. Scroll to the *Value section* at the bottom of the list.
36. Change the *Buffer Size* to **64**, and change the *Calccount*—samples per pixel—to **32**.
37. Exit *Presentation Mode.*
38. Connect the left outlet of the *Attack* dial to the second inlet of **adsr~**.
39. Connect the left outlet of the *Release* dial to the rightmost inlet of **adsr~**.
40. Connect the outlet of the **~* object connected to **plugout~** to the left inlet of **scope~**. *Scope* will receive the same audio that is being sent back to Live.
41. Save your work! We will be referring to this instrument as "Chippy" throughout the rest of the chapter.

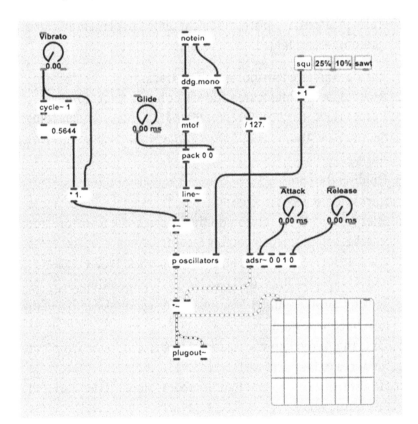

FIGURE 10.12

Finished patch.

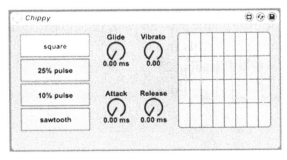

FIGURE 10.13

Finished patch in Device View (and Presentation Mode).

Using the Custom Chip Sounds

Now that we have made a great custom chiptunes generator, there are a few options for how to proceed with writing the parts. We could:

a. Go on to make Chippy polyphonic by learning how to use the *poly~ object* (difficult).

b. Use Chippy to write only monophonic parts (works, but harmony can be clunky).

c. Resample Chippy's unique sounds to achieve polyphony (easy).

There are more technical and possibly elegant ways to make a custom polyphonic synth, but the quickest and most convenient way to make a sound conveniently polyphonic is to record a C3 onto a separate unused audio track, then drag the resulting clip into Simpler. Once Simpler is set up, that is the track where the actual parts will be written. The example file uses a combination of direct Chippy tracks and sampled tracks—the audio quality difference is not noticeable except at extreme pitch shifts. The ability to play chords far outweighs the downsides of resampling.

1. Ensure you have a working Chippy track.
2. Right-click in a blank area and select *Insert Audio Track*.
3. Ensure the small *IO* button on the right of *Session View* is lit.
4. On the new *Audio track*, under *Audio From* choose your *Chippy track*.
5. Holding the command (or control) key, arm both the *Chippy track* and the new *Audio track*.
6. Hit the *stop all clips* button on the master track to ensure nothing else will play when you hit record.
7. Click a *clip record* button on the *Audio track*. Play a *C3* for a couple seconds. Press the *spacebar* to stop recording.
8. In your Browser, under *Instruments*, drag *Simpler* into a blank area in your session.
9. Drag the Audio clip you recorded in step 7 into the *Drop sample here* area of Simpler.
10. Adjust the start and end handles to line up with the start and end of the note.
11. Set the *Volume* to 0.00 dB.
12. Locate the dials on the left-hand side of Simpler. Turn on the *Loop* button next to this area.
13. Set the *Loop* dial to about 25%.

14. Set the *Fade* dial to 100%. This creates an infinitely looping region at the end of the sample, and neatly fades the loop so it is less detectable. This allows playing the sound for longer durations than were initially recorded.

15. Chords are now playable on your Chippy sound.

FIGURE 10.14

Routing audio from the Chippy track into an Audio track—recording on this track will only "hear" the Chippy track.

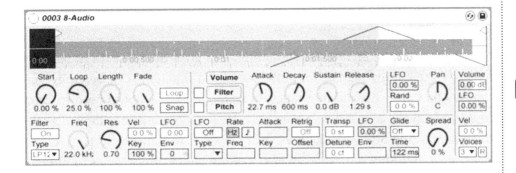

FIGURE 10.15

Simpler using the resampled Chippy note, enabling polyphonic playing.

Auto-Chords and MIDI Reuse

Due to the simplistic nature of chiptune timbres, much of the creativity in this genre comes from the ingenuity and resourcefulness of the musician. In the early days of computer music, tracker programs were used to painstakingly hard-code MIDI sequences in 16-beat grids. Due to the tedium of this work, shortcuts were made to reduce the amount of hand programming needed to create credible music with elements like chord progressions, broken chord patterns, and bass accompaniments. We will explore three methods a chiptune musician might use to lighten their workload and enable quick creativity without needing lots of technical skills.

First, we will set up our polyphonic Simpler Chippy to perform our chord progressions for us.

16. In your Browser, under *MIDI effects*, locate *Scale* and click the *disclosure triangle* to reveal the presets for Scale.

17. Choose a *Scale* (our example uses C minor). Do not be concerned about keys other than C. We can change that once the effect is in place.

18. Scale shows input note on the X-axis versus output note on the Y-axis. When an output note does not match the input, the nearest note will be chosen. Try playing a chromatic scale— the only notes you should hear are those in a C minor scale.

19. Go back to the Browser and locate *Chord*. Click its *disclosure triangle*.

20. Locate *Major Chord* —drag and place this effect *to the left* of *Scale* in the device panel. It does not matter that this plug-in is Major, and the other is Minor. In this case, the Chord effect is going to split a single note into a Triad with a third and fifth. The Scale plug-in will shift those extra notes to "correct" notes in the scale.

21. Play some chords. Notice that the chords are diatonic, and do not play out of key.

From a music theory standpoint, this is a great device chain to use. Not only do the chords play diatonically, but chord functions can be easily performed by simply playing root notes. In fact, one does not even need to know the names of the notes! If you want a I – IV – V progression, simply play the first, fourth, and fifth white keys on your keyboard to achieve this pattern. The plug-ins will do the rest. You can also look up chord progressions to modern songs using a resource like http://hooktheory.com and use the roman numeral analyses you find in the same way.

In addition, we can generate all of our background parts from this original chord progression.

22. Duplicate the Simpler track by right-clicking the track title and selecting *Duplicate*.

23. Right-click the Duplicate track's title, and rename the track *Chippy Bass*.

24. Remove the Major Chord device from the track by selecting it and pressing *Delete*.

25. In your Browser, locate *MIDI effects*, then *Arpeggiator*.

26. Drag *Arpeggiator* onto the *Simpler track*.

27. In the *Scale* device, set the *Transpose* to -24 st.

28. Play the *MIDI clip* on the Chippy Bass track.

The clip that used to be a chord pattern now sounds like a straight eighth-note bass pattern. This can be mixed and matched with your other clips, or act on its own as well. Using the Arpeggiator we can make another variation of this idea with a faster, sweeping blips track. In the example, the track using this technique is called "Chippy Arp" (it is made using the same technique as the bass, but with a higher note range and a faster Arpeggiator rate setting).

Sampled Chip Sounds

We can get sounds from other sources as well. For instance, we can record an actual video game system's audio output, and use those sounds in Simpler as well. There are many ways to record the output of an NES system, but there are relatively few ways to run custom software on the actual hardware. In this example, we will use an emulation program and a custom NES ROM designed to play simple scales.

Since there are a great deal of emulator programs and methods to record, we will not cover any of them exhaustively. There are a great deal of ROMs designed for producing sound. In this example I used a basic ROM written to play scales using the three main wave types on a Nintendo Entertainment System: Square, Sawtooth, and Triangle. The emulation software (Nestopia in this case) has an audio recording feature, so a wave file can be generated simply by pressing record and running the ROM. In other cases, software such as Soundflower by Cycling '74 might be used to route audio from the emulator into Live. Another crude option is to simply run an audio cable from the headphone jack of your computer back into an audio input, but this is not recommended as it reduces the "direct" nature of chip sounds.

After generating an audio file, dragging the file into Simpler works very much the same way as it did in steps 1–15 (Using the Custom Chip Sounds). The important thing is to make sure that your synth is sounding the same note as the MIDI keyboard is playing; samples played in Simpler aren't necessarily in tune—it simply assigns the imported sound to C3. This can be quickly remedied using the Spectrum device and visually tuning the note using the Transp. control.

8-Bit Drums

Drums are much easier to reproduce. Since early synths and drum machines used noise channels to simulate percussion instruments, we can quickly imitate the sounds by reducing the audio quality. Actual white noise is a fairly high resolution sound, and noise on a 1980s computer was very crude and "crunchy" sounding. To simulate an old noise-based drum kit, we will actually start with a high resolution kit and work backward.

29. In your Browser, click *Drums*. Locate *Kit-Core 808.adg* and drag it into a blank part of your session.
30. In the *Drum Rack device*, delete all of the pads except for C1 (Kick 808), D1 (Snare 808), and F#1 (Hihat Closed). Early synths did not have enough memory to accommodate a large library of samples, and after we apply the reduction effect, most of these sounds would sound similar anyway.

31. In the Browser, click *Audio Effects*. Locate *Redux* and drag it onto the device panel after Drum Rack. Redux is a digital audio-quality reducer.

32. Set the *Downsample* dial in Redux to 30.

33. The drum samples now have a very gritty quality. Note: there are no cymbals in most chiptune music, since cymbals require a very high frequency noise sample. Thus, you will likely be using your *hihat closed* as the snare sound, and the *snare 808* as a lower snare sound.

34. Double-click on each sample in the Drum Rack. We need to shorten these sounds so they do not overlap. Unfortunately, Drum Rack does not have an easy way to specify number of voices. Use the *Length* dial in the enclosed sampler to shorten the time of each clip, specifically the *Kick 808* sample, which is far too long.

35. Write some drum parts. Keep the loops simple and short. See the example set project file for pattern ideas.

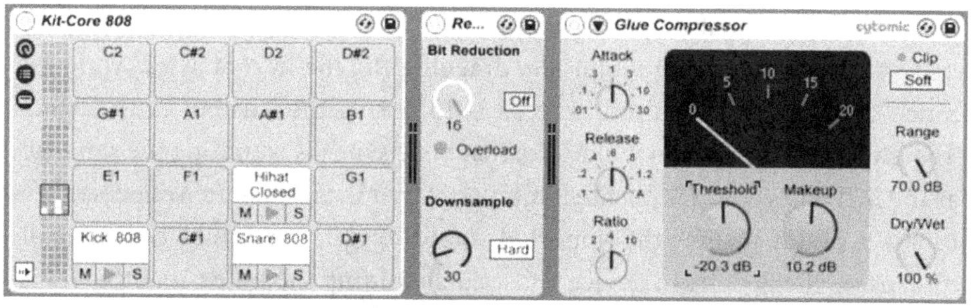

FIGURE 10.16

Chiptune drum track, Reduxed to skip every 30 samples. Since this reduces the overall pitch, it is possible to use a closed hi-hat in place of an actual snare drum sample.

Two factors determine digital audio quality: sample rate and bit depth. Sample rate is how many times per second the audio is measured. Since the highest frequency humans can hear is around 20,000 Hz, audio must be sampled at a much higher rate to be able to reproduce waveforms with cycles going that fast (CD-quality audio is sampled at 44,100 Hz). *Bit depth* is how many different steps can be used to measure the audio; 16-bit audio has sixteen volumes between "off" and "all the way loud"; 1-bit audio would only have speaker on and off clicks, and would not be able to make much difference between a square wave or Pavarotti's singing. To make an analogy to video, sample rates are like frames per second, and bit depth is like the resolution of the video. Lowering either value will make the video either choppier in motion or more pixilated. Using Redux allows creative control over audio reductions and can bring some retro flavor to recorded sounds.

Form and Structure

Earlier in the chapter we discussed some of the stylistic tropes of chiptune music (strong melodic hooks, faster speed, simple structure, etc.). These are not mandatory by any means, but for the example set we will adhere to these guidelines.

The example set is written at a speedy 180 BPM and attempts to only allow a maximum of three clips to play at any given time. The session is designed as such:

Scenes 1–3: A section
Scenes 4–6: B section
Scenes 7–8: Bridge section

Each section has a corresponding melodic line not exceeding eight bars in length, a chord progression not exceeding eight bars (usually only four bars), and a drum beat not exceeding one bar. In more detail, the melodic segments are designed around a one-bar hook that repeats and varies only slightly during the melodic line.

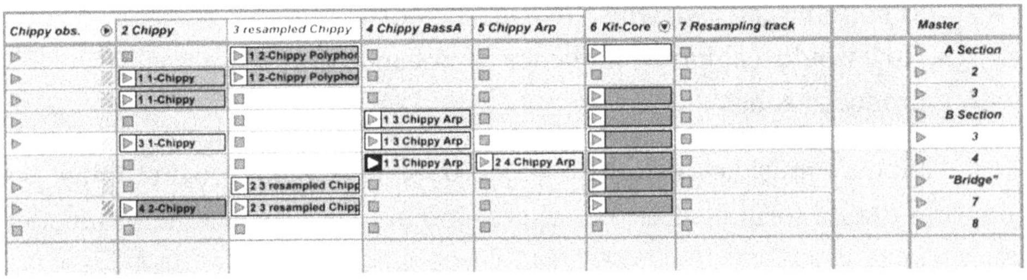

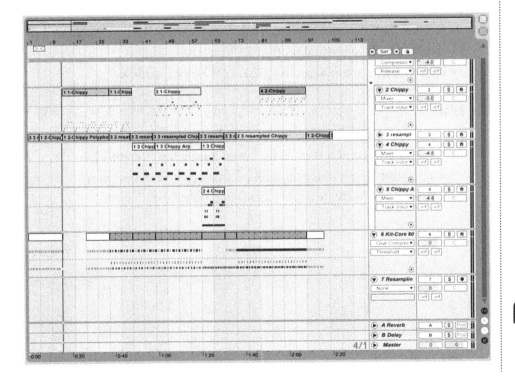

FIGURE 10.17

Completed song in Session View.

FIGURE 10.18

Completed song in Arrangement View.

On Your Own

We have covered quite a bit in the chapter on both creating custom instruments in Max and recreating a specific genre. However, the best tool we learned was the *auto chord* function, which just might change the way you write music. Now try this:

- Look up roman numeral chord progressions of existing songs, and use those numbers on the white piano keys to recreate those progressions—use this trick in other songs to immediately get a harmonic structure in your song.
- Try recreating a known song by stripping it down to its bare melodic, bass, and drum tracks, then use Chippy (or sampled chip sounds) to give the song a chiptune makeover.
- Try writing a version of Chippy that uses the *poly~* function to produce polyphonic sounds, or maybe a version that lets you draw your own wavetables.
- How might one make a chiptune song using authentic tools, such as portable game systems, to make sounds?
- How would a chiptune influence complement a conventionally produced song?

Chiptune music used to be a necessary evil of game programming, but now it is a valid form of electronic expression in music and a valid production technique.

In Live

- Review the Live documentation on *Simpler* from the Live manual.
- Review the Live manual section 23.1 on *Arpeggiator*.
- Read the Live manual section 32.1.3 on *Track Freezing*.

In Max

- Read the help files for the objects used in the example.
- Experiment with UI layouts for your Chippy instrument—how might your layout make the tool easier/harder for a new user?
- Explore how to create subpatches using polyphony for *Poly~*.

11

Granular Synthesis and Advanced Sampling

G ranular synthesis is not so much a genre as it is a sound design technique. The idea of repurposing recorded sounds using technology in an unusual way goes back to Hugh Le Caine's *Dripsody*, composed in 1955 using only reel-to-reel tapes and countless overdubs (the song was composed using a single recording of a drip from his faucet). In the late 1980s and 1990s, granular synthesis developed as an alternative use case for standard MIDI samplers. Many samplers, even early ones, had a loop function that allowed a triggered sample to be repeated. Since the audio processing in these machines was quite responsive at the audio rate, the sample could be cropped to create very quick repeats. When a sample is repeated quickly enough, a type of blurred waveform emerges—not quite a pure waveform cycle but not a recognizably recorded sample either. This clouded, blurry result is defined as "granular synthesis": using a "grain" of sound as the basis for a synthesized instrument.

Granular synthesis is a standard part of most electronic musicians' toolkits, but artists rarely use it exclusively. Those who do use it tend to create works of an experimental nature or a study piece to determine the extreme limits of the technique.

In our example we will create a song reminiscent of artists who use granular synthesis extensively, and we will also create the entire song from one voice sample.

Suggested Listening

Hugh Le Caine: *Dripsody*
Monolake: "Unstable Matter"
Boards of Canada: "A Is to B as B Is to C"
BT: "The Internal Locus"
Future Sound of London: "Life Form Ends"
Laurel Halo: "Wow"

Artist Profile: Monolake

Robert Henke, a.k.a. Monolake, was one of the founding engineers of Ableton Live. His career ranges from the relatively straightforward Berlin techno of the mid-90s to some very esoteric ambient music, often made in collaboration with visual and performance artists.

Live was originally developed as a solution for musicians attempting to perform using sound processed interactively in realtime on a laptop computer. Earlier solutions involved creating custom software for the task, and Live began its life as such software for use in Monolake performances. This chapter will heavily use one of Henke's later contributions to Max for Live, his Granulator II device.

Basic Sampling

We will start by recording a sound. In the example, this is the author saying the word "punch." This word was chosen for its wide range of timbres, from the plosive "p" to the sibilant "ch." If we are to limit ourselves to one sound, we might as well make it a versatile one.

1. Create a new Live set.
2. Arm an audio track.
3. Choose a clip slot and press the small circular *record* button in the slot.
4. Say "Punch" (or another word of your liking).
5. Press the stop button.
6. Double-click the clip you just recorded.
7. Drag the start position handle so it lines up with the transient spike in the waveform. Zoom in if necessary.
8. Make sure *Loop* is not turned on.

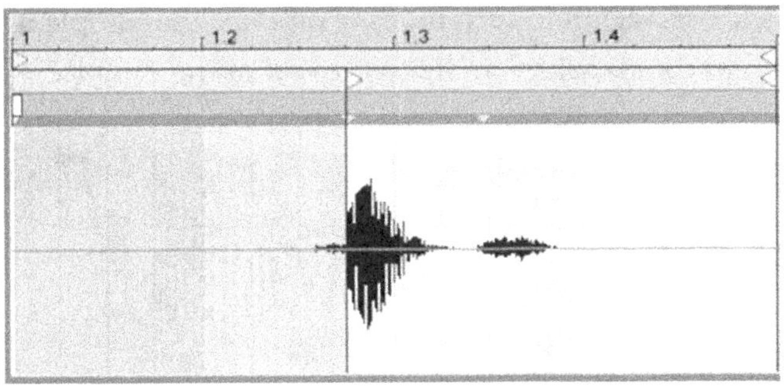

FIGURE 11.1

"Punch" recorded sample, with adjusted start position.

We now have a sample to use for our set, and we are ready to make a basic Simpler instrument.

9. In your Browser, click *Instruments*.
10. Locate *Simpler*, then drag it into a blank area of your set.
11. Drag the recorded audio clip into *Simpler's Drop Sample Here* box.
12. Arm the *Simpler* track—the sound should now be playable. (If you do not hear sound right away, try holding down a key on your piano—you should see a pale orange playhead scrub across the waveform in *Simpler*.)

We now need to get the sample in tune. Remember, *Simpler* (or *Sampler*) does not analyze for pitch content, and blindly assigns the sample to C3. Since it is likely our sound is not a C3, we need to use Spectrum to analyze it ourselves, and transpose it to the correct pitch.

13. In your Browser, click *Audio Effects*.
14. Click the disclosure triangle next to *Spectrum*.
15. Select *Pitch* and drag it onto your Simpler track.

When notes are played now, Spectrum will show the harmonic content of the sample. However, it may be quite difficult to determine the exact pitch of a spoken word as the pitch may modulate as the word is spoken. Nonetheless, we must try to be accurate because our entire song is based on this sample. We will temporarily loop the sample to make this possible.

16. Click *Loop* in Simpler.
17. Hold down a *C3* on your keyboard.
18. Drag the end-point handle toward the start point while playing the note, until the sound becomes steadier in pitch.
19. Spectrum should be showing a stable readout of fundamentals and overtones for this note.
20. Click *Transp* in Simpler. While playing a note, use your arrow keys to move up or down so the first spike (the fundamental) in Spectrum is lined up with *C3*. Use the *Detune* box for finer adjustments.

21. Click *Loop* again to turn looping off once the sample is in tune.
22. Drag the end-point handle to the end of the sample.

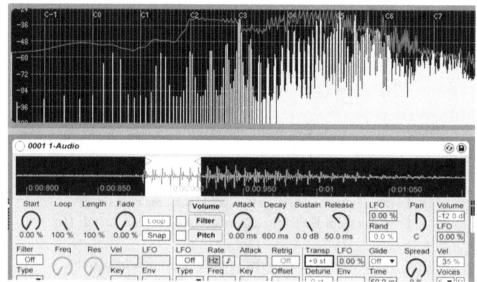

Looped vocal sample, with visible Spectrum showing a harmonically complex sound with a prominent tone on C3, used as the fundamental.

Since Simpler gives the track a default name matching that of the audio sample (1 1-Audio in our case), we should change the name to better reflect our sampling method for this track.

23. Select the *Simpler track*'s title.
24. Right-click and choose *Rename*.
25. Name the track *Simple*, since this is the simplest form of sampling we will be using.

The simple sample is going to beget the next few tracks and serve as a basis for further manipulation. In this example we are also going to use the Scale filter to ensure that we do not play out of key on future tracks, and we want our subsequent tracks to match that as well.

26. In your Browser, choose *MIDI effects*.
27. Click the triangle next to *Scale*.
28. Select *C Minor* and drag it onto the *Simple* track.
29. Right-click the *Simple* track and choose *Duplicate*.
30. Right-click the *Duplicate track*'s title and choose *Rename*.
31. Change the track name to *Looped*.

Now we will make a sustaining sound by looping the sample on this track. These steps are similar to those we followed to get the first sample in tune.

32. Click *Loop* in Simpler.
33. Hold down a *C3* on your keyboard.
34. Drag the end-point handle (a small triangle pointing to the right located at the end of the waveform) toward the start point

while playing the note, until the sound becomes steadier in pitch and sounds more like a sustained note.

35. Set the *Loop* dial to 50%.

36. Set the *Fade* dial to 100%.

37. Readjust the end-point handle as needed until the sound is sustained and sounds like it holds a stable pitch.

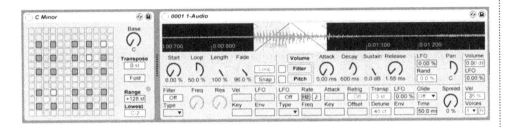

FIGURE 11.3

Looped sample with Scale MIDI effect.

Wavetable Synthesis with Simpler

We now have two simple-sampled voice instrument tracks. Using Simpler, we can go a step further and make a sample-based wavetable out of our voice. There is a very thin line between a wavetable (a single-period audio cycle used as a basis for sound generation) and a looped sample. In fact, we can easily locate one period of our recording's sound wave by zooming in to a sample-rate scale in Simpler.

38. Right-click the *Looped* track and select *Duplicate*.

39. Right-click the *Duplicate* track and select *Rename*.

40. Name the *Duplicate* track *Wavetable*.

41. In this track's Simpler, set *Loop* to 100%.

42. Set *Fade* to 0%.

43. Click and drag on the *waveform* and move your mouse down to zoom in.

44. Zoom until the end-point handle is almost off-screen. When it gets close to being off-screen, drag it closer to the start point.

45. After doing this once or twice, the individual cycles of the waveform should be visible.

46. Locate the lowest point of the cycle; set the start point at one end and the end point at the exact same point in the next cycle.

47. Play a *C3*. The note should sound like a cheap synthesizer (this is due to the minimal resolution of the wavetable to which we reduced this sample),

48. Use the *Spectrum device* to determine the fundamental pitch.

49. Use *Transp* and *Detune* to move the pitch of this instrument to C3 on *Spectrum*'s graph.

181

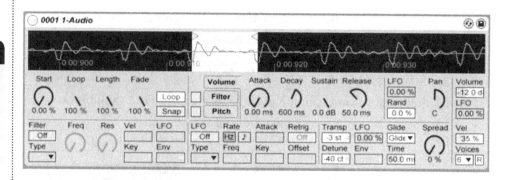

FIGURE 11.4

Wavetable synthesis using Simpler—the loop is set to exactly one wave cycle within the word "Punch." Note the loop length: six-thousandths of a second.

Now we will design an instrument that uses more advanced sampling techniques to achieve a wider sonic palette.

Granular Synthesis with Granulator II

For a true granular synthesis experience, we will turn to a Max for Live patch developed by one of the original inventors of Ableton Live, Robert Henke (also known by his stage name, Monolake). Granulator II at its heart works in a manner similar to our looping Simpler track, but instead of only looping one point, this patch has built-in variability and can create much more haunting and complex timbres from an audio file.

First we will need to install Granulator II.

50. Visit http://www.monolake.de/technology/granulator.html and download the *Granulator II* device.
51. Drag the downloaded file into your Live window.
52. In your Browser, click Max for Live.
53. Select *Granulator II* and drag it into a blank region of your *Session View*.
(Note: Granulator II takes longer to load than most Ableton devices.)
54. Drag the *Punch* audio file into the black *Drop Sample Here* region of Granulator II.

Before we dive into recreating the sounds in the example, it is worth noting the main difference between Granulator II and Simpler—the *FilePos* and *Grain* size are both variable by Live control dials. In Simpler, these controls were part of the waveform view, and they were not available for automation or external control. In Granulator II, we can assign LFOs and automation curves to these variables, allowing for a much greater range of possibilities in the timbre of our instrument. We will be combining this device with another Max device (*LFO MIDI*) for automatic modulation of these parameters.

55. Adjust the *FilePos* in Granulator II to fall in the middle of your recording's waveform.
56. Adjust the *Grain* dial to around 14 Hz.

57. In your Browser, click *Audio Effects*, then *Spectrum*.
58. Click the *triangle* next to *Spectrum*, then drag *Pitch* onto the *Granulator II* track.
59. Click the *Grain* box underneath the word *View* in Granulator II.
60. Play a *C3* on your keyboard.
61. Adjust the box under the label *Pitch* until the largest leftmost spike in *Spectrum* is close to *C3*.
62. Use the *Fine* box underneath *Pitch* to align the spike with *C3* further.

     (Note: Since this is not a single pitch but rather a "cloud" of many pitches, perfection may not be possible with your sample. Get as close as you can to intonation, and do not hesitate to revisit the *Pitch* box as needed during this project.)

Now we will add another track that allows exploitation of the *FilePos* and *Grain* dials, two controls now available to external control.

The next steps outline developing a quick Max object to add an LFO-style control to any of the Granulator objects (or any other parameters, for that matter).

63. Right-click the *Granulator II* track and select *Duplicate*.
64. Right-click the duplicate track and select *Rename*.
65. Name the duplicate track *Granulator Chords*.
66. In your Browser, click *Max for Live*.
67. Drag *Max MIDI Effect* onto the *Granulator Chords* track.
68. Click the *Edit* button to open a *Max Patcher* window.
69. Press *N* to make a new object.
70. Name the object **bpatcher M4L.SignalToLiveParam** and press *Enter*.
71. A square with a partially obscured set of buttons will appear—drag the lower right corner of this box to reveal the entire UI. This object can send a control signal to any device in a Live project. This includes every dial and setting on every device, on every track (excluding Max UI objects).
72. Press *N* to make another new object.
73. Name the object **live.dial** and press *Enter*.

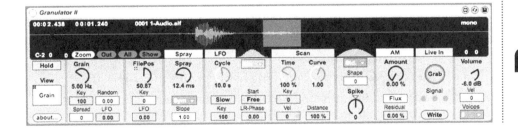

FIGURE 11.5

Granulator II with automated FilePos and Grain controls.

74. Right-click this dial and choose *Inspector*.
75. Scroll down to the *Parameter* group in the *Inspector*.
76. Set *Range/Enum* to **0. 1.** (Don't forget the decimal points!)
77. Set *Unit Style* to **Float**.
78. Close the *Inspector*.
79. Press *N* to make a third object.
80. Name the object **cycle~** and press *Enter*.
81. Connect the left outlet of **live.dial** to the left inlet of **cycle~**.
82. Connect the outlet of **cycle~** to the left inlet of the *bpatcher object* (located above the *Curve* dial).
83. Close and save the patch as **LFO all the things.amxd**.
84. Set the *Output rate* to 1.00 milliseconds (ms).
85. Adjust the *live.dial*—the graph should show a slowly moving sine wave pattern.

FIGURE 11.6

Max Inspector settings for the Live.dial controlling the cycle~ object.

Before we move on, note that the *cycle~* object used in this patch is the same one used to generate sound in the chiptune chapter. The difference is that the input frequency here is well under 20 cycles per second, placing it in the subsonic range. Thus, we have made a truly "low-frequency" oscillator, suitable for time-based control of other parameters.

We will now assign our LFO to a Granulator parameter.

86. On the right of *LFO All the Things*, locate the three pulldown menus.
87. Click *This Track* and choose *This Track* at the top of the list.
88. Under device choose *Granulator II*.
89. Under *Parameter* choose *GrainSpread*.
90. Adjust the *live.dial* to a desired speed; the sound of the chords should now fluctuate as the sine cycle adjusts the value of the *Spread* dial in *Granulator*.
91. Set the *Max* box to something between 50% and 70%—the effect will be mitigated a bit this way to preserve pitch content in the chords.

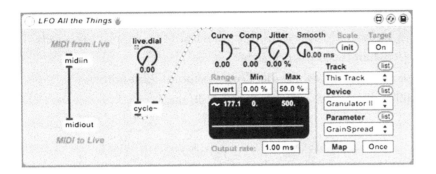

FIGURE 11.7

Custom LFO Max MIDI patch completed; notice the track list on the right—the list buttons can be used to refresh the lists of track devices.

If we wanted to go further and assign an external sound or mic input to control parameters, we could do that too, but this will do fine for this example and definitely gives the chords a unique modulated sound.

Before we move on to creating drum sounds from our recording, we should recap what we have so far. We have an audio track with the original recording, a "normal" Simpler track that simply repitches the sample on a keyboard, a "looped" Simpler track that sustains on a vowel sound, a Wavetable Simpler that loops the periodic cycle of the vowel sound, and the Granulator II device track which makes SFX-like sound. Note that as you make your own version, you can create as many variations as needed. For example, you might find the Wavetable tracks to suit your needs, but would like some to be harsher, have more release, or less treble frequency content. Feel free to make as many as fit your needs.

Drums from a Voice

Rather than using the Drum Rack, which we use almost any time we want a programmable drum track, we will be using the older Impulse device to make these drums. The main reason is the "stretch" function, which is a somewhat granular feature in itself—a pitch-insensitive speed adjustment for samples. Drum Rack is based on Simpler, which simply uses the repitch algorithm to achieve pitch change, which in turn speeds or slows the sample. Impulse is able to stretch and pull the length of the sample, which can achieve some very idiomatic results for a song based on granular techniques.

92. In your Browser, click *Instruments* and locate *Impulse*.
93. Drag *Impulse* to a blank area of your arrangement.
94. Double-click on your original audio clip of the word ("punch" or whatever you recorded instead).
95. Drag the start position handle to a "plosive" sound in the clip, such as a "p" or "d" sound.
96. Drag the audio clip into the first clip slot inside of *Impulse*.
97. Make sure the *Impulse* track is armed by clicking the *arm* button—it should be lit up red.

98. Press the *A* key on your (typing) keyboard—while doing this repeatedly, adjust the *Start* dial until the clip plays precisely when the key is pressed.

99. Adjust the *Transp* dial down to about -22 semitones.

100. Adjust the *Decay* dial to about 40 ms.

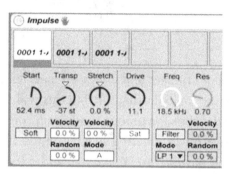

Kick Drum settings in Impulse.

This should produce a low, popping sound not unlike an extremely deadened kick drum. If it is not sounding like a kick drum, continue adjusting the transposition and decay length until it does. Assuming the initial sound was indeed plosive (think air being puffed into an unshielded microphone), this sound should be achievable.

Now we will make two sibilant drum sounds—the snare and cymbal.

101. Double-click on your original audio clip of the word ("punch" or whatever you recorded instead).

102. Drag the *start position* handle to a sibilant sound in the clip, such as a "ch" or a "ss" sound.

103. Drag the audio clip into the second clip slot inside of Impulse.

104. Make sure the *Impulse* track is armed by clicking the arm button—it should be lit up red.

105. Press the *S* key on your (typing) keyboard—while doing this repeatedly, adjust the *Start* dial until the clip plays precisely when the key is pressed.

106. Adjust the *Transp* dial down a bit—around -10 semitones.

107. Adjust the *Stretch* dial up, until the clip sounds like it has an unnatural, glitchy reverb.

108. Adjust the *Decay* to about 1.14s.

109. Double-click on your original audio clip of the word ("punch" or whatever you recorded instead).

110. Drag the audio clip into the third clip slot inside of Impulse.

111. Press the *D* key on your (typing) keyboard—while doing this repeatedly, adjust the *Start* dial until the clip plays precisely when the key is pressed.

112. Adjust the *Transp* dial up a bit—around +2 semitones.

113. Click Impulse's *Filter* button to activate filtering.

114. Change *Mode* to *HP 1*.
115. Set the *Freq* dial to about 7.39 kHz.
116. Adjust the *Decay* dial to about 252 ms.
117. Increase the volume as needed. Note that Impulse has two volume controls—one for the clip and one for the entire Impulse device. They are located very close to each other—the one on the left adjusts the selected drum sound only.

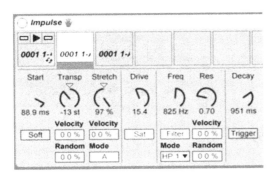

FIGURE 11.9

Snare drum Impulse settings; the waveform start point was also trimmed before dragging into Impulse.

Now that we have three somewhat convincing drum sounds made from our original audio recording, we are free to use them to write our song. We will use the standard method for writing our clips.

118. Double-click in a clip slot on your *Impulse track*.
119. Click the *pencil* icon in the top right of Live's window to enable *Draw Mode*.
120. Draw your desired drum patterns.

Mixing

Standard mixing techniques apply in this example, such as grouping drum and non-drum tracks, applying Glue Compressor on the groups, and Limiting the master track.

187

Original	2 Group	Simple	Looped	Wavetable	Granulator	Granulator Chords	8 Impulse	9 Operator	Master	
1 1-Audio	▷	▷ 1 Simple	▢	▢	▷	▷ 1 Granulator Chords	▷	▢	▷	1
1 1-Audio	▷	▷ 1 Simple	▷	▢	▷	▷	▢	▢	▷	1
▢	▷	▢	▢	▢	▷	▷	▷	▢	▷	2
▢	▷	▢	▢	◉	▷	▷	▷	▢	▷	3
▢	▷	▢	▷ 1 Looped	▷	▷	▷	▷	▢	▷	4
▢	▢	▢	▢	◉	▢	▢	▷	▢	▷	5
▢	▷	▢	▢	▷	▷	▢	▢	▢	▷	6
▢	▢	▢	▢	▢	◉	▢	▢	▢	▷	7
▢	▢	▢	▢	▢	◉	▢	▢	▢	▷	8

FIGURE 11.10

Completed set in Session View.

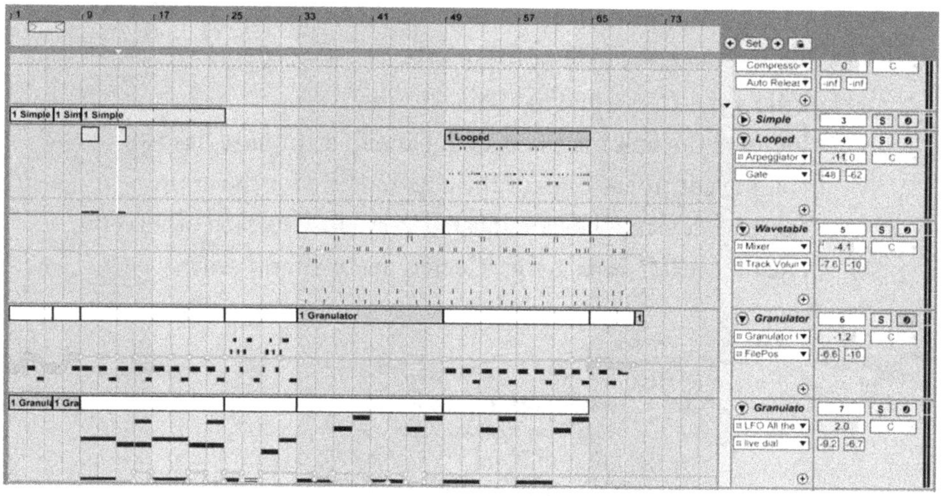

FIGURE 11.11

Completed song in Arrangement View.

On Your Own

Granular synthesis is not so much a genre as it is a technique for sound design. That being said, the types of music that employ granular synthesis more heavily are usually of an experimental nature. This technique would work well in ambient music and its relatives—trip-hop, acid jazz, chillout, and the like. The listening examples given at the beginning of this chapter should serve as a jumping-off point for further exploration into artists who use the technique.

The example provided with this book attempts to create an homage to groups such as Boards of Canada (warm, detuned synths), but try creating sounds for other styles using these methods. Using advanced techniques for sampling can set your music apart and create truly original sonic environments.

- Try using sounds other than vocal recordings to produce grains.
- Note other differences between Granulator II and Simpler—when would either be the more appropriate tool?
- Try using Sampler (it's less simple than Simpler) —the key feature of setting key zones for different samples is very useful for live performance.

In Live

Review the Live documentation on *Simpler* from the Live manual.

Review the *Max for Live Essentials* lesson in Live's Help View.

Review the *Synthetic Sounds, Acoustic Samples* lesson in Live's lessons Table of Contents.

Review the *Granulator II by Monolake* Free Pack lesson, found in Live's lessons Table of Contents.

In Max

Read the *help* file for the *M4L.SignaltoLiveParam object.*

12

Dubstep

Dubstep is a U.K. electronic dance style started in 2005, often cited as beginning with the Skream track "Midnight Request Line" then later Americanized into a very different style with the same name. We will explore the differences between U.K. and U.S. Dubstep in a bit. The name "dubstep" is a portmanteau of two other electronic music subgenres: "dub" music and "2-step" or "2-step garage." There are also significant influences in the genre from the United Kingdom's Grime subgenre of hip-hop, and some significant contributions from drum and bass. Here is a short recipe for dubstep music, using ingredients from each of these subgenres.

From dub we will need the aesthetic of "wobbles," but we will be achieving them in a way totally unrelated to dub music. Dub, an electronic offshoot of reggae, was predictably a product of the Caribbean, which is a hot tropical climate. DJs of the late 1980s and early 1990s often used quickly pressed records called "dub plates" to make loop records and other tools for mixing on the fly. These records were made of material with a lower melting point than standard vinyl or cassette tape, which made the records warp quite reliably. Thus, when played simultaneously with a vinyl record, the samples would be out of sync and sound "wobbly." This became a key part of the dub sound and was popularized mainly by the artist King Tubby. Dub music also is usually downtempo, washy-sounding music with plenty of reverb and pad synths.

From 2-step we will be swiping the drum patterns. The 2-step garage style is a U.K. production style created as a response to regular U.K. Garage, which shares many similarities with house music including the 4-on-the-floor kick drum pattern. 2-step allows the kick drum to play quick, syncopated patterns that have plenty of groove but are a bit less danceable.

From Grime we need the gritty, dirty bass synthesizers used in many U.K. hip-hop recordings. "Bonkers" by Dizzee Rascal is a good example of this sound. These synths share a bit of an aesthetic with the Reese bass from chapter 9, but instead of getting their complexity from lack of intonation, they simply get it by modulating waves until the timbre is complex and dirty-sounding.

Take one part of each ingredient above, then mix together using DJs and venues accustomed to playing and hearing drum and bass music. Apply the common intro-build-drop form using only the ingredients listed above. This is the mindset of making a good dubstep track. Now we will examine in depth how to start a basic track in this genre.

Artist Profile: Skrillex

Sonny Moore was a niche rock artist, specializing in post-hardcore sounds with his band From First to Last before he started experimenting with production. His initial releases used some of the more aggressive production ideas happening in transatlantic dubstep recordings of Flux Pavilion and Datsik and took their dirty, complicated nature to new extremes.

His production style features a very Ableton-centric workflow, involving a general concept of a line or phrase followed by a great deal of one-shot sampling, effect plug-ins, resampling, and combining back into a phrase. The production technique will be covered in this chapter, albeit with one original sound source versus the myriad outboard equipment used in Skrillex productions.

Suggested Listening

U.K. Style:

Skream: "Midnight Request Line"
Benga: "Crunked Up"
Excision & Datsik: "Deviance"

U.S. Style:

Freestylers: "Cracks" (Flux Pavilion remix)
Benny Benassi: "Cinema" (Skrillex remix)
Nero: "Promises"

Drum Patterns

1. Before you do anything else, set your tempo to 135.00 BPM. This is the average tempo for dubstep songs (most fall between 130 and 140 BPM).

2. Click *Drums* in your Browser. Drag a default (blank) *Drum Rack* into your set.

3. We need six sounds: 2 *kicks*, 2 *claps/snares*, a closed *Hi-Hat*, and a *Crash cymbal*. These can be easily found by typing the name of the instrument into the search box above the Browser. The Browser will only show items with that keyword in their name.

4. When developing clips for dubstep, start by double-clicking to make a blank clip, and set the length to at least 2.0.0. This is necessary because dubstep drum patterns are almost always in half-time, necessitating two measures to complete the minimum time cycle.

5. The typical "full" pattern in most dubstep songs usually involves a *snare* on beat 3 (of both measures), *syncopated kicks* between beats 1 and 3 of both measures (but usually not during beats 3–4), and complex, near-random *Hi-Hat* patterns. See Figure 12.1 for an example. We will be layering the two sounds chosen for the *kick* and the *snare*—this will create an even heavier sound.

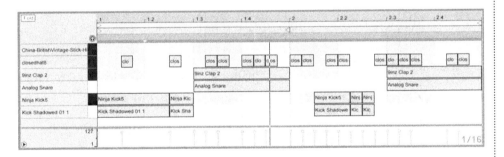

FIGURE 12.1

Typical dubstep drum pattern. Note layered kicks/snares, and lack of kick drum after beat 3.

6. Create 2–3 drum clips in this vein, creating varying degrees of complexity.

7. Turn up the *A Send* dial, which by default gives the track a bit of reverb.

191

Bass Instruments and Resampling

8. We will start by making a variety of bass loops. Many dubstep producers have a large library of interesting bass sounds, some rhythmically modulated, others extremely harsh or smooth. Like other elements of EDM construction, these can be recycled and reused for different songs and do not have to be made from scratch for every composition. For this example, we are going to create a couple bass loops focused in low frequencies and a couple focused in high frequencies.

9. Begin by dragging an *Operator* from the Browser to bring up a new FM synthesizer instrument. Operator has four tone generators that can be routed to either be audible or act as *modulators* for another tone generator.

10. Set the *Wave* type of *Oscillator A* to *Saw D*. This creates a *Sawtooth wave* that is mathematically calculated for the maximum number of overtones.

11. On *Oscillator B*, set the *Coarse* setting to 0.5, and set the *Level* to -15 dB.

12. On *Oscillator C*, set the *Coarse* setting to 2, and set the *Level* to -15 dB.

13. On *Oscillator D*, set the *Coarse* setting to 5, and set the *Level* to -15 dB.

14. Play a *C1 note* (if you are using the computer's keyboard, this requires hitting the *octave down* or *Z* key twice and playing a *C* (the letter *A* for typing).

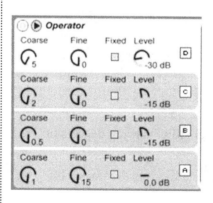

FIGURE 12.2

Operator bass settings. Note: Osc A is a Saw D wave, the rest are default sine waves.

Now that we have a very gritty, grimy sound, we will add some modulation and filters to our sound.

15. Click the box under *LFO* on the right-hand side of *Operator*. Keep in mind, an LFO makes no sound—it is simply an automated knob-turning device. We will use this to turn two knobs in particular.

16. In the second drop-down box, change the setting to *Sync*. This makes the LFO interpolate between the minimum and maximum at a musical note rate.

17. Set the *Rate* knob to *1* (whole notes).

18. Set the *Amount* knob to *100%*.

19. In the black center window of *Operator*, locate the *Dest. A* and *Dest. B* controls. These signify to which knobs the LFO's control is being routed. By default, A–D are turned on, causing the LFO to bend their pitch up and down.

20. Turn off A–D under *Dest. A*. This eliminates the pitch bending.

21. Turn on *Fil* under *Dest. A*. This will cause the Filter Frequency to interpolate between the lowest frequency of its range and the cutoff frequency we choose in the next step.

22. Under *Dest. B*, change the setting from *Off* to *Vol B*. This will cause the *Level* knob on *Osc. B* to interpolate between –inf dB and -15 dB.

23. Turn on the box next to *Filter*. Change the setting to *Low SVF*, and set the *Freq.* to 2.00 kH.

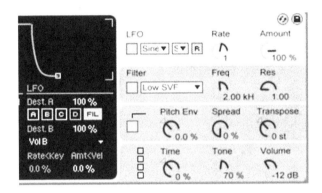

Operator LFO and Filter settings. Dest A is set to the low-pass Filter, and Dest. B is set to the volume level of Osc. B.

A modulator essentially causes an up-and-down pitch bend to occur on the generator with which it is paired. The pitch will bend in the manner depicted next to the *Wave* setting in *Operator*'s settings window. For instance, if the modulator (e.g., *Osc. B*) is set to *sine wave*, it will bend *Osc. A*'s pitch smoothly up and down at the rate specified by the note played. If an A=440 is played on the keyboard, Oscillator A will play a sine wave at that rate, and Oscillator B will bend A's pitch up and down at 440 cycles per second. This effectively changes the timbre of Oscillator A and makes a much more complex waveform. We're going to exploit this feature to make some nausea-inducing bass patterns.

Right now we have a gritty, grimy synth. With Osc. B's level all the way down we have a quite powerful bass synth, and with Osc. B's level all the way up we have some serious high-frequency noise. This will represent the sonic range of our wobble bass instrument.

You may prefer a bit more power to your sound. Here is a quick way to achieve that "massive" sound you might be looking for:

24. In the Browser, under *Audio Effects*, add a *Saturator* to your bass clips track. *Saturator* works as a very basic analog distorter, not dissimilar to a guitar amp. Turn the *Drive* setting up

193

a bit. *Saturator* has a built-in limiter, so you will not clip—but you shouldn't overdo it either.

25. Also under *Audio Effects*, add a *Simple Delay* to your bass clips track. Some dubstep drops have a wide stereo field, and Simple Delay is a quick way to achieve a doubled sound without changing the timbre too much.

26. Change both channels' *Sync* buttons to *Time*.

27. Set the *L channel* time to 40.0 ms.

28. Set the *R channel* time to 4.00 ms.

29. Set both *Feedback* and *Dry/Wet* to 30%.

30. You should hear a fat, spread-out character to your bass clips now.

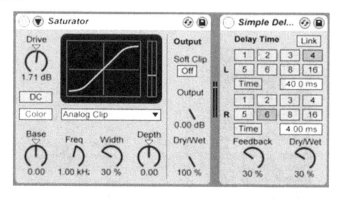

FIGURE 12.4

Audio Effects on the wobble bass Operator.

We now have the basic settings for creating a good, slightly aggressive wobble sound. The sound we are achieving in this example falls somewhere between the early, relaxed U.K. dubstep basses and the extremely aggressive U.S. dubstep bass sounds. The key here is that this Operator will not actually be performed in our song. We will use this instrument to create one-bar samples, then play back those samples in an interactive way to create the complex-sounding drop. Here we will sample a basic low, slow wobble:

31. Double-click in a blank clip slot on the Operator we made in the last step.

32. Draw in a *C1* that lasts for the duration of the clip (one measure by default).

33. Right-click the track title and select *Freeze Track*. This temporarily disables editing and makes any clips in the track into rendered audio clips.

34. Right-click and select *Insert Audio Track*.

35. Drag your *C1* clip onto the audio track. Double-click the clip to ensure that it is now audio.

In the included example, the drop is composed of six to seven clips made in this manner. Each one was made by creating a MIDI clip with slightly different LFO rates, filter types, and MIDI notes; freezing the track; dragging the clip

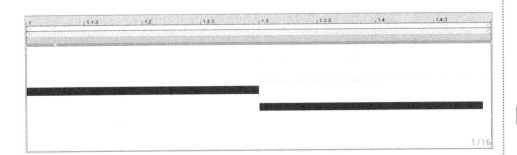

FIGURE 12.5

Operator MIDI Clip.

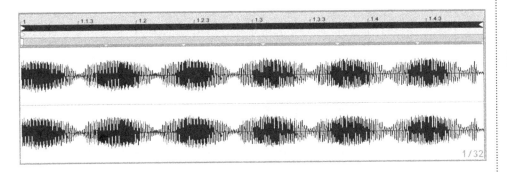

FIGURE 12.6

The same clip, after freezing the Operator track and copying to an audio track. The sound is identical in both figures 12.5 and 12.6.

onto a neighboring audio track; and then unfreezing the track and repeating the process. The best practice here is to obtain a variety of interesting rhythms and timbres, covering frequencies ranging from slow to fast and low to high. Some ideas might be:

LFO rate: whole note, C1.
LFO rate: 1/8 triplet, C2.
LFO rate: 1/4 note, C1, high-pass filter.
LFO rate: 1/4 note triplet, C#1.
Something not using the filter, as a non sequitur—possibly a synth
    pad chord on only *Osc. A*.

Note that selection is usually limited to a root note, a perfect fifth, and possibly a half-step above the root note. Music theorists might refer to this as the Phrygian Mode, but one doubts popular dubstep artists are writing in that context.

Now we will stitch together and perform the clips. We need a better way to trigger the audio clips dynamically than simply clicking each clip's *play* button individually, and we definitely need to be able to change clips more quickly than once every measure. This is how to set up a more dynamic way of launching clips:

36. Double-click on one of your audio clips to switch to *Clip View*.
37. Holding the *shift* key, select the first and last of your bass audio
    clips.
38. In *Clip View*, click the small *L* in the lower-left of the window.
    This reveals the *Clip Launch* preferences.

195

FIGURE 12.7

Five bass audio clips selected, with Launch option shown. Quantization for just these five clips is set to quarter notes, while the rest of the set still triggers at the global 1-bar value.

FIGURE 12.8

Key assignment mode is now active. To use this mode properly, turn off the piano keys icon to allow the entire keyboard to be available for assignment.

196

FIGURE 12.9

Key assignments on each MIDI clip. Clips have been renamed to reflect sonic content.

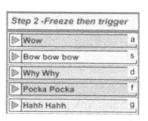

39. Under *Quantization*, choose *1/4*. This allows these clips to trigger at a different rate than the rest of the set. Now a new clip from this group can be triggered every beat rather than every four beats.

40. If you are using a device like the Launch-pad or APC40, triggering these clips will work similar to playing a quantized drum rack, except that they will interrupt each other rather than playing as separate layers.

41. If you have no such control surface, here is a great workaround: in the top right of the window, click the *piano keys* button next to *KEY* to turn it off.

42. Click the *KEY* button. Your project will now be highlighted in orange. This mode allows the computer's (typing) keyboard buttons to be assigned as triggers in your set.

43. Click the first bass audio clip, and type the letter *A*. An *A* appears next to the clip, signifying that pressing the letter *A* will activate the clip.

44. Assign other letters to the other clips. A logical suggestion might be to organize the clips by pitch, then assign the lower-pitched clips to letters on the left of the keyboard and higher-pitched clips to the right.

45. Click *KEY* to exit *Key assignment mode*. Try triggering clips—they should play quantized to quarter notes, and seem to fit together rhythmically.

Now it is time to stitch together these disparate sounds into a 16-measure phrase, suitable for a *drop* section. Since our bass clips are quantized and trigger-ready, it is simply a matter of routing the audio from our audio track with the bass clips into another audio track's clip.

46. Check that the *IO* circle on the extreme lower-right of the Ableton session panel is lit.

47. Right click and select *insert audio track*.

48. Under *Audio From* select the audio track with your bass clips. This will make it so recording on this track will "record" audio from that track rather than from your microphone. This process is essentially lossless; it is technically similar to bouncing from *Arrangement View*, but much more elegant.

49. Arm the new audio track.

50. Click one of the circles on a blank clip on the new audio track. As soon as Live starts recording, trigger your bass samples. Try to reserve the lowest sounds for the beginning of the measure (as one would use a kick drum), but use your musical sense to judge the best way to play these samples.

51. After 16 measures have passed (the timer at the top of the window will indicate how many measures have gone by if you lost count), press the *space* bar to stop recording.

52. Double-click the new clip on your new audio track. In the *Clip detail panel*, check that the *Length* is 16.0.0 and that no numbers are lit orange (indicating a non-integer clip length).

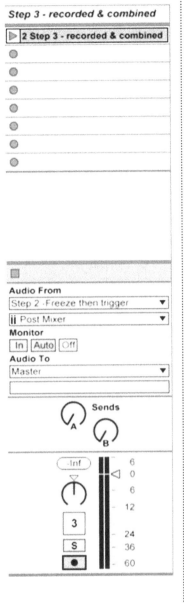

FIGURE 12.10

A third track, capturing audio from the second track. Audio is recorded directly from the Freeze track when routed in this way.

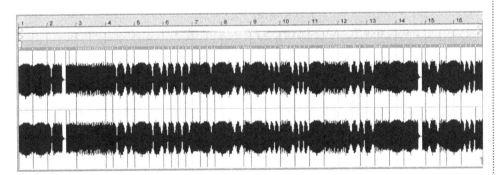

FIGURE 12.11

16-bar consolidated bass drop, composed of multiple combinations of frozen audio clips.

197

Treble Leads

In dubstep, the bulk of work goes into the sound design of the bass loops. Most early dubstep recordings included very little beyond a mood-setting drum beat and a few key bass grooves. Most recordings, however, have some treble elements to set the introductory section apart from the bass-heavy drop section. In our example we will add some arpeggiated leads, paying homage to some early U.K. dubstep tunes. We will also begin the mixing process with track grouping and sidechain compression.

53. Right-click the title of your original Operator instrument and click *Duplicate*.
54. On the new copy of Operator, change the *Coarse* setting of *Osc. B* to *1*.
55. Deactivate *Osc. D* (click the orange *D* button").
56. Set the *Filter* to about 2.00 kHz. The sound should be much brighter and simpler. Play a *C3* and tweak the *Osc. B* and *C* levels as desired—we are aiming for a bright, stabby sound.
57. In the Browser, under *MIDI Effects*, add *Arpeggiator*.
58. Also under *MIDI Effects*, disclose the presets for *Chords*, and add *Minor*. Be sure to place *Chord* to the left of *Arpeggiator*.
59. Play the *C3* again. There should be a smooth broken-chord pattern playing. Adjust the rate of *Arpeggiator* to a desired setting (1/16 is usually a good choice here).
60. Double-click a blank clip slot on your *Arpeggiated Operator track*.
61. Set the length of this clip to four measures.
62. Record a pattern using four to five long notes. Keep it simple—like the bass loop we should be using roots, sharp roots, and fifths as our main melodic elements. That being said, feel free to experiment. Try changing to a different note for part of a pattern, or changing the *Style* setting of *Arpeggiator* to fit your song better.

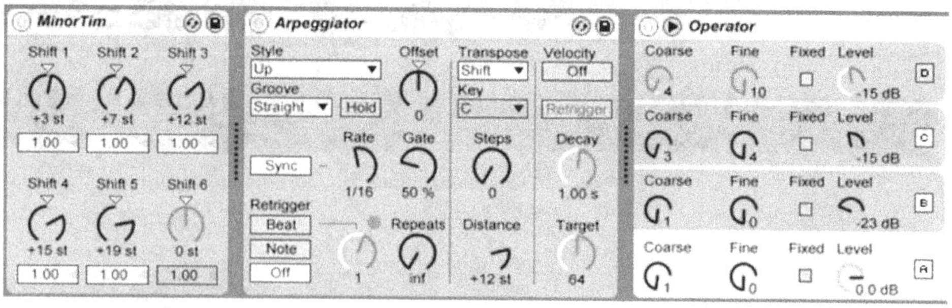

FIGURE 12.12

A duplicate Operator, adjusted for arpeggiated treble leads.

Risers

Like drum and bass music, dubstep uses the familiar EDM trope of the long "riser" buildup and drop form. The drop in dubstep music is considered as the climax of the song and key memorable moment. Thus, a dramatic build can add excitement to a mix. Conversely, a shorter buildup section can "get to the point" more quickly and might be a better fit for your song. Some supplemental listening might help you choose how you want this section to sound. For a quick, no-nonsense buildup, Flux Pavilion's "Bass Cannon" is a good example. For an extremely long and borderline absurdist buildup, try Porter Robinson's "The State." In our example we will do the shorter variety with the understanding that a key mechanism for making a longer buildup is to simply do everything we are doing here—but for a longer duration and with more layers.

63. On the *Drum Rack* instrument, double-click in a blank clip slot to make a new one-measure clip.
64. Set the clip's length to 8.0.0.
65. In the top-right of Live's window, click the *Pencil* icon to change to *drawing mode* for MIDI.
66. Right-click in the MIDI grid panel, and set the fixed grid size to *1 Bar*.
67. Draw in four notes on all drum tracks.
68. Right-click again and set the fixed grid size to *1/2*.
69. Draw in four more notes on all drum tracks.
70. Right-click again—set the fixed grid to *1/4*.
71. Draw in four more notes.
72. Right-click again—set the fixed grid to *1/8*.
73. Draw in four more notes.
74. Right-click again—set the fixed grid to *1/16*.
75. Draw in four more notes.
76. And so on.

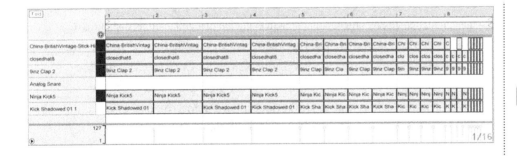

FIGURE 12.13

Accelerating drum pattern for buildup.

We will also want some interesting sound effects during our buildup. Now we will make a generated white noise sweep.

77. From the Browser, drag a new *Operator track* into your session.

78. Under *Wave* set it to *Noise White*. This will generate pitchless white noise, no matter what key is pressed.

79. Double-click in a clip slot on the Noise track we just made. Set the length of the clip to 8.0.0 (eight measures), and either program or record a note lasting through the entire duration of the clip.

80. In the Browser, click *Audio Effects*, then drag *Auto Filter* onto your noise track. We will not actually be using any of the automatic features of this effect, but the setting is a convenient way to add a filter.

81. Change the filter type to the third setting (*Band*).

82. Double-click the clip to show *Clip Detail* on the bottom panel. In the very bottom left of this panel are three buttons, the rightmost being a letter *E*. Click the *E* to show automation parameters for the clip.

83. We want an exponential curve for this noise, starting from a very low frequency and only letting higher sounds pass near the very end of the clip. To do this, we first need to select *Auto Filter* in the top parameter box, and then *Frequency* in the lower parameter box. This will show the automation line for the knob that controls where the cutoff frequency for our filter is.

84. Double-click on the line near the beginning of the clip, and again near the end of the clip. The first dot should be dragged all the way down, and the second should be dragged all the way up. This creates a linear ramp of the filter frequency when played.

85. To make a nice exponential curve, place your mouse near the line where you want the knee of the curve to be. Holding the *Option* key, drag the line down to make the desired curve. We want this noise effect to increase most of the way during the last two measures of the clip. Now we have an interesting sweep effect that is really only loud during the end of the clip, but somewhat present throughout the buildup.

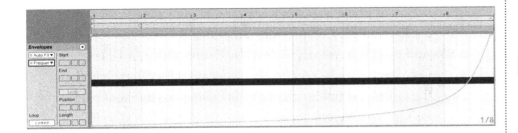

FIGURE 12.14

8-Bar White noise, with Auto Filter's frequency rising exponentially.

Another appropriate sound to pair with the white noise is a lead synth with some sort of applied pitch bend.

86. Duplicate your *Arpeggiated lead track* from steps 53–62.
87. Double-click in a blank clip slot to create a new MIDI clip. Set the length to 8.0.0.
88. Record a chord, preferably in the same key as the song, that lasts the duration of the clip.
89. Click the *E* button under the clip detail panel to show the automation parameters for the clip.
90. Set the first box to *MIDI Ctrl* and the second box to *Pitch Bend*.
91. Add a breakpoint at the beginning and end of the clip by double-clicking in both locations on the pink line. Drag the first point all the way down and drag the second point all the way up.
92. This should apply an extreme pitch-bend to your chord, and should line up nicely with the accelerating drum pattern and the filtered noise sweep.

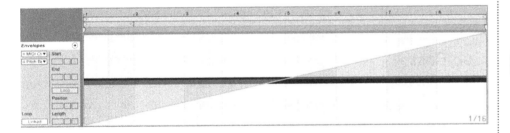

FIGURE 12.15

Minor chord with linear rising Pitch Bend during buildup.

Initial Mixing

201

We need to group the tracks and set some initial track relationships to make the drums pop out and the drop effective. Here is a list of some mixing element we will use as we work to polish up our scenes.

93. Group the Non-Drum tracks, including all synths, the drop, and any other sound effects.
94. Add a *Compressor* to the drum track. Set the *Threshold* to about -10.0 dB and the ratio to *inf*. We need these drums to be very loud, but not distorted—using a Limiter instead of the Com-

pressor is possible, but in track-level mixing it is usually best practices to use Compressors rather than Limiters.

95. Add two Compressors to the Non-Drums group: A Glue Compressor, and a regular one. You can technically use both of the same type, but for clarity we are using two different plugins for two different goals.

96. The Glue Compressor will be used to achieve uniformity among the non-drum parts. It will also enable us to add some Sub bass later without overpowering the drop. Set the *Threshold* to -14 dB and the *Makeup* to 8.41 dB.

97. The standard Compressor will be used to achieve ducking by sidechaining from the Drum Rack. Click the *Triangle* button in the top left of Compressor to show the *Sidechain* controls.

98. Change *Audio From* to *Drum Rack*, and the second box to *Kick Drum—Post FX* (your titles may vary).

99. Turn up the input *Gain* knob below the *Sidechain* button.

100. Turn *Ratio* all the way up to *inf:1*. This produces a reliable gain reduction whenever the threshold is crossed.

101. Lower the *Thresh slider* to about halfway.

102. Play a clip from the *Drum Rack*. You should see the *GR* meter pulling down in orange every time the kick drum plays. If you play any track inside the non-drums group, you should also hear the volume ducking down significantly whenever the kick drum hits.

103. Finally (for now) place a Limiter on the Master track. This will prevent any accidental clipping that may occur.

Sub Bass

In an ironic reversal, our bass instrument we made earlier has less bass content than one would expect. This is mainly due to the large amount of overtones and other timbral complexity we added to the sound. We may want to add in a supportive sub-bass instrument to add some low end to our sound.

Recording into Arrangement View

Unlike some other examples, we will be doing a bit of postproduction work in this example, so absolute perfection is not necessary when recording into *Arrangement View*. It is necessary to organize into at least three scenes: Introduction, Buildup, and Drop.

The scenes are set up as such in our example:

Scene 1:   Intro   Arpeggiated synth lead only
Scene 2:   Add Hi-Hat and Snare
Scene 3:   Add Full drum beat
Scene 4–5:   (used only for bass clips—unused in arrangement)
Scene 6:   Buildup
Scene 7:   Drop

Like the drum and bass example in chapter 9, when recording this example you should cycle through the Buildup and Drop scene twice for a standard-length dubstep tune.

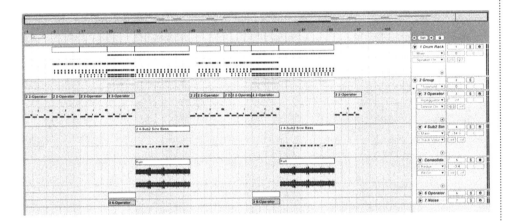

FIGURE 12.16

Completed song in Arrangement View.

On Your Own

Dubstep, one of the more recently invented styles in this book, may or may not be seen as a passing fad by music enthusiasts. Regardless of dubstep's legacy, what remains are the new production techniques invented by producers of this music, namely the creative use of FM chains to produce bizarre "bass" sounds, and the aggressive resampling of said sounds to create impossibly complex-sounding instruments. This technique could be applied to other styles as well—picture something like a processed voice or guitar sound being treated in the same way the bass sounds in this example were treated. Some things to try:

- Try changing Operator's routing to creating more/less complex bass tones for resampling.
- Create a song that uses the dubstep bass techniques outlined in this chapter but does not use the tempo and groove of dubstep; house music especially works well with this technique.
- Instead of manually drawing clip automations, try assigning the parameter to a MIDI controller and recording the automation directly into the clips.

203

- Figure out an interesting way to perform dubstep music live— what elements could be varied in a performance environment and what must remain preprogrammed?

In Live

Review the Live documentation on *Operator* from the Live manual. Review the *Operator* lessons in Live's help panel.

Remixing and Loop Sampling

n this chapter we will be creating not one but three projects. We have chosen to focus on three here because the first two are not so much projects as they are quick studies in how to pull off a common DJ-centric task. Before we begin, we should lay down two quick definitions: (1) a *simple remix* is when you take an acapella track of a song and make the background instrumentals different; and (2) a *mashup* is when you take one or more acapellas and one or more instrumentals and combine them to form a sort of two-headed song. Often, mashups involve two songs and use some instrumental and vocal material from both.

The *complex remix* we will do at the end of this chapter will involve creating a song entirely out of samples from other songs. This "frankensong" will yield a more original-sounding production and provide quite a bit of practice in sampling, warping, beatmatching, and pitch-matching techniques.

Artist profile: DJ Shadow

Josh Davis, a.k.a. DJ Shadow, is most famous for his debut album "Endtro-ducing...," composed entirely of sampled material but creatively morphed into something new and unheard. To date it is considered one of the most influential electronic recordings, and it earned a Guinness World Record for being the first record made entirely from samples.

His production method was one of the first to explore the power of the Akai MPC sampler, in 1993 still a very new product. He plays samples from vinyl into the MPC (which functions in ways similar to both Ableton's Drum Rack and its Session view, depending on the length of the clip), then uses the MPC to rearrange the variety of samples. He still uses this method today, but in Live shows, especially those with synchronized lights and video, he will use an Ableton set due to its improved stability over traditional turntables and/or CDJ decks.

Listening Examples

DJ Shadow: "Endtroducing . . ."
Cut Chemist: "The Audience's Listening"
DJ Danger Mouse: "The Grey Album"
DJ Rashad: "Double Cup"

Simple Remixing

A simple remix might involve the use of an acapella vocal track and a set of precalculated loops. In this example we will need to match Live's global tempo to that of the acapella track and simply add loops from any loop collection to match. We will keep this one simple and only use drum loops, since later in the chapter we will go deeper into pitch-sensitive mixing.

1. Choose an acapella vocal track to remix; try to pick something fairly modern that has likely been recorded to a metronome.
2. Drag the audio file into your project.
3. After dragging in the acapella track, double-click the clip.
4. Turn *Warp* off in the *clip detail panel*; now the global song tempo will not affect the acapella track.
5. Set the *Start* position triangle to where *Beat 1* should be at the beginning of your song.

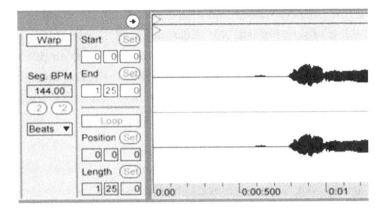

FIGURE 13.1

Warp turned off, and start position manually set to where Beat 1 is.

6. Trigger the acapella clip. While the song is playing, continually press the *TAP* button in the upper left of the Live window to the beat of the song. The global tempo will automatically change as you do this.

7. After eight or so bars, you can stop the clip.

8. Set the global tempo to the closest integer number to its post-TAP setting; for example, change 144.37 to 144.00.

9. At this point you may want to consult a web search verifying your tempo choice—many modern songs have a documented BPM number that is readily accessible online.

10. Turn the metronome on.

11. Trigger your acapella again—the metronome *should* line up with your song. If it does not, you may need to do some tricky manual warping or simply choose a different song.

Now that our acapella is synced to Live's tempo, all we need to do is add some premade loops.

12. In your Browser, click the *Clips* category.

13. Type *drum* into the search box.

14. Select a few drum loops.

15. Trigger the loops along with your song—they should match the speed of the acapella.

Mashups

Mashups are a bit trickier because the element of key is involved. The general task of matching a suitable instrumental with an acapella is sometimes frustrating, especially when a great idea to combine two songs does not seem to actually work in practice. Some great mashups occur when two songs of similar topic or artistic background are chosen, and other great mashups occur when two completely unrelated songs get together as one (see *The Grey Album* by Danger Mouse for a good example of this). We will take our acapella track from

207

earlier, and this time we will add an instrumental of a complementary song to serve as the background music. We will avoid complicated things like mixing verses and choruses from two songs for now, and just focus on riding the vocal on top of a synced instrumental. Since our method relies on an unsynced acapella (warp is still turned off), we should pick an instrumental track that has a tempo somewhat close to the acapella track's tempo.

16. Pick an instrumental track.
17. Drag the audio file into a second track in your Live set.
18. Double-click the instrumental clip to bring up the *Clip Detail* panel.
19. Drag on the clip's timeline to zoom in; try to locate beat 1 of the song.
20. Once you locate beat 1, double-click the transient mark above the note to create a warp marker.
21. Right-click the warp marker and select *Set 1.1.1 Here* to make the clip start in the correct spot.
22. Turn the metronome on.
23. Play the instrumental clip—the metronome should line up with the song.
24. If it does not, try right clicking the warp marker and selecting *warp from here* (*straight*).
25. If it still is not synced to the metronome, see the paragraph below step 51 later in this chapter.
26. Click the *Record* button on the top of Live's window.
27. Play both clips together.
28. Switch to *Arrangement View* to see the result.

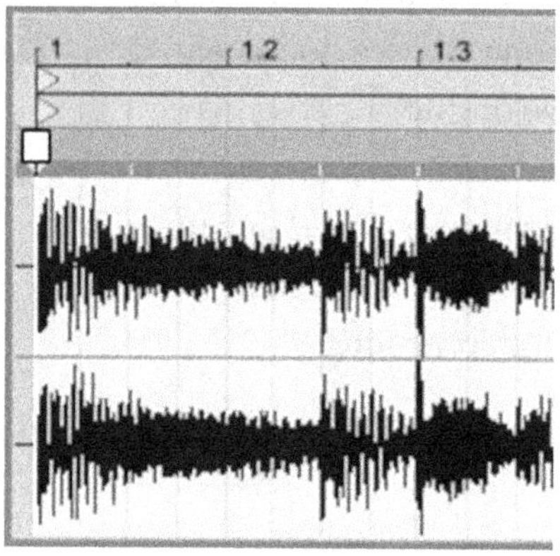

FIGURE 13.2

Warp marker placed manually on beat 1 of Instrumental track.

FIGURE 13.3

Right-click menu on warp marker.

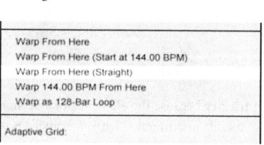

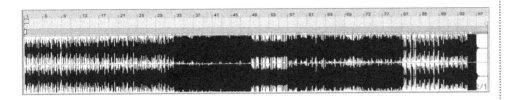

FIGURE 13.4

Warp From Here (Straight) removes all warp markers except the first one; it assumes the tempo never changes during the song.

We now have an instrumental and an acapella synced together. Whether they sound great together or not will heavily depend on what songs were selected. In the next steps we will learn how to gain fine control over aspects such as pitch and form sections, and we will also combine pieces of more than two songs into a totally new composition.

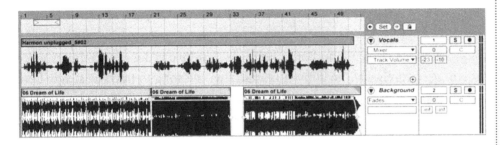

FIGURE 13.5

Acapella playing in sync with Instrumental in arrangement view (postrecording).

Sampling Loops from Preexisting Songs

In our example we will be finding songs with various instrumental attributes. You might want to do some research through your own music collection—this example works best using songs with which you are already familiar. Also note that while it is totally fine to use copyrighted works in private for learning purposes, you will want to get permission before posting anything you make using this tutorial online and especially before using it in your commercial works. If you get sued for posting a song with unlicensed samples, you are on your own—this book is not to blame.

29. Create a new Live set.
30. Delete any MIDI tracks—you should have two audio tracks now (if you do not have these, make them now).
31. Right-click the first audio track; click *Rename* and name it *Drums.*
32. Right-click the second audio track; click *Rename* and name it *Not Drums.*
33. Locate a song with a good drum intro—try to avoid anything with pitched sounds.
34. Drag the audio file onto the *Drums* track.
35. Repeat with three to four more songs, all with clean drum intros.
36. Locate a song with a good non-drum instrumental intro—it can be guitar, piano, Indonesian gamelan, etc. (but no vocals yet).

209

37. Drag the audio file onto the *Not Drums* track.
38. Repeat with three to four more songs with non-drum instrumental intros.

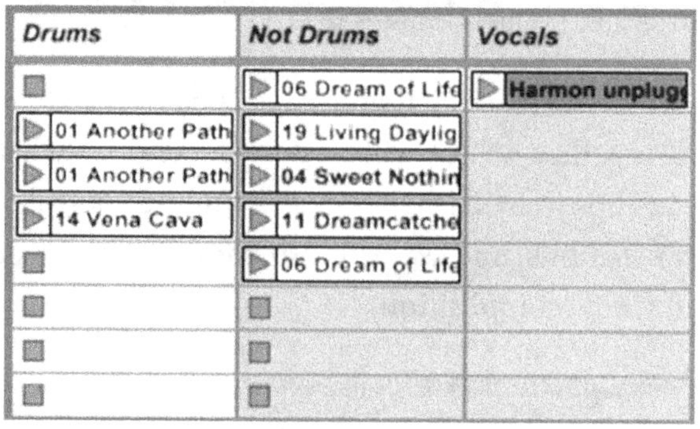

Drums	Not Drums	Vocals
▢	▷ 06 Dream of Life	▷ Harmon unplug
▷ 01 Another Path	▷ 19 Living Daylig	
▷ 01 Another Path	▷ 04 Sweet Nothin	
▷ 14 Vena Cava	▷ 11 Dreamcatche	
▢	▷ 06 Dream of Life	
▢	▢	
▢	▢	
▢	▢	

FIGURE 13.6

Variety of sampled loops on separate tracks.

The key to this method of sampling is that Live is doing two things when you drag in foreign audio clips: it is analyzing the song to find the steady beat, then it warps the clip to match the global tempo in the top left of the window. Many people doing this for the first time are alarmed when their clips sound quite different from the original when dragging them in—for instance, a song originally going at 90 BPM will now play faster if Live's global tempo is at 120 BPM. This is good—we want them all to match so they can exist in the same song together.

To meet this end, we now need to bracket off the loops in the songs that we plan on using. Notice that no actual editing is being done—we are not cutting anything out of the songs. That said, we will effectively cut and loop only the few bars at the beginning of the song that we want to hear in our example.

Since your loops will vary from the ones demonstrated here, we will show two different types of loop scenarios—one "ideal" case in which Live analyzes the file with few errors, and another "not ideal" case where Live makes a few mistakes that we have to manually fix.

First, the ideal case—we will use a drum loop for this one. Usually Live calculates the clip's tempo correctly but needs to be shown where the actual beat 1 is located. After setting that, the loop basically works right away.

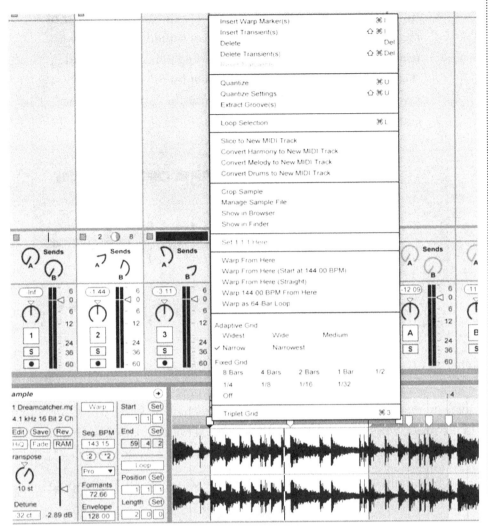

Insert Warp Marker(s)   ⌘ I
Insert Transient(s)   ⇧ ⌘ I
Delete   Del
Delete Transient(s)   ⇧ ⌘ Del
Reset Transients

Quantize   ⌘ U
Quantize Settings   ⇧ ⌘ U
Extract Groove(s)

Loop Selection   ⌘ L

Slice to New MIDI Track
Convert Harmony to New MIDI Track
Convert Melody to New MIDI Track
Convert Drums to New MIDI Track

Crop Sample
Manage Sample File
Show in Browser
Show in Finder

Set 1.1.1 Here

Warp From Here
Warp From Here (Start at 144.00 BPM)
Warp From Here (Straight)
Warp 144.00 BPM From Here
Warp as 64-Bar Loop

Adaptive Grid
    Widest   Wide   Medium
  ✓ Narrow   Narrowest
Fixed Grid
    8 Bars   4 Bars   2 Bars   1 Bar   1/2
    1/4   1/8   1/16   1/32
    Off

Triplet Grid   ⌘ 3

FIGURE 13.7

Manually setting 1.1.1 in the middle of a song to isolate a two-bar loop.

39. Double-click your clip to show it in the *Clip detail panel.*
40. Hover your mouse over the timeline strip in the *Clip Detail panel*—the cursor should look like a magnifying glass.
41. Drag down to zoom in so Beat 1 of the loop you want to sample is enlarged, and the warp markers are visible above each transient spike.
42. Right-click the warp marker above Beat 1.
43. Select *Set 1.1.1 Here* to reset the timeline to start on this note—when you trigger this clip, it will start exactly here.
44. Click the *metronome* button in the top left of your Live window.
45. Trigger the clip; assuming Live calculated the tempo correctly, the metronome should be in sync with the beats in the clip (if they aren't in sync, use the next example on how to fix this manually).
46. Click the *Loop* button in the *Clip Detail panel.*
47. Set the *Loop Position* to 1.1.1.

48. Adjust the first number under *Length* to the desired number of measures—the second and third boxes should almost always read "zero." (Note: if a number is colored orange in this area, that means the value is not exactly that number and would involve decimal places to show its position—simply type the correct number in the box to fix this.)

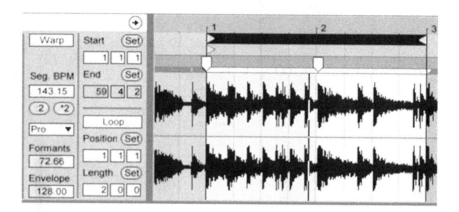

FIGURE 13.8

Correctly warped sample.

The method listed above usually works well for drum-based loops. If the clip has weaker transients, or simply is not warping correctly, we will need to do some manual fixes. The following steps assume that you know where the counts in the music you sample should go. They also serve as a reminder that computers cannot currently replace all straightforward musical knowledge.

49. Complete steps 11–20—this example will show a 1-bar loop, so you may want to set your length to match.
50. Turn *Loop* off for now.
51. Turn the *Metronome* off.
52. Trigger the clip and be ready to watch the *playhead* scroll over the clip.
53. Stop the clip when the *playhead* reaches the beginning of the second measure in the music; note which spike lines up with Beat 1 of Bar 2.
54. Double-click the *transient mark* over that spike to create a warp marker.
55. Drag the *warp marker* you just made to line up with *2.1.1* or simply *2* on the Timeline; this makes actual measure 2s start in the music lineup with Live's measure 2 on the timeline.
56. Turn on the metronome—it should click with the track through the first measure.
57. Turn *Loop* back on.
58. If you hear a skip when the clip loops, zoom in further and check that Beat 1 of Bar 2 isn't inside the looping bracket.

A third level of sampling might involve warping an entire song, measure-by-measure. While it may be tempting to manually adjust many points in a song, it may be easier to place warp markers every eight measures while eliminating any preplaced markers. Right-clicking a warp marker brings up some tools to attempt to recalculate the speed of the song from that position. They include:

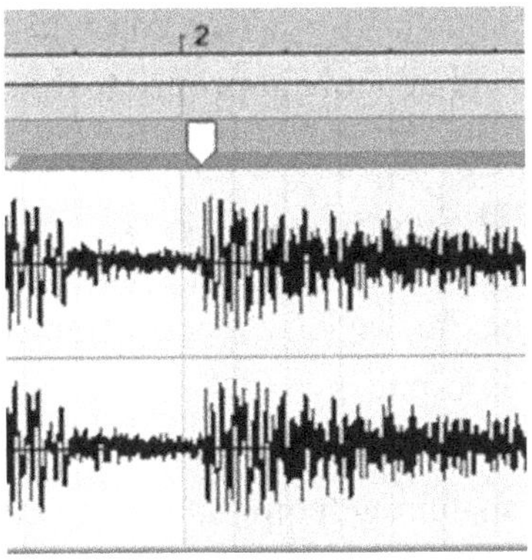

FIGURE 13.9

Warp marker automatically placed in the wrong spot—it should be on Beat 2.

Warp From Here: recalculates using normal method, but ignores anything before the marker.

Warp From Here (Start at xxx BPM): recalculates assuming the global tempo should match the clip.

Warp From Here (Straight): calculates an average speed assumption and places no further warp markers on the clip—useful for warping acapella tracks that essentially do not work well with any method.

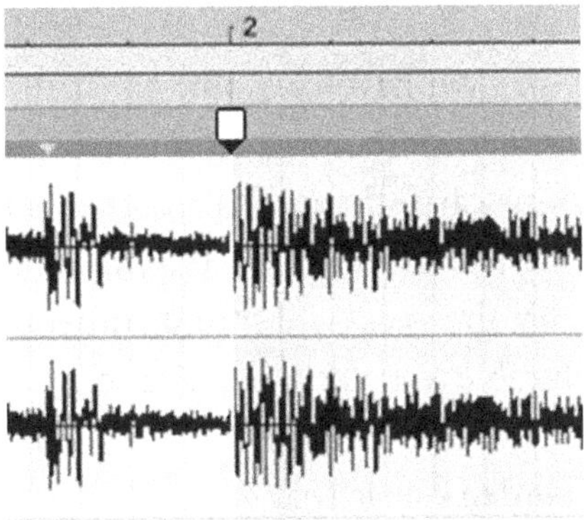

FIGURE 13.10

Dragging the yellow marker to line up with Beat 2 fixes the timing issue.

Warp XXX BPM From Here: Similar to Straight but assumes the global tempo already somewhat matches the clip.

Warp as a XX bar loop: Attempts to space the beginning and end points between a regular power-of-two number of measures and creates a loop.

A combination of these may be useful in warping a difficult clip, and the reader should realize that not all songs warp cleanly. If your sampling is proving difficult and frustrating, simply practice with a different clip—you will

Set 1.1.1 Here

Warp From Here
Warp From Here (Start at 144.00 BPM)
Warp From Here (Straight)
Warp 144.00 BPM From Here
Warp as 64-Bar Loop

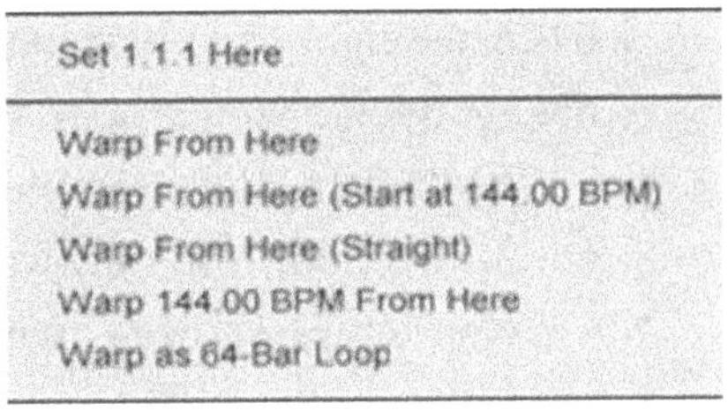

FIGURE 13.11

Warping right-click menu options, showing multiple warp strategies.

find that most songs will warp somewhat sensibly while a few will be extremely difficult to conform. Songs recorded without a metronome will generally need manual fixing, while modern pop with metronomic precision will simply need a start point to be defined.

Now that we have a collection of clips with which to work, we can start matching them. Since we started by organizing our clips into *Drums* and *Not Drums* from the beginning, we should be able to play anything from the first column and anything from the second column and, in theory, they should match. In practice you will prefer some combinations over others, and some will be more appropriate than others for the various form sections in your song.

Remixing an Acapella

So far we have a collection of loops that may or may not be loosely organized into pairings that sound complementary. If we want to incorporate these elements into an actual song, we will need to conform all of the disparate clips to a matching tempo and pitch center.

59. Choose an *acapella vocal track* to remix.
60. Drag the *audio file* onto a third audio track in your project.

We have two options at this point; we can warp the acapella manually, which can be very tedious (but sometimes this is the only option); or we can "un-warp" the acapella clip, manually set the start point, and manually adjust the rest of the song's tempo around that. The key advantage to this method is that the vocal will sound authentic. The key disadvantage is that we will not yet be able to make the entire song any other tempo than the original.

Note that the "un-warp" trick generally only works on professionally recorded music that *definitely has been recorded using a metronome.* Keeping this in mind, we can get started.

61. After dragging in the *acapella track*, double-click the clip.
62. Turn *Warp* off in the *clip detail panel*; now the global song tempo will not affect the acapella track.
63. Trigger the acapella clip. While the song is playing, continually press the *TAP* button in the upper left of the Live window to the beat of the song; the global tempo will automatically change as you do this.
64. After eight or so bars, you can stop the clip.
65. Set the global tempo to the closest integer number to its post-TAP setting; for example, change 144.37 to 144.00.
66. At this point you may want to consult a web search verifying your tempo choice—many modern songs have a documented BPM number that is readily accessible online.
67. Turn the metronome on.
68. Trigger your acapella again—the metronome *should* line up with your song. If it does not, you may need to do some tricky manual warping or simply choose a different song.

Now that the song is in sync with the loops, we will need to manually adjust the pitch of each pitched loop to put it in tune with the song. There is no automatic tool in Live to help with this task, and the Pitch Spectrum device we used previously in the granular synthesis chapter is only useful for pure tones, not harmony-rich samples.

We must rely on our own ear training to tune these samples. Since this book assumes technical experience, but not necessarily music school experience, here are two ways of going about this task.

Untrained Musician's Method for Pitch Matching

69. Double-click a *not drums* loop to see the *Clip Detail panel*.
70. Trigger this loop and the acapella at the same time; there is roughly an 83% chance of it not sounding good together (12 keys, 2 relatives = 6:1 chance of being in an unrelated key).
71. Click the *Transpose* dial in the *Clip Detail panel*.
72. Using the up and down arrows on your keyboard, adjust the loop up by 1 semitone (st) and replay both clips together.
73. Continue until either the song suddenly sounds like a good match or you hit +6; if you reach +6 without a match, try starting at -1 st and going down to -6 (one of these is the correct key).
74. If the loop starts to sound choppy, try changing the warp mode from *Beats* to something else, like *Texture* or *Complex*.
75. To tell if it matches or not, ask a simple question: "Does it sound like the singer is singing the wrong notes?" If it does, then your loop is still out of tune. Keep trying.
76. Remember the possibility that your loop simply will not match, due to stylistic issues or exotic key signatures. Try another loop—like the *not drums* looping earlier, most songs will work with this method, but not all.

Method for Pitch Matching Using Classical Ear Training

These steps are meant as a supplement to steps 41–47 and can help speed along the process.

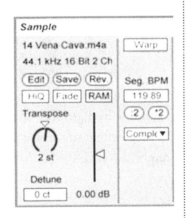

FIGURE 13.12

Transpose dial used to match instrumental clip to key of acapella.

215

77. Listen to your acapella and find the solfege note *Do* to be aware of the pitch center.
78. In your Browser, drag an instrument such as Grand Piano out into a fourth track.
79. Play the *Do* note on the instrument; this is the root note we are trying to match.

80. Trigger your loop and listen for *Do* in the loop while continually playing the pitch on your instrument.

81. Adjust the *Transposition* dial on the clip up or down to match the pitch you played on the instrument, again only using +6 or -6 (too much pitch adjustment will distort the clip but on the other hand could make for an interesting effect—use your discretion here).

82. In the event of a Major song and Minor loop or vice versa, remember that the relative Minor is three semitones below the Major. So instead of matching *Do* to *Do* you may be matching *Do* to *La*; sometimes there are enough chromatic notes that this will not work, but it should get you pretty close to the correct key.

For both types of musician, repeat the process until all non-drum loops are pitch-corrected to the acapella. Now we will organize our song and make the loops playable in form sections without interrupting the acapella.

83. Organize the loops into scenes matching the different form sections of the acapella (verse, chorus, prechorus, bridge, etc.).

84. Right-click the scene (row) on the master track that holds the acapella.

85. Select *Duplicate*.

86. Delete the *Acapella* on the duplicate scene.

87. Select all blank slots on the acapella track by holding the *shift* key and clicking each of them.

88. Right-click on any of the selected blank slots.

89. Select *Remove Stop Button*; this will prevent the acapella from being stopped when changing the clips playing in the background.

90. Try playing through your song, changing scenes using the scene triggers on the Master track; make adjustments as needed.

Most songs will start with a Verse and alternate with Choruses and sometimes Pre-Choruses. Generally Verse sections should use softer and thinner-sounding backgrounds than the Chorus sections.

Now that the scenes all seem to work properly, we will record our heavily remixed song onto the Arrangement View.

91. Double-click the *stop* button on the top of the Live window to reset the timer.

92. Press the *stop all clips* button on the Master track (located under the scene triggers, resembling a blank unlabeled square).

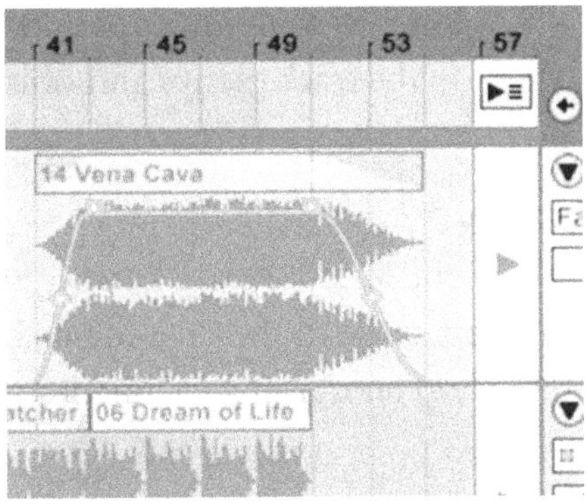

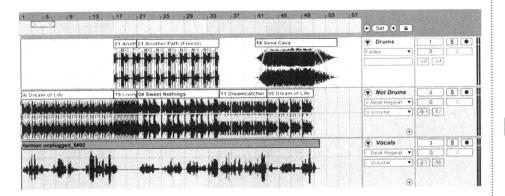

FIGURE 13.13

Turn off the unlabeled orange button to "unlock" Arrangement View.

93. Press the *global record* button at the top of the Live window.

94. Trigger your scenes; be sure not to trigger the scene containing the acapella more than once, or else the song will restart

95. After recording, press *Tab* to switch to *Arrangement View*.

96. Unlock *Arrangement View* by pressing the orange *play clips* button on the timeline.

97. Make any final edits to your song and export.

FIGURE 13.14

Completed arrangement of song using parts of seven different songs.

On Your Own

The example provided in this book did not use any well-known songs as its source material. Taking remixing further might involve combining popular songs on the fly in front of an audience (as DJs often do) or give a more danceable groove to an indie rock song (an increasingly common practice for newer bands).

- Practice looping isolated sections of a larger song to use as a basis for your remix.
- Find two acapella tracks, then use the verses from one and the choruses from the other; mash them together into one coherent song (bonus points for mashing two feuding artists together).
- Change the feel of a song entirely by placing its vocals atop half-time instrumentals, or over instruments not found in the song's genre.

217

• Simplify your remix performance potential by adding live effects to the track groups and/or master track.

In Live

Follow the *Instant Remix* Racks lesson in Live's *Help* panel for adding live effects to a remix. Read the Live Manual section 9.2 on Time-Warping Samples for more info on warping techniques.

Mastering

astering, the "black art" of audio engineering, is an oft-romanticized and misunderstood process. In the days of vinyl LPs, a mastering engineer's job was to simply decide on a proper track order for the master disc. Since LPs could hold roughly 22 minutes per side, these technicians made crucial decisions about the flow of an album. In addition, the medium of vinyl allowed different maximum signal levels for wider or narrower paths on the record, dictating songs of loud or soft volume levels to be placed in physically complementary parts of the record.

In modern recording, the mastering engineer's job is to take the finished stereo mixdowns from producers and ensure they work well on multiple sets of speakers. Doing an online search for "Mastering Suite" reveals some exotic-looking studios, replete with dozens of speakers at all price points. A major-label mastering producer makes sure the product will be effective on everything from the lowest-end car stereo to the highest-end audiophile speakers.

Most electronic music is self-produced, and there is no extensive budget for such top-shelf operations. Thus, many electronic producers will master their music themselves. Before diving into some basic mastering techniques, it is helpful to note that it is sometimes difficult to properly master one's own music. A key advantage of having another person master your tracks is to have a fresh perspective from another trusted professional.

Caveats aside, mastering one's music is mandatory, whether by yourself or by another. Maybe you have heard a track from a bedroom producer that sounds much softer or weaker than a professional track played from a CD. Maybe your own mixes, when combined on a playlist with other "real" tracks, sound much softer and leave one fiddling with the volume knob to balance the wide difference between tracks. This chapter will address some very simple ways to make a track sound mastered and have it fit in well sonically with professional tracks.

Generic Mixing Technique

Each example in the book has its own mixing steps delineated, and the astute reader will notice an overall pattern to mixing as portrayed in this book. For reference, here is a step-by-step review of our mixing method in Live:

1. Group all drum and bass tracks.
2. Group all synth/non-drum instrument tracks.
3. Group all vocal tracks—try to have as few groups as possible.
4. Add Equalizer (EQ) to the kick drum and snare drum tracks to bring out characteristic qualities.

   a. Snare drums have a "wham" around 400 Hz and a "snap" around 10,000 Hz.
   b. Kick drums have a "boom" around 100 Hz and a "thwock" around 1000 Hz.
   c. Depending on your recording, there may be undesirable qualities between these two frequencies.
   d. Do not overadjust the EQ—keep your adjustment under +/- 6 dB.

5. Glue compress the drums group—lower the Threshold and increase the Makeup until the group's overall dynamics are around -5 dB.
6. Glue compress the synths group—lower the Threshold and increase the Makeup until the group's overall dynamics are around -5 dB.
7. Adjust the level of the synths group to fit well with the level of the drums group. Do not go over 0 dB when using the group volume faders.
8. Glue compress the vocals group—lower the Threshold and increase the Makeup until the group's overall dynamics are around -5 dB.
9. Add *sends* 1 and 2 (delay and reverb) as needed.

FIGURE 14.1

Mix groups in Arrangement View.

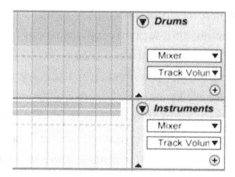

Why Group Tracks

Many audio tutorials will suggest using *aux* or *send* tracks to do your complex mixing. Groups are simply another visualization for the same thing. The audio being processed on the group track is a mixdown of everything inside the group, with the added visual benefit of having this processing bus attached to your tracks. In other programs, the mix bus or send tracks method is reminiscent of using a physical mixing board, and it is a bit of skeumorphism at play. Live allows this method, but views *sends* as a sort of "shared effects" bus rather than as a tool used for mixing. Mixing in groups makes more visual sense, and there is no sonic difference from the way that many pros use their tools.

The key is that using this method should get you very close to a final sound—if a problem exists in the mix, it will continue to exist during the mastering process. Assuming your song already sounds pretty good, we will move on to mastering the song.

The Master Track

In Ableton Live, the master track should be seen as the last possible chance to do anything to the audio signal before it is sent to the headphones. Located on the extreme right of the window in *Session View* and the extreme bottom in *Arrangement View*, it lacks the clip slots and *send* controls found on other tracks, and includes audio input/output (IO) settings for stereo output and cue assignment.

We have discussed using the scene triggers on the master track in previous chapters, but we will be using the track exclusively in *Arrangement View* during this chapter. The assumption is that mastering generally occurs at the end of a song's workflow, and thus the song will already have been recorded in *Arrangement View*.

The Limiter

First and foremost, producers should be aware that Ableton Live does not automatically limit your music. Some other DAW programs have a sort of "safety" limiter on the master track to prevent clipping or overloading the maximum signal level. Live does not include this, and additionally it performs a slightly more aggressive summing of the mix than that found in other programs. Be assured that the master track is indeed showing an exact summation of what is going on in the other tracks.

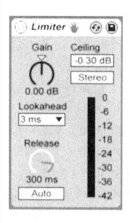

FIGURE 14.2

The Limiter—set it and forget it.

Limiters are a type of compressor that are generally used as a type of "safety" rather than as an effect (although their aggressive nature can surely be used to great effect creatively). A limiter has one setting: Gain.

In a way, the Limiter has a Threshold setting, but it is called "Ceiling" instead because it is designed to hold threshold at almost—but not quite—0 dB. Ceiling works the same here as it does on other dynamic plug-ins, such as Gates and Compressors. When audio levels are above the threshold, the Limiter kicks in. The "effect" of the Limiter is that audio that crosses the ceiling is simply not allowed to get any louder. In contrast to the compressor, which gently "squeezes" audio toward the threshold, the Limiter acts as a "wall" that the signal simply cannot cross. Sometimes Limiters are referred to as "brick-wall" limiters for this reason. We employ Limiters on the master track because we do not want our final mixdown to cross 0 dB since that will constitute clipping and be an inaccurate and unprofessional result. (If an intentional clipping effect is what we're after, there are better ways to achieve that sound without clipping the master track. Try using a Saturator if that's the kind of thing you want.)

The Limiter's *Gain* control (sometimes referred to as "limit gain") is a type of makeup gain adjustment that occurs before the actual limiting of the signal. Adjusting the *Gain* dial will adjust the track prior to being limited and can be used as an upward "makeup" effect if desired. Raising the gain will make the Limiter's presence obvious and the overcompression of a hard ceiling will be apparent. Usually we can achieve this by smart compression on track groups rather than by doing it here, but it is technically possible to do at this stage.

We can begin a generic mastering process by keeping it simple:

1. In your Browser, click *Audio Effects*.
2. Locate *Limiter* and drag it onto the *Volume Fader* of the master track (dragging it to the clip area is not allowed, unlike other tracks).
3. There is no step 3—set it and forget it. At this point your track will no longer be allowed to clip.

This does little to actually make the track sound better, but will at least be a safety mechanism for an amateur. *Do not actually use this Limiter to make your track louder.* If this Limiter is showing regular gain reduction when your song plays, your individual tracks are probably too loud.

You might say: *But my tracks don't sound loud at all!*

This is due less to the *volume* being too soft and more to the *average volume level* being too soft. More on this in the "compression" part of this chapter.

For now, consider our first step like a safety net—nice to have, but you do not want to actually have to use it.

The Mastering Chain

Disallowing clipping (especially for very quick and rough exports) is an acceptable beginning step but will hardly make a difference on the average well-mixed track. Next we will explore some basic options for mastering beyond limiting the maximum volume.

4. In your Browser, click *Audio Effects*.
5. Click the disclosure triangle next to *Audio Effect Rack*.
6. Click the disclosure triangle next to *Mixing & Mastering*.
7. Note the location of these for future exploration after completing the basic mastering tutorial here.

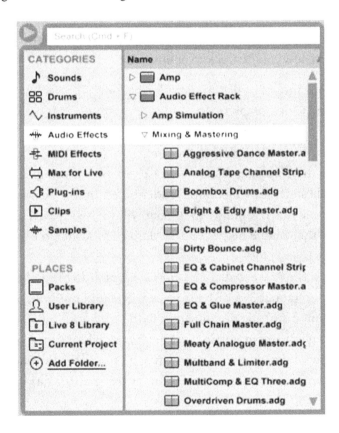

FIGURE 14.3

There are many preset options in the Browser for mastering.

The *Full Chain Master effect*, for example, includes a basic selection of mastering utilities that might be applied to any production. The effects included are *EQ Eight*, *Glue Compressor*, *Overdrive*, *Utility*, *Limiter*, and *Spectrum*. We will explore how each of these is used in a mastering situation manually, but in a pinch the preset mastering chain will suffice.

The Limiter we just added is the very last device in the mastering chain. We will now jump back to the beginning of the mastering chain.

223

Compression on the Master Track

In mastering, the compressor can be used to bring the average volume level of a track closer to 0 dB and to even out the dynamic range between loud and soft parts of a song. This is desirable for two reasons. Tracks with less dynamic range tend to play well on a wider range of equipment from low-end earbuds to high-end PA systems. Another reason for compressing at the master stage is to make your track slightly louder without clipping, so it fits in with other professionally produced music in playlists and mixes.

A note on effect order: whether to equalize before compression is a hotly debated topic. Conventional mixing boards tend to allow insert effects (like compressors) before the channel EQ, but on the master track the order is pretty much up to you. In mastering, since subtlety is key, we can avoid overly EQ-ing our track by compressing first, and then EQ-ing, which will allow a subtler EQ to get the sound we want. Another option we will explore is the use of a multi-band compressor, which combines aspects of EQ and compressor into one unit.

We will add a compressor to the master track and adjust it to bring the average volume level of the track to about -5 dB.

8. In your browser, click *Audio Effects*.
9. Locate *Glue Compressor*.
10. Drag it onto the *Master Track*.
11. Press *play* to start playing the song.
12. Drag the *Threshold* dial on *Glue Compressor* down until the needle starts moving on the louder notes. In the included example this is around -15 dB, but will vary with each set.
13. Note the volume output on the *Master Track* should be notably softer than before.
14. Adjust the *Makeup* dial on *Glue Compressor* to bring the level back up (about 3–4 dB); the track will sound uniformly louder, without distorting or going past 0 dB.
15. For a gentler compression, set the *Ratio* dial to *2*; this will only attenuate signal by a 2:1 ratio when it crosses the threshold (likewise, for harder compression try using a 10:1 ratio).

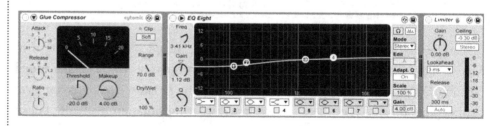

FFIGURE 14.4

Our simple mastering chain.

Equalizing on the Master Track

The main idea with equalization on the master track is to keep things subtle, and think about "sweetening" the track rather than making any large changes to the overall frequency spectrum. Remember, your adjustments for the mix and overall character of your song have already been completed—if you feel that you need big changes to bass/mids/treble at this point, you may need to go back and fix your mix.

The EQ Eight in Full Chain master is by default set to a slight 1–2 dB gain on the 70 Hz and 8,000 Hz bands—this will have the effect of making the track slightly punchier and brighter so that it can be experienced on a wider range of audio hardware. Your track needs to be heard on everything from cheap headphones to car stereos to high-end monitors. A common mistake is to make large adjustments (especially in the bass range) during the mastering process, then being surprised to hear that the mix is very bass-heavy on a "regular" stereo or headphones.

An extra trick can be borrowed from other Mastering chains that include a "tone" EQ setting. This extends the range of experienced sound by exaggerating the opposite ends of the frequency spectrum. Here we will expand the use of the Full Chain Master group to include the tonal range control.

16. In your Browser, click *Audio Effects*.
17. Locate *EQ Eight*; drag it onto your *Master Track* between *Glue Compressor* and *Limiter*.
18. Press *play* to hear your song.
19. Adjust dots #1 and #4 to balance the bass and treble in your track; do not adjust more than +/- 3 dB.
20. Listen for kick and snare drums—are they too loud/not loud enough?
    a. Adjust these using dots #2 and #3.
    b. Snare drum lives in the 500–5,000 Hz range.
    c. Kick drum lives in the 100–500 Hz range.
    d. If you find yourself adjusting more than 3 dB in any direction, go back and fix your mixing in the tracks. Mastering is a place for small adjustments, not big fixes.

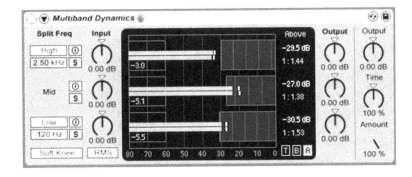

FIGURE 14.5

Multiband Dynamics effect—the boxes near the right of the audio signal meters are where the actual compression takes place (the Input and Output dials do not actually do any compression).

225

Multiband Dynamics

Multiband compression is a viable option for Mastering, but to many users it is confusing and misused. This section will attempt to demystify the Multiband Compressor and give at least one use case that is difficult to accomplish without its use.

The Multiband Compressor's signal process starts like this: (1) Signal goes in; (2) Signal is split into high-, mid-, and low-frequency bands; and (3) *Input* dials allow gain adjustment before compression.

Many amateur Live users will simply adjust the *Input* dials, hear a result, and move on. However, this procedure does not actually give us a compression effect—it could have also been achieved with EQ Three, which is probably the more appropriate tool for that type of operation.

Once the audio is inside the *graph* area, watch the levels as the track plays. If they are not hitting the dark blue box area on the right side of the graph, they are not being compressed. The dark blue boxes can be adjusted by dragging the left edge (for setting the threshold) and inside of them (for setting the compression ratio).

One use case of a Multiband Compressor could be to "de-ess" a track with lots of sibilance. Sometimes a vocalist will pronounce their "s" syllable in a way that triggers a microphone's natural sympathetic frequency and usually occurs in the 10,000 Hz range. If we only use the Multiband Compressor's high-frequency compressor, we can attenuate the instances of sibilance without affecting the rest of the track unduly.

To de-ess something, if needed:

21. Add the Multiband Dynamics effect to the track you want to de-ess.
22. Turn off the Low and Mid Compressors by clicking the tiny *power* icons to the right of the words *Low* and *Mid* in the device.
23. Using the drag handles on the uppermost dark-blue box, move the Threshold (left edge) so it intersects where the *ess* syllables are occurring in the audio signal.
24. Drag down on the blue box until the orange numbers read *1 : 4.00.*
25. The signal should now have less prominent sibilance.

FIGURE 14.6

Multiband dynamics set as a de-esser. Note only the high is active at 6 kHz, and the threshold box will definitely catch any peaks in that range.

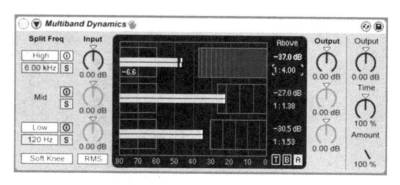

The Loudness War

When mastering, it is becoming more and more commonplace to simply think of this phase of the music creation process as the "make it louder" stage. While in many ways this is correct, now is our chance to thicken the track as a whole and make it more uniform and sturdy. Mastering does indeed provide its gelling effect by making the track more uniform and thus louder-sounding.

However, it is a mistake to simply make tracks louder as a rule. First of all, the louder the average volume of a track, the closer the audio signal is to 0 dB. Assuming we are not clipping (even if we are, actually), this naturally begins to result in a track with less and less dynamic range—that is, the signal-level difference between the loudest and softest points of the track.

As was mentioned earlier, a big focus of mastering is to make a track sound good on a wide variety of equipment. This focus can hurt the process too—if you mix your track on laptop speakers, for instance, a louder signal instantly sounds better than a softer one, since there is not much definition to begin with. Playing the same signal on good equipment reveals a lifeless track with less direction and range.

Many songs in the pop genres tend to overcompress in the mastering stage to be easier to hear over other tracks on equipment with poor reception; others do the same thing with cheap earbuds in mind. In turn, the next round of songs compete to become a bit louder overall, and the average volume of all tracks starts to increase. The effect is most notable on remastered editions of classic albums from the 60s and 70s. Each time the album is rereleased, the overall loudness is increased.

In short, do not abuse the Mastering chain by "simply" making things louder. We want the track to sound appropriately loud, and we still want it to have room in its dynamic range to breathe.

Exporting

To export your finished track to an uncompressed audio file, the process is straightforward.

26. In *Arrangement View*, make sure the view is unlocked (there should not be an orange button lit to the right of the timeline and no tracks should be greyed out).
27. Press *command-A* to select the full range of the song.
28. Click *File*, then click *Export Audio/Video*.
29. Set *Rendered Track* to *Master* (if you want to export each individual track or group, choose the *All Tracks* option instead).

30. Live will automatically choose an appropriate Sample rate and Bit Depth for your export, but you can change these to scale up or down for further processing if desired.

31. *Dither Options* presents an interesting list of strange algorithms that add imperceptible randomness to the resampling that occurs during export to avoid unintentional audio artifacts. For the average person, the default *Triangular* setting is fine.

32. Turn *Normalize* to *off*—we have already mastered the track, so we do not want any additional changes made to our signal.

33. Double-check that the exported range is correct—the Export dialogue lists this near the top of the window (if you have a clip selected it will only export the selected range).

34. Click *Export*.

35. Listen to your exported audio—does it sound exactly how it did in Live? (It should.)

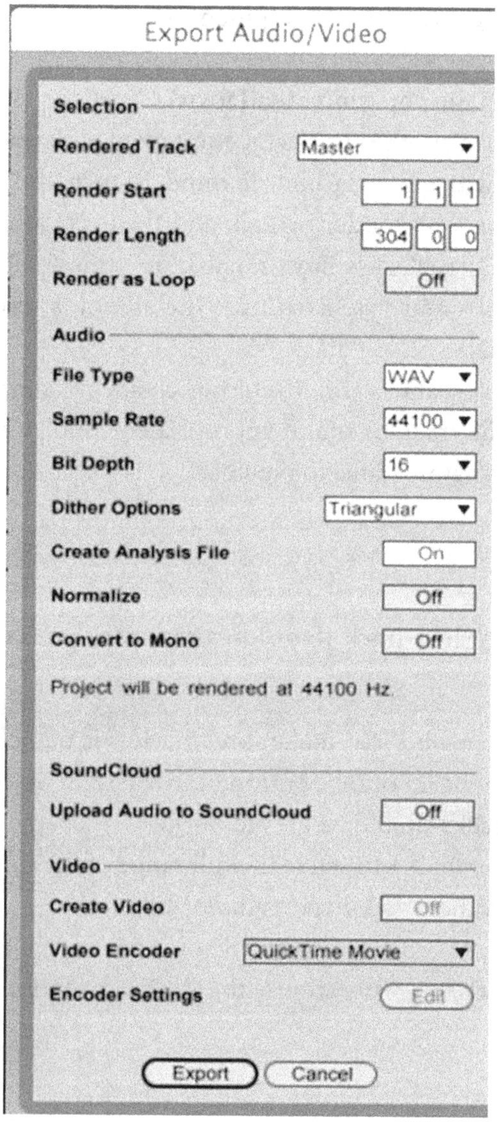

FIGURE 14.7

Live's export dialog.

On Your Own

In this chapter we have explored some general finishing techniques for your tracks. Some things to try as you use these techniques to complete your own works:

- Does it work better for you to equalize first, then compress? Give it a try and see if you can tell the difference.
- How loud is too loud? Try pushing your volume level in an extreme way upward to test the limits of the Limiter and see where audible overcompression occurs.
- Try exporting the stems of your song (just the track groups), then reimporting them into clip slots to allow live remixing in a performance setting.
- Read more about the Loudness War—many gallons of virtual and literal ink have been spilled on this topic, both for and against the use of brickwall limiters in mastering.

In Live

Review Section 5.2.3 *Exporting Audio & Video* in the Live manual.

Analysis of Projects

In this chapter, we will look at some larger-scale projects in Live. Many of the projects involve some heavy-duty Max programming, so don't worry if some aspects of them are unclear. We will describe the portions of the Max for Live patches that take advantage of using Live and allow it to function in novel ways.

Live Rig

Let's begin by looking at a variation of the Live set we used in chapter 5 while discussing rock and pop music.

1. Open the file *Live Rig* from the *Live Rig Project* folder in *Chapter Examples.*
2. Ensure that you are in *Session View.*

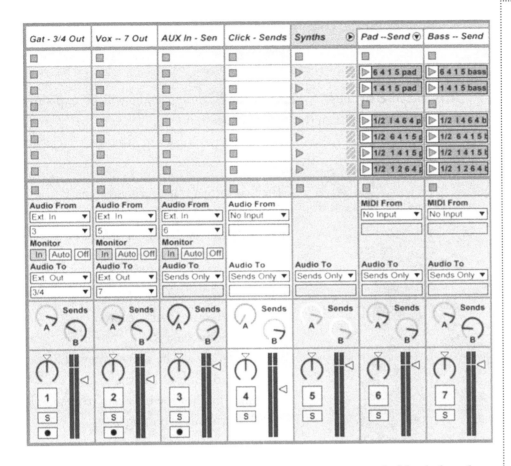

Gat - 3/4 Out	Vox -- 7 Out	AUX In - Sen	Click - Sends	Synths ⊙	Pad --Send ⊙	Bass -- Send
☐	☐	☐	☐	☐	☐	☐
☐	☐	☐	☐	▷	▷ 6 4 1 5 pad	▷ 6 4 1 5 bass
☐	☐	☐	☐	▷	▷ 1 4 1 5 pad	▷ 1 4 1 5 bass
☐	☐	☐	☐	☐	☐	☐
☐	☐	☐	☐	▷	▷ 1/2 1 4 6 4 p	▷ 1/2 1 4 6 4 b
☐	☐	☐	☐	▷	▷ 1/2 6 4 1 5 p	▷ 1/2 6 4 1 5 b
☐	☐	☐	☐	▷	▷ 1/2 1 4 1 5 p	▷ 1/2 1 4 1 5 b
☐	☐	☐	☐	▷	▷ 1/2 1 2 6 4 p	▷ 1/2 1 2 6 4 b
☐	☐	☐	☐	☐	☐	☐
Audio From	**Audio From**	**Audio From**	**Audio From**		**MIDI From**	**MIDI From**
Ext. In ▾	Ext. In ▾	Ext. In ▾	No Input ▾		No Input ▾	No Input ▾
3 ▾	5 ▾	6 ▾				
Monitor	**Monitor**	**Monitor**				
In Auto Off	In Auto Off	In Auto Off				
Audio To	**Audio To**	**Audio To**	**Audio To**	**Audio To**	**Audio To**	**Audio To**
Ext. Out ▾	Ext. Out ▾	Sends Only ▾	Sends Only ▾	Sends Only ▾	Sends Only ▾	Sends Only ▾
3/4 ▾	7 ▾					

FIGURE 15.1

Tracks in Session View for Live Rig.

By examining the session for a moment, you can probably deduce how this patch may be used in live performance:

- On the first track, live guitar input is received from the soundcard.
  - The guitar signal is processed in a variety of ways.
  - The signal is sent to *Sends* and to dedicated *Output Channels* o the sound card.
- On the second track, a vocal signal is received from the soundcard.
  - The vocal signal is processed in a variety of ways.
  - The signal is sent to *Sends* and to dedicated *Output Channels* of the sound card.
- On the third track, a channel marked *AUX In* receives some other signal; the signal could be a monitor mix or some offstage communication with the sound engineers.
  - The *AUX* signal is sent to *Sends Only*.
- On the fourth track, a channel marked *Click* receives no input.
  - The *Click* signal is sent to *Sends Only*.
- On the fifth track, a group track marked *Synths* contains two MIDI tracks marked *Pad* and *Bass*.

- The MIDI tracks contain simple four-bar chord patterns in the key of C Major.
- The signal is sent to *Sends Only*.

The purpose of these tracks and their configuration will be explained shortly. There are two return tracks for this session.

The two return tracks are used in a variety of ways:

FIGURE 15.2

Return tracks.

- The first return track receives signals sent on *Send A*.
  - These signals will be sent through the soundcard's output 1 to the house mixing console for the audience to hear through the house PA.
- The second return track receives signals sent on *Send B*.
  - These signals will be sent through the soundcard's output 2 to the in-ear monitor mix for the musician to hear while performing on stage.

The purpose of this set is to allow a musician to play guitar, sing, trigger synth loops, and send that signal to the house via *Return A*, while monitoring each signal on stage using a personal monitor of some kind via *Return B*. There are a few interesting features employed in this session, which we will discuss.

Improving the Metronome

As you know, Live's metronome can be enabled to beep according to the tempo and time signature of the session. There are a few limitations as of the time of writing this—specifically, the signal can only be routed to the *Cue* on the master track. But what if you find that it's necessary to send the metronome signal to several output channels? It simply doesn't have the *Send/Return* options that a normal track does. For this reason, we've used Max for Live to create an improved metronome on the *Click* track.

3. Double-click the *Click* track to reveal the M4L patch in *Detail* View for this track.
4. Click the *Test Click* button to trigger a *click* sound.

Notice that the click sound only comes through *Return B* as a result of the signal routing for this track. Also notice that the *Cue* volume on the master track has been muted.

5. Enable the metronome by clicking on the *metronome* icon at the top left of the screen.
6. Press the *space bar* to begin playback.

Notice that the metronome plays back through the *Click* track.

7. Press the *space bar* to stop playback.

Let's examine the M4L patch to see how this was accomplished.

8. Click the *Edit* button on the *Click M4L Device* on the click track.
9. Put the patch in *Patching Mode* by clicking the *Patching Mode* button at the bottom of the patch.

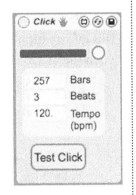

FIGURE 15.3

Click M4L patch.

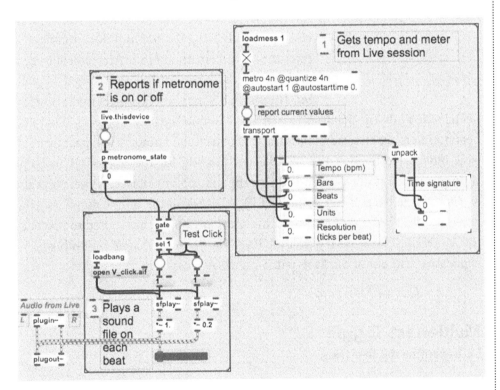

FIGURE 15.4

Inside the Click M4L patch.

This patch is fairly simple and has been divided into three sections. Max has an object named *transport* that is used within Max to standardize timing objects around a traditional DAW-styled timing system. In Live, the *transport* object is slaved to Live's transport. This means that tempo and meter changes that take place in Live are reflected in the *transport* object. The first section of this patch simply polls Live's metronome for information via the *transport* object.

233

The second section of this patch reports if Live's metronome is on or off. This information is used to ensure that the click is not sounding constantly even when the metronome is turned off.

10. Lock the patch.
11. Double-click the **p metronome_state** object.

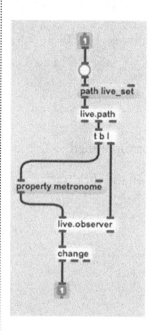

The *metronome_state* subpatcher simply observes the *metronome* property in this patch and reports any change from *off* (0) to *on* (1). To summarize what these objects are doing: the *live.path* object tells the patch where the activity is happening, and the *live.observer* object notes the location and observes the *metronome* property. The *live.device* object outside of this subpatcher sends a bang to this subpatcher when it is loaded in order to initialize this activity.

In the third section of this patch, we can see that the *on/off* state of the metronome will open or close a *gate* allowing the bar and beat numbers to pass through from the *object*. An audio file of a click sound has been created and named *V_click. aif*. This file exists in this set's project folder and has been loaded into the patchers two *sfplay~* ("sound file play") objects. If bar and beat numbers are allowed to pass the *gate* object, the numbers will pass through a *sel* object. Notice that the *sel* object is looking for the number 1 to come through. When it does, it sends a 1 to the first *sfplay~* object, which plays the *V_click.aif* file back at full volume (1.0), whereas all the non-1 numbers, triggered by weak beats reported from the *transport* object, are routed to playback the *V_click.aif* file at partial volume (0.2) via the second *sfplay~*. Both *sfplay~* signals are sent out of the M4L patch via the *plugout~* object.

12. *Close the M4L patch.*

Multieffect Toggle

Let's examine the first track.

13. Double click the *Gat* track to reveal *Detail View* for this track.

One concept of this set is to allow the musician to see all the information needed while performing and to control various parameters "hands-free" through foot pedals and other MIDI controllers. After all, the guitarist has his hands in use while performing! The first few devices on this track, *Amp*, *Cabinet*, and *Looper*, are related to the guitarist's sound. You can substitute these for any effects you see fit. The real features on this track are the *MultiDevice Switcher* and *Transposer Control* Max for Live patches.

The *MultiDevice Switcher* patch toggles the state of multiple devices on the *Vox* track. The *Transposer Control* patch sets the key of the MIDI synth loops. Let's first look at the *MultiDevice Switcher*.

14. Double-click on the *Vox* track and observe that all of the effect devices are on.
15. Double-click on the *Gat* track.
16. Click the large orange button in the *MultiDevice Switcher* patch so that it reads *FX Bypass*.
17. Double-click on the *Vox* track once again, and observe that some of the effect devices are now off.

A feature like this is useful if you are a singer and prefer to sing with multiple effects on in some configuration. It is also useful if you want to quickly switch to another configuration that, for example, might be better suited to speaking to the audience; while speaking to the audience, you might not want your reverb and delays on.

Let's look at the inside of this patch.

18. Double-click on the *Gat* track.
19. Click the *Edit* button for the *MultiDevice Switcher* M4L device.
20. Switch the patch into *Patching Mode*.

MultiDevice Switcher M4L patch.

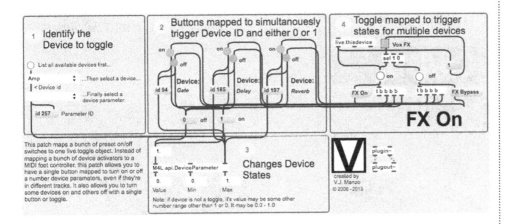

Inside the MultiDevice Switcher M4L patch.

This patch is broken up into four sections. The first section polls all devices used in your set and identifies all of their individual parameters.

21. Select *Vocal Hall* from the first menu. This is a device on the *Vox* track.
22. From the menu that populates below, select one of the parameters for this device.

235

Notice that the second menu reports the device ID number when a parameter is selected. We will send this ID number along with a 1 or 0 to turn devices on and off, respectively.

In the second section of the patch, buttons have been mapped to device ID messages and 1s and 0s. Notice that a single button triggers one device ID message and either 1 or 0.

The third section of the patch receives the device ID messages and the message to turn the parameter on or off (1 or 0). Please note, some devices report either *0* or *1* integer values as parameter states, while others report floating-point values between 0.0 and 1.0. For example, you might not want a *Wet/Dry* parameter value for a reverb to be either all the way on (value of 1) or off (value of 0), but somewhere in between, like *.7*.

The fourth section of the patch maps a single *live.toggle* object to the desired configuration of device *on* and device *off* messages. To change what is enabled or disabled in the two states, simply reconnect the *t* objects in the section 4 patch to the *on/off* buttons in section 2.

23. Close this patch.

Simple Transposer

Let's now take a look at the *Transposer Control* M4L patch used to allow the performer to change the key of the MIDI loops on the fly.

FIGURE 15.8

The Transposer_Control M4L patch.

24. On the *Gat* track, click the *Edit* button for the *Transposer Control* M4L device.
25. Switch the patch into *Patching Mode*.

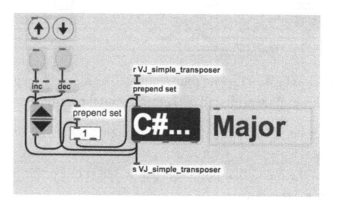

FIGURE 15.9

Inside the Transposer_ Control M4L patch.

This patch is pretty simple: a *umenu* object exists containing all 12 possible tonal centers for a key. When a key is selected by either clicking on the *umenu* or clicking the two *live.button* objects connected to *incdec*, the tonic is sent through the *s* (*send*) object named *VJ_simple_transposer*. It is received by all *r* (*receive*) objects with the same name. Let's look at the location of those *receive* objects.

26. Close this patch.
27. Double-click on the *Pad* track in the *Synths* group folder track.
28. Click the *Edit* button for the *Simple Transposer* M4L device.
29. Switch the patch into *Patching Mode*.

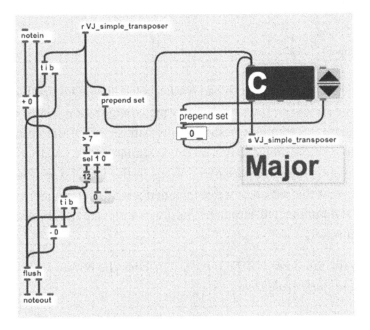

FIGURE 15.10

Tonal center data is sent between tracks via M4L patches using send and receive objects.

This patch is not unlike the very first Max for Live patch we made in chapter 3. Notice how the tonic value is received from the *receive* object and is used to transpose incoming MIDI notes. There's some fanciness in this patch that detects if the transposition is greater than seven and, if it is, also transposes the notes down one octave. Other than that aspect, this is a very simple, but useful, patch. The performer can easily trigger loops in whatever key he or she is performing in.

30. Close this patch.
31. Close this set.

Pedalman Pro

Pedalman Pro is a set that allows an instrumentalist to use MIDI pedals (bass pedals) to play full chords on a synthesizer by triggering the root note with their feet. The software would then intelligently harmonize the note according to the key specified in the software. For example, if a guitarist is playing in the key of C Major and hits an F# with his foot, the software will know what chord to harmonize that note with. Based on the default settings, the note will be harmonized with an F# diminished chord, but this can be changed to any other chord or even set to randomly choose between a few chords.

32. Open the file *Pedalman Pro* from the *Pedalman Pro Project* folder in *Chapter Examples.*
33. Ensure that you are in *Arrangement View.*

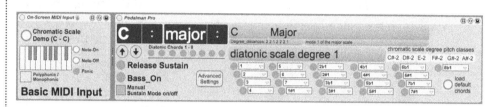

The Pedalman track devices in Detail View.

This patch contains a synth pad track labeled *Synth Out* that receives MIDI data from the *Pedalman* track's MIDI routing configuration. There is also a *Bass Out* track that receives the lowest note of whatever MIDI the *Pedalman* patch produces via a *receive* object patcher. This is similar to the way that we sent and received key information to the MIDI loops in the *Live Rig* session. To get the full idea of what this set does, we've included a small demo patcher called *On-Screen MIDI Input* that will simulate a performer playing the chromatic scale on a MIDI controller.

34. In the *On-Screen MIDI Input* patch, click the button labeled *Chromatic Scale Demo.*

Notice that the *Pedalman Pro* patch harmonizes each note according to their function in the C Major scale using a set of external Max objects included in the *EAMIR Software Development Kit* (SDK) called the *Modal Object Library.* These report that F# in the key of C Major is a "raised scale degree four," whereas the same note in the key of D Major will be reported as the "diatonic scale degree three." If this terminology is a little over your head, just know that using the default settings will allow you to play any note in the scale and harmonize it in a reasonably acceptable manner. From the *Pedalman Pro* patch, you can change the chords used to harmonize each diatonic or chromatic scale degree by choosing a different chord from the menus.

35. Click 8 buttons marked *Diatonic Chords 1–8* to quickly play each chord in the selected key.
36. Click the *Bass_On/Bass_Off* button to enable the lowest MIDI note produced in this track to be sent to the *Bass* instrument.

The real fun with this patch is not just that it harmonizes MIDI notes at any octave with these chords but that all of the controls can be mapped easily to

MIDI controls. For example, the performer can choose to have notes sustain infinitely when they are played, or notes can sustain manually according to how long they're held on the MIDI controller. Toggling this feature is as simple as mapping a MIDI control to the *Manual Sustain Mode On/Off* toggle. The *Advanced Settings* button allows you to make changes to the way the chords are voiced.

Though this set is somewhat complicated in terms of the Max programming, in essence it's quite simple: the Max patch plays some chords and the MIDI data is routed to a synth track and a bass track.

37. Play around with this track with a MIDI keyboard.
38. Close the set.

Wrap-Up

We hope that you have enjoyed this book. As you continue to work with interactive music, remember the techniques we've discussed. Remember that signal flows can get confusing, whether in the real world with cables and mixers, in the DAW world with channels and routing, or in Max with patch cords. Take your time and draw things out if necessary.

As with many creative works, if you get stuck for ideas, it's sometimes helpful to visualize the audience that is going to receive your work. It could be your friends, your family, or just yourself; consider these people and what is going to reach them. Use notes, gestures, multimedia, sounds, visuals, and more to facilitate your idea.

Consult the Ableton and Cycling '74 forums regarding questions. This is also a great way to stay informed as to what others like you are doing creatively. Please also consider reading other books in this genre: *Max/MSP/Jitter for Music* and *Foundations of Music Technology*, both published by Oxford University Press.

On Your Own

- Create a composition that uses one of these two larger projects in some capacity.

Bibliography

Arfib, D., J. M. Couturier, L. Kessous, and V. Verfaille. 2002. Strategies of mapping between gesture data and synthesis model parameters using perceptual spaces. *Organised Sound: Cambridge University Press* 7, no. 2: 127–144.

Broadbent, D. E. 1958. *Perception and communication*. New York: Macmillan.

Butler, D. 1989. Describing the perception of tonality in music: A critique of the tonal hierarchy theory and a proposal for a theory of intervallic rivalry. *Music Perception* 6: 1219–1242.

Butler, D. 1990a. A study of event hierarchies in tonal and post-tonal music. *Psychology of Music* 18: 4–17.

Butler, D. 1990b. Response to Carol Krumhansl. *Music Perception* 7: 325–338.

Carterette, E. C., and R. A. Kendall. 1989. "Human Music Perception." In R. J. Dowling and S. H. Hulse, eds., *The Comparative Psychology of Audition: Processing Complex Sounds*, 131–172. Hillsdale, NJ: Lawrence Erlbaum.

Chomsky, N. 1957. *Syntactic Structures*. The Hague: Mouton.

Chomsky, N. 1965. *Aspects of the Theory of Syntax*. Cambridge, MA: MIT Press.

Chomsky, N. 1968. *Language and Mind*. New York: Harcourt Brace Jovanovich.

Crowe, B. J. 2004. Implications of technology in music therapy practice and research for music therapy education: A review of literature. *Journal of Music Therapy* 41, no. 4 (Winter): 282–320.

Cuddy, L. L. 1982. On hearing pattern in melody. *Psychology of Music* 10: 3–10.

Cuddy, L. L., A. J. Cohen, and D. J. K. Mewhort. 1981. Perception of structure in short melodic sequences. *Journal of Experiments in Psychology: Human Perception and Performance* 7: 869–883.

Demorest, S. M., S. J. Morrison, D. Jungbluth, and M. Beken. 2008. Lost in translation: An enculturation effect in music memory performance. *Music Perception: An Interdisciplinary Journal* 25, no. 3: 213–223.

Deutsch, D., and R. C. Boulanger. 1984. Octave equivalence and the immediate recall of pitch. *Music Perception* 2, no. 1 (Fall): 40–51.

Deutsch, D., F. R. Moore, and M. Dolson. 1984. Pitch classes differ with respect to height. *Music Perception* 2, no. 2 (Winter): 265–271.

Dowling, W., and D. Harwood. 1986. *Music Cognition*. Orlando, FL: Academic Press.

Elliott, D. 1995. *Music Matters: A New Philosophy of Music Education*. New York: Oxford University Press.

ETS. 2010. *Music: Content knowledge (0113)*. Retrieved from http://www.ets.org/Media/Tests/PRAXIS/pdf/0113.pdf

Farnsworth, P. R. 1969. *The Social Psychology of Music*. 2d ed. Ames: Iowa State University Press.

Fletcher, H., and W. A. Munson. 1933. Loudness, its definition, measurement and calculation. *Journal of the Acoustical Society of America* 5, no. 2 (August): 82–108.

Gillmor, Alan M. 1988. *Erik Satie*. Boston: Twayne, 325–326.

Green, L. 2002. *How Popular Musicians Learn*. Aldershot, UK: Ashgate.

Green, L. 2008. *Music, Informal Learning and the School: A New Classroom Pedagogy*. Surrey, UK: Ashgate.

Greene, Jo-Ann. 1995. "Happiness Is Slavery." *Musician Magazine* (August): n.p.

Goudeseune, C. 2002. Interpolated mappings for musical instruments. *Organised Sound: Cambridge University Press* 7, no. 2: 85–96.

Hunt, A., and M. Wanderly. 2002. Mapping performer parameters to synthesis engines. *Organised Sound: Cambridge University Press* 7, no. 2: 97–108.

Koehler, M. J., and P. Mishra. 2008. "Introducing TPCK." In J. A. Colbert, K. E. Boyd, K. A. Clark, S. Guan, J. B. Harris, and M. A. Kelly et al., eds., *Handbook of Technological Pedagogical Content Knowledge for Educators*, 1–29. New York: Routledge.

Krumhansel, C. L. 1979. The psychological representation of pitch in a musical context. *Cognitive Psychology* 11: 364–374.

Krumhansel, C. L., J. J. Bharucha, and E. J. Kessler. 1982. Perceived harmonic structure of chords in three closely related musical keys. *Journal of Experimental Psychology: Human Perception and Performance* 8, no. 1: 24–36.

Krumhansel, C. L., J. J. Bharucha, and E. J. Kessler. 1982. Perceived harmonic structure of chords in three related musical keys. *Journal of Experimental Psychology: Human Perception and Performance* 8, no. 1: 24–36.

Krumhansel, C. L. 1990. *Cognitive Foundations of Musical Pitch*. New York: Oxford University Press.

Krumhansel, C. L., and E. J. Kessler. 1982. Tracing the dynamic changes in perceived tonal organization. *Psychological Review* 89, no. 4: 334–368.

Levitin D. J., S. McAdams, and R. Adams. 2002. Control parameters for musical instruments: A foundation for new mappings of gesture to sound. *Organised Sound: Cambridge University Press* 7, no. 2: 171–189.

Lipscomb, S. D. 1996. The Cognitive Organization of Musical Sound. In D. A. Hodges, ed., *Handbook of Music Psychology*, 2d ed., 133–175. San Antonio, TX: IMR Press.

Lundin, R. W. (1967). *An objective psychology of music (2nd ed.)*. New York: Ronald Press.

Manzo, V. J., and R. Dammers. 2010. *Interactive music technology curriculum project (IMTCP)*. Retrieved from http://www.imtcp.org.

Manzo, V. J., M. Halper, and M. Halper. 2011. Multimedia-based visual programming promoting core competencies in IT education [tools and environments]. In *Association for Computing Machinery SIGITE National Conference*. Vol. 1, *Proceedings of the 2011 ACM special interest group for information technology education conference*, 203–208. West Point, NY: Association for Computing Machinery.

Manzo, V. 2005. *Cliché Progressions*. Retrieved from http://www.clicheprogressions.com

Manzo, V. 2006. *The Modal Object Library: A Collection of Algorithms to Control and Define Modality*. Retrieved from http://www.vjmanzo.com/mol.

Manzo, V. 2007. *EAMIR* [The electro-acoustic musically interactive room]. Retrieved from http://www.eamir.org.

Manzo, V. 2007. *The EAMIR Software Development Kit (SDK)*. Retrieved from http://www.eamir.org.

Manzo, V. 2010. *Computer-aided Composition with High School Non-music Students*. Temple University, Philadelphia. Retrieved from http://www.vjmanzo.com/automata.

Manzo, V. 2011a. *Polyphony as Bias in Determining Harmony*. Temple University, Philadelphia. Retrieved from http://www.vjmanzo.com/clients/vincemanzo/scores/abstracts/Polyphony_as_Bias_in_Determining_Harmony.pdf.

Manzo, V. 2011b. Software-assisted composition instruction for non-music students. *TI:ME News* 3, no. 1: 3–9. Retrieved from http://www.vjmanzo.com/clients/vincemanzo/TIMENews_Winter2011.pdf.

Manzo, V. 2011c. *Max/MSP/Jitter for Music*. New York: Oxford University Press.

Meyer, L. B. 1956. *Emotion and Meaning in Music*. Chicago: University of Chicago Press.

Meyer, L. B. 1967. *Music, the Arts and Ideas*. Chicago: University of Chicago Press.

Meyer, L. B. 2001. "Music and Emotion: Distinctions and Uncertainties." In P. N. Juslin and J. A. Sloboda, eds., *Music and Emotion: Theory and Research*, 341–360. Oxford: Oxford University Press.

Mursell, J. L. 1937. *Psychology of Music*. New York: W. W. Norton.

Oteri, F. J. 1999. "Interview with Todd Machover." In *Technology and the Future of Music*. Retrieved May 25, 2011, from NewMusicBox: http://www.newmusicbox.org.

Pask, A. (Interviewer), and P. Oliveros (Interviewee). 2007. *The Adaptive Use Instruments Project*. Retrieved July 11, 2011, from Cycling '74: http://cycling74.com/2007/12/07/the-adaptive-use-instruments-project/.

Radocy, R. E., and J. D. Boyle. 2003. *Psychological Foundations of Musical Behavior*. 4th ed. Springfield, IL: Charles C Thomas.

Robinson, D. W., and R. S. Dadson. 1956. A re-determination of the equal-loudness relations for pure tones. *British Journal of Applied Physics* 7, no. 5: 166–181.

Rowe, R. 1993. *Interactive Music Systems*. Cambridge, MA: MIT Press.

Rudolph, T., F. Richmond, D. Mash, P. Webster, W. I. Bauer, and K. Walls. 2005. *Technology Strategies for Music Education*. Wyncote, PA: TI:ME.

Scarth, G. 2013. *Goldie*. Attack Magazine. Retrieved Aug. 23, 2014, from http://attackmagazine.com/features/interview/goldie.

Schenker, H. 1979. *Free Composition*. Ed. and trans. E. Oster. 1935; Reprint, New York: Longman.

Schogler, B. 2010. *Skoog Music*. Retrieved Oct. 24, 2011, from http://www.skoogmusic.com.

Serafine, M. L. 1983. Cognitive processes in music: Discoveries and definitions. *Council for Research in Music Education* 73: 1–14.

Sheldon, D. A. 1999. The effects of live accompaniment, intelligent digital accompaniment, and no accompaniment on musicans' performance quality. *Journal of Research in Music Education* 47, no. 3: 251–265.

Shepard, R. N. 1964. Circularity in judgments of relative pitch sequences. *Journal of the Acoustical Society of America* 36, no. 12: 2346–2353.

Sloboda, J. A. 1985. *The Musical Mind*. Oxford: Clarendon Press.

Sloboda, J. A. 1991. Music structure and emotional response: Some empirical findings. *Psychology of Music* 19, no. 2 (October): 110–220.

Sloboda, J. A. 2005. *Exploring the Musical Mind*. New York: Oxford University Press.

Taylor, J. A. 1976. Perception of tonality in short melodies. *Journal of Research in Music Education* 24, no. 4 (Winter): 197–208.

Terhardt, E. 1987. "Gestalt principles and music perception." In W. A. Yost and C. S. Watson, eds., *Auditory Processing of Complex Sounds*, 157–166. Hillsdale, NJ: Lawrence Erlbaum.

Thomas, R. B. 1970. *MMCP Synthesis: A Structure for Music Education*. Bardonia, NY: Media Materials.

Watson, C. S. 1973. "Psychophysics." In B. B. Wolman, ed., *Handbook of General Psychology*, 275–306. Englewood Cliffs, NJ: Prentice-Hall.

Watson, S. 2005. *Technology Guide for Music Educators*. Boston: Artist Pro.

Watterman, M. 1996. Emotional responses to music: Implicit and explicit effects in listeners. *Psychology of Music* 24, no. 1 (April): 53–67.

Wel, R. V. D. 2011. *My Breath Music Foundation.* Retrieved July 5, 2011, from My Breathe My Music Foundation: http://www.mybreathmymusic.com.

West, R., P. Howell, and I. Cross. 1985. Modelling perceived musical structure. In P. Howell, I. Cross, and R. West, eds., *Musical Structure and Cognition*, 21–52. London: Academic Press.

Index

acapella, remixing, 209, 209f, 214–17
Acoustic Arpeggio, 77–78
acoustic instruments, 101–2
add interval, 55, 55f
Air Project, 91–92
algorithmic composition, 100–101
aligning, patch cords, 51
Allan, Andi, 78
Ambient music: adding timing, 66–69; calm
    piano, 60–61; controls, 73–74; defining, 57;
    diatonic, 72–73; Dissonant piano, 61–62;
    Eno, 59, 60; form, 63; generating auto-
    matically, 63–64; other instruments of,
    60–62; RAT, 67, 67f–69f; synthesizing
    MIDI numbers in, 64–65; Synth Pad,
    57–60; tempo, 69–72; Wooden Room
    reverb, 59, 59f
Amount parameter, 110–11
Amp, 78, 234
analog delay, 97
analysis, of projects, 230–39
Andy C., 142, 148
Arduino microcontroller, 116
arguments, 49, 51, 64, 68, 68f
Arm Arrangement Recording switch, 18
Arm Session Recording button, 30, 30f
Arpeggiator, 126, 127f, 172, 198, 198f
Arrangement Loop, 22, 22f
Arrangement Record Button, 42f
Arrangement View, 6; Breakbeat/Drum and
    Bass music, 158, 158f; Chiptune music,
    175f; Dubstep, 203f; granular synthesis,
    188f; Master Track, 221; mixing groups in,
    220, 220f; recording in, 35; recording to,
    41–42, 42f, 131, 140, 140f, 202–3; remixing,
    217, 217f; toggle, 6f
artifacts, 94
Attack, 168
attack value, 58
audio, 31–35, 32f–34f, 62
Audio Device, 31
Audio Effects, 3, 3f; adding, 37–39, 37f;
    enhancing recording with, 75–78;
    permanently applying, 88; signal chain
    of, 62. See also specific effects
Audio From, 33–35, 34f
audio interface, 33. See also soundcards
Audio Preferences, 32–33, 32f–33f

Audio To, 33–35, 34f
Audio Tracks, 7, 7f
Audio/Video, importing, 23–24, 28
auto-chords, 171–72
Auto Filter, 153–54, 154f, 200–201, 201f
Automation, 79–81, 80f, 106f, 111, 111f
Auto-Warp Long Samples, 28
aux tracks, 221

Basic Monitor Mix Out 5, 88
basic setup, 2. See also Browser
bass: Dubstep, 192–97, 192f–197f; electro-bass
    synth, 135–37, 136f–137f; figure drawn
    using MIDI Note Editor, 17, 17f; Hip-Hop
    bass lines, 123–24; mixing and, 225;
    Operator settings for, 192, 192f; Reese,
    148–51, 148f–151f; 16-bar consolidated
    bass drop, 197, 197f; sub, 150–51, 202;
    Sub2 Sine Bass.adv., 123–24, 124f; wobble,
    194, 194f
"Bass Cannon," 199
Beat 1, 206–7, 207f
Beats Per Minute (BPM), 22, 22f, 213, 214.
    See also tempo
Benassi, Benny, 133, 190
Benga, 190
Bianchi, Fred, 115–17, 116f
binary code, 36
bit crusher, 61–62
bit depth, 62, 174
bit rate, 36
blank.mp3, 104–7, 105f–106f, 113, 113f
bleed, 34
book content, 6
boutique FX, 99
BPM. See Beats Per Minute
Breakbeat/Drum and Bass music: adding MIDI
    Drums, 146–47, 146f–147f; advanced drum
    looping in, 145–46; Arrangement View,
    158, 158f; buildups, 153–55, 155f; defining,
    142; Drum Rack, 146–47, 146f; form,
    157–58, 157f–158f; Goldie, 142, 143, 148;
    kick drum, 156, 156f; kick/snare patterns,
    147f; mixing, 155–56, 156f; other instru-
    ments, 151–53; Reese bass, 148–51,
    148f–151f; sampled drums, 145; sampled
    loop creation, 143–48, 144f; sampled
    sirens, 151–53; Session View, 157, 157f;

Breakbeat/Drum and Bass music (*continued*)
    sub bass, 150–51; subgenres, 157; suggested
    listening, 142; Warping, 144, 144*f*–145*f*
breakbeats, 145
Browser, 3–4, 3*f*–4*f*. *See also specific menu items*
Brushed Bell Hits Bells, 63, 72
Bug Music Project, 115
buildup patterns, 125–26, 126*f*, 153–55, 155*f*.
    See also risers
built-in internal microphones, 32, 32*f*
button object, 115

call-and-response clip firing, 115
call fire, 114–15
calm piano, 60–61
CD-quality audio, 62, 174
channels, 32–33, 32*f*–33*f*, 33, 83–84, 92–93, 93*f*.
    See also recording
chipmunk vocals, 129–31, 130*f*
Chippy, 169, 171*f*
chip sounds, 170–71, 171*f*, 173
Chiptune music: Arrangement View, 175*f*;
    auto-chords, 171–72; custom chip sounds,
    170–71, 171*f*; defining, 159–60; designing
    custom instrument, 161–69, 162*f*–165*f*,
    167*f*–169*f*; 8-bit drums, 173–74, 174*f*; form,
    175, 175*f*; MIDI reuse, 171–72; sampled
    chip sounds, 173; Session View, 175*f*;
    suggested listening, 160; YMO, 159, 160.
    See also Chippy
chord progressions, 172
chord sequences, 126–27, 127*f*
Chorus, 38–39, 97, 103
Clap, 122, 122*f*
cleaning up sets, 22–23
Click track, 89–90, 232–34, 233*f*–234*f*. *See also*
    Metronome
clips, 4, 4*f*; editing, 30–31, 30*f*; keystroke
    assignments to, 130*f*; MIDI, 9–15, 10*f*, 12*f*,
    15*f*, 154, 154*f*, 195–96, 195*f*–196*f*; record-
    ing, 30–31, 30*f*; slots, 27–30, 27*f*–28*f*, 30*f*;
    Stop All Clips Button, 29, 29*f*, 42
Clip View, 10, 10*f*, 15, 17, 17*f*, 31, 105, 105*f*
Coarse Frequency, 136–37, 137*f*, 150, 150*f*
commenting, 55
companion website (Oxford), 6
complete remix, 205
Complex, 94, 215
Complex Pro, 94, 109
composition, 100–101, 114–19, 114*f*, 116*f*, 131,
    131*f*
compression, 98, 103, 201–2, 224, 225*f*–226*f*,
    226, 227
Compressors: Drum Rack and, 123, 138, 138*f*;
    Glue, 187, 202, 224, 225; Sidechain, 156,
    156*f*

computer-generated sounds, 108–11, 109*f*–111*f*
Computer MIDI Keyboard, 18, 18*f*, 40–41
Computer Parts, 117
computers, 32, 32*f*, 33*f*, 39, 82, 88, 119
Computer Sounds, 110–13
Configure button, 81
Connection diagrams, 148*f*
Consolidate, 110, 110*f*
Contextual menu, 110, 110*f*
copying and pasting, 9, 12–13, 12*f*
Core library, 4–5, 5*f*
counterpoint, with MIDI loops, 13
CPU usage, 39, 88, 119
Creating a Loop, 143
Crystal Castles, 160
Current Project, 26–27, 27*f*
custom chip sounds, 170–71, 171*f*
Cut Chemist, 206
cycle, 167–68, 184, 184*f*

Dada Life, 133, 139
Daft Punk, 133, 134, 139
Dance Dot Org, 46–47, 47*f*
Datsik, 190
Davidovsky, Mario, 100, 101
Davis, Josh. *See* DJ Shadow
ddg.mono, 162–63, 162*f*–163*f*
Decay Time, 59, 59*f*
delay: analog, 97; digital, 97; in Electroacoustic
    music, reverb and, 103–4, 103*f*; Ping Pong
    Delay, 37, 37*f*; Simple Delay, 77–78, 86,
    103; Sucker Delays, 126, 127*f*
Dest A, 193, 193*f*
Dest B, 193, 193*f*
Detail View, 8–9, 47, 47*f*
detune settings, 152
Devices, 2; Activator, 38; Audio, 31; Chooser,
    106; Deactivator, 78; in Detail View, 47,
    47*f*; Drop Area, 58; Drop Files and, 91;
    finding installed, 3; live.device object, 234;
    in MIDI Sync tab, 40–41, 40*f*; MultiDevice
    Switcher, 234–35, 235*f*; Pitch, 149*f*; Title
    Bar, 39, 47; Vertical Limit, 48, 54; View, 37,
    37*f*, 61*f*
diatonic Ambient music, 72–73
digital delay, 97
dirty South style, 120–21
Dissonant piano, 61–62
Dither Options, 228
Dizzee Rascal, 190
DJ Danger Mouse, 206, 208
DJ Rashad, 206
DJ Shadow, 206
draw mode, 122
Draw Mode, 11
Dr. Dre, 120

Dripsody, 177, 178
Driver Type, 31
drop, 199
Drop Files and Devices, 91
Drum and Bass. *See* Breakbeat/Drum and Bass music
drum patterns: accelerating, 155*f*, 199–201, 199*f*, 201*f*; Dubstep, 191, 191*f*; Dubstep risers, 199–201, 199*f*, 201*f*; Hip-Hop Music, 122–23, 122*f*–123*f*; House music, 135*f*; kick drum, 123–25, 124*f*; sub kicks, 123–24, 124*f*
Drum Rack, 18, 122, 124; Breakbeat/Drum and Bass music, 146–47, 146*f*; Compressor and, 123, 138, 138*f*; drum samples within, 19–20, 19*f*; 16-bar accelerating buildup pattern, 155*f*
drums: advanced looping of, 145–46; 8-bit, 173–74, 174*f*; EQ, 220; MIDI, 18, 146–47, 146*f*–147*f*; non-drum tracks, 155–56, 156*f*; samples, 19–20, 19*f*, 145; from voice, 185–87
Drums, 3, 3*f*, 18, 19–20, 19*f*, 122, 213. *See also* Quantization
Dry/Wet parameter knob, 38, 40, 61, 80, 80*f*, 104, 236
Dubstep: aesthetic, 189; Arrangement View, 203*f*; bass, 192–97, 192*f*–197*f*; Compressors, 201–2; defining, 189; drop, 199; drum patterns, 191, 191*f*; Grime, 189–90; kick drum, 191, 191*f*; mixing, 201–3; Quantization, 196, 196*f*; resampling, 192–97; risers, 199–201, 199*f*, 201*f*; Skrillex, 190; sub bass, 202; subgenres, 189–90; suggested listening, 190; treble leads, 198, 198*f*; U.K. style, 190, 194; U.S. style, 190, 194; white noise, 200–201, 201*f*
Dupl. Loop button, 124

EAMIR Software Development Kit, 238
ear training, 215–17
Edit button, 47
editing clips, 30–31, 30*f*
Edit menu, 9, 21
8-bit, 36
8-bit drums, 173–74, 174*f*
Electroacoustic music: blank.mp3, 104–7, 105*f*–106*f*, 113, 113*f*; composition examples, 114–19, 114*f*, 116*f*; computer-generated sounds, 108–11, 109*f*–111*f*; Davidovsky, 100, 101; defining, 100; delay and reverb in, 103–4, 103*f*; Envelope window, 105, 105*f*; form, 104–7, 105*f*–107*f*; musical aspects of, 102; performance, 111–13, 111*f*–113*f*; *Synchronisms*, 100, 101; technical aspects of, 102. *See also* algorithmic composition

electro-bass synth, 135–37, 136*f*–137*f*
Eno, Brian, 59, 60
envelope filter, 96
Envelopes, 105, 105*f*, 123
Equalizer (EQ), 220, 224, 225
Excision & Datsik, 190
experimental computer music, 159. *See also* Chiptune music
Export Audio/Video, 23, 23*f*, 227–28, 228*f*
external soundcard, 32, 32*f*

feedback, 81–82
File Folder, 4
FilePos, 182–83, 183*f*
Filter, 149
Filter Freq macro knob, 150–51, 150*f*–151*f*
filter sweep, 125, 126*f*
finished patch, 169, 169*f*
Firing_Clips Project folder, 114
First Chirp, 115
Fixed Grid, 122
flanger, 98, 103
Float, 167, 184
Flux Pavilion, 190, 199
Fold button, 12, 31
Follow Action, 111–13, 112*f*, 117
form: Ambient music, 63; Breakbeat/Drum and Bass music, 157–58, 157*f*–158*f*; Chiptune music, 175, 175*f*; Electroacoustic music, 104–7, 105*f*–107*f*; House music, 140; scenes, 29–30, 30*f*
Francis, Dillon, 121
Freestylers, 190
Freeze Tracks, 88, 194–95, 195*f*, 197*f*
frequencies, 19, 162, 162*f*
Frequency Shifter, 110
Fujii, Minae, 160
Full Chain Master effect, 223, 225
funk music, 145
fuzz, 99

Gain control, 222
Gain Reduction meter, 155, 156
gate object, 234
Glide, 166, 167*f*, 168*f*
Glide indicator, 150*f*
Global Record Button, 20, 20*f*, 140, 217
global tempo, 206, 210, 214
Glue Compressor, 187, 202, 224, 225
Goldie, 142, 143, 148
Grain, 182–83, 183*f*
granular synthesis: Arrangement View, 188*f*; defining, 177; drums from voice, 185–87; with Granulator II, 182–85, 183*f*; mixing, 187–88, 187*f*–188*f*; Monolake, 178; "punch," 178–79, 179*f*, 182, 182*f*; sampling, 178–81,

granular synthesis (*continued*)
179f–181f; Session View, 187f; suggested
listening, 178; wavetable synthesis with
Simpler, 181–82, 182f
Granulator II, 182–85, 183f
gravity.mp3, 108
Grime, 189–90
Group, 83, 112–13, 113f
Grouped folder track, 90f
Grouped Operators, 150, 150f
grouped track folder, 75–76, 76f, 84f
Guitarist Mix Out 6, 88
Guitar Live, 86
guitar processors, 76

Hansen, Beck, 160
"Harlem Shake," 128
harmoniser, 96
harmonization, of MIDI pitches, 51
headphone icon. *See* Preview headphone
button
Help file, 28
Help menu, 45
Help patchers, 49–50
Henke, Robert. *See* Monolake
hidden controls, 111, 111f
Hip-Hop music: bass lines, 123–24; buildup
patterns, 125–26, 126f; chipmunk vocals,
129–31, 130f; chord sequences, 126–27,
127f; cinematic feel in, 127; composition
examples, 131, 131f; dirty South, 120–21;
drum patterns, 122–23, 122f–123f; futuristic feel in, 128; hype tracks, 129; lasers,
128–29, 129f; roots of, 120; shouts, 129–31,
130f; stabs, 127–28, 128f; sub kicks,
123–24, 124f; suggested listening, 121
HiQ button, 105
House music: Daft Punk, 133, 134, 139; drum
pattern, 135f; electro-bass synth, 135–37,
136f–137f; essential elements of, 134–35;
form, 140; kick drum in, 134–35, 135f,
138f; mix groups, 138; Sidechain ducking,
138, 138f; snare in, 135f; subgenres of, 139;
suggested listening, 133; tempo, 134, 141
House PA Mix Out 1 & 2, 88
hype tracks, 129

Import Audio/Video, 23–24, 28
Impulse, 185–87, 186f–187f
Info View, 2, 2f, 37
inlets, 47, 51
"Inner City Life," 143
In/Out Section, 33–34, 33f–34f
Input Config, 32–33, 33f
Insert Audio Track, 34
inserting, new MIDI clips, 14–15, 15f

Insert MIDI track, 63
Inspector, 55, 184, 184f
Installation for Foghorn, 115–17, 116f
Institute de Recherche et Coordination
Acoustique/Musique. *See* IRCAM
Instrument Browser, 46
Instrument Dry, 117–19
Instrument FX, 117
Instrument Rack, 57–58
instruments, 3, 3f; acoustic, 101–2; Breakbeat/
Drum and Bass other, 151–53; calm piano,
60–61; designing custom Chiptune,
161–69, 162f–165f, 167f–169f; Dissonant
piano, 61–62; M4L, 63; Max for Live
default, 161, 161f; substitute sounds for
missing media, 9. *See also specific
instruments*
Instrument Track, 107, 110
IO button, 33, 33f
IRCAM (Institute de Recherche et Coordina-
tion Acoustique/Musique), 159

Just Blaze x Baauer, 121

Key assignment mode, 196, 196f
Key Map Mode, 39–41, 39f
Key Mappings, 40, 111, 111f
Keystroke assignments, 130, 130f
kick drum: Breakbeat/Drum and Bass music,
156, 156f; Dubstep, 191, 191f; EQ, 220;
House music, 134–35, 135f, 138f; Impulse
settings for, 185–86, 186f; patterns, 123–25,
124f; sub kick patterns, 123–24, 124f
King Tubby, 189
Kit-Core 808, 123, 123f
Kondo, Koji, 160
Kraftwerk, 159, 160

lasers, 128–29, 129f
Launch window, 111–12, 112f, 196, 197f
LeBarton, Brian, 160
Le Caine, Hugh, 177, 178
Legato, 124
Length, 212
LFO all the things.amxd, 184–85, 185f
library, 2, 3
licensing samples, 209
Limiter, 221–23, 222f, 225
line, 166, 168
Live browser. *See* browser
live.device object, 234
live.dial, 166, 167, 184, 184f
Live Instruments, 87
Live library. *See* library
live.menu object, 71–74, 72f
live.numbox, 52, 52f, 54f, 55–56

live.object, 114
live.observer object, 234
Live Packs, 4, 4f–5f
live.path object, 114, 234
Live Rig: improving metronome of, 232–34, 233f–234f; multieffect toggle, 234–36, 235f; Session View, 230–31, 231f; Simple Transposer, 236–37, 236f
live.slider, 68–69, 69f, 70, 71f, 73–74
live.tab, 164–65, 165f
live.toggle, 73–74
Locators, 90–92, 90f
Loop Points, 90
Loop Position 1.1.1, 211, 211f
loops: advanced drum, 145–46; MIDI, 12–13, 12f–13f, 17–18; sampled loop creation, 143–48, 144f; sampling, 209–14, 210f–213f; vocal sample, 179, 180f
Loop Selection, 22
Loop Switch, 22, 22f, 90
loudness war, 227
low pass, 150f
LTJ Bukem, 142, 148
Luger, Lex, 125, 131

M4L instrument, 63
M4L patch, 115–19, 118f, 233–34, 233f, 235f–236f
Macro knob. See Filter Freq macro knob
Major Lazer, 121
makenote object, 65–66, 68–70, 71
Map button, 151f
Markers, 90
mashups, 205, 207–9, 208f–209f
mastering, 219; chain, 223, 223f–224f; common mistakes, 225; exporting and, 227–28, 228f; Full Chain Master effect, 223, 225; loudness war, 227; Multiband Dynamics, 225f–226f, 226; options, 223, 223f. See also Master Track; mixing
Master Track, 29, 29f; Arrangement View, 221; Audio From, 33–35, 34f; Audio To, 33–35, 34f; compression on, 224; EQ, 225; Limiter, 221–23, 222f, 225; monitoring and, 89–90; output channel of, 83–84; play buttons, 29, 29f; Return track output set to, 86, 86f; Session View, 221. See also mastering
Max for Live, 3, 3f–4f; adding objects, 48–49, 48f–49f; add interval, 55, 55f; basic objects, 114, 114f; Browser, 46, 46f; commenting, 55; default instrument, 161, 161f; designing custom Chiptune instrument in, 161–69, 162f–165f, 167f–169f; devices in Detail View, 47, 47f; Granulator II, 182–85, 183f; Help menu, 45; Help patchers, 49–50; inlets, 47, 51; Inspector, 55, 184, 184f;

installation of, 44; Instrument Browser, 46; live.numbox, 52, 52f, 54f, 55–56; Max MIDI Effect, 45, 45f, 47, 47f, 63; MultiDevice Switcher, 234–35, 235f; outlets, 47, 51; patch cords, 45, 47–48, 49, 51; Patcher Inspector, 55, 161, 161f; Patching Mode, 49–50, 54, 233, 235; Patching View, 49; Presentation Mode, 54–55, 54f–56f, 164–65; programming, 45; segmented patch cords, 47–48, 49; signal-flow diagram, 45, 45f; simple math, 51–54; Transposer Control, 234–37, 236f; writing MIDI program, 45–56. See also objects
Max MIDI Effect, 45, 45f, 47, 47f, 63
Max patch, 48f
message box, 114–15
message object, 71, 71f
Metronome, 20, 20f, 84, 232–34, 233f–234f. See also Click track
metronome_state subpatcher, 234, 234f
metro object, 66–69, 66f, 71
microphones, 32, 32f, 81–82
MIDI: clips, 9–15, 10f, 12f, 15f, 154, 154f, 195–96, 195f–196f; controllers, 18, 30, 30f, 39, 81, 237–39, 238f; data, 7–8; devices in MIDI Sync tab, 40–41, 40f; drums, 18, 146–47, 146f–147f; editing panel, 122; Effects, 3, 3f, 71–72; files, 7–9; foot controller, 76; information, 19; Keyboard Computer, 18, 18f, 40–41; loops, 12–13, 12f–13f, 17–18; Map Mode, 41, 41f, 111, 111f; mapping, 39–41; messages, 47, 53, 53f, 65, 65f; Note Editor, 10–15, 12f, 15f–17f, 17, 21, 21f, 147; notes, 7f, 21, 21f, 51, 162, 162f; numbers, synthesizing, 64–65; patterns as clips in Current Project, 27f; pedals, 237–39, 238f; pitches, 51, 72f; plug-ins, 126–27; program, writing, 45–56; reuse, 171–72; samplers, 19, 177; samples, 19; synthesis, 19; Values, 64; Velocity Editor, 11–12, 11f
midiformat object, 53, 53f–54f
midiin object, 46–49, 47f, 49f–50f, 52f
midiout object, 46–49, 47f, 50f, 53f–54f
midiparse object, 48–50, 48f–49f, 52f–54f
MIDI tracks, 7f; adding, 7, 14; adding drums on, 18; arming for recording, 18, 18f, 30; Insert, 63; mixer, 14, 14f; naming, 22–23; recording and editing, 30–31, 30f; selecting region, 15, 15f; volume, 14
"Midnight Request Line," 189
Mirage, 61
missing media, substitute sounds for, 9
mix groups, 138
mixing: bass and, 225; Breakbeat/Drum and Bass music, 155–56, 156f; Dubstep, 201–3;

mixing (*continued*)
EQ, 220, 224; generic technique for, 220–21; granular synthesis, 187–88, 187*f*–188*f*; in groups, 221; groups in Arrangement View, 220, 220*f*; track mixer, 14, 14*f*. *See also* mastering
Moby, 133
Modal Object Library, 238
Modes. *See* Arrangement View; Session View
monitoring, 34–35, 81–82, 81*f*, 86–90, 89*f*
Monkey FX Guide, 78, 96–99
mono, 32, 33
Monolake, 178
Moombahton, 139
Moore, Sonny. *See* Skrillex
Multiband Dynamics, 225*f*–226*f*, 226
multichannel concepts, 92–93, 93*f*
MultiDevice Switcher, 234–35, 235*f*
multieffect toggle, 234–36, 235*f*
multiple sessions, in one session, 90–92, 91*f*–92*f*
Musical styles. *See* specific styles
My Live Projects, 4, 4*f*–5*f*, 22–23

naming tracks, 23
Nero, 121, 190
NES ROM, 173
nil Project, 117–18
Nine Inch Nails (NIN), 79, 79*f*
Nintendo Entertainment System, 173
Noise White, 153–54, 200
non-drum tracks, 155–56, 156*f*
Normalize, 228
Not Drums, 213
notein, 162, 162*f*
noteout object, 65–66, 66*f*
note value abbreviations, 74. *See also* MIDI
number, 167–68
number boxes, 50, 51, 64–65, 65*f*
number object, 50, 50*f*, 52, 70

Oakenfold, Paul, 133, 139
objects, 45; adding, 48–49, 48*f*–49*f*; basic, 114, 114*f*; button, 115; comment, 55; pitches and, 52, 52*f*. *See also* specific objects
On-Screen MIDI Input patch, 238
Open in Presentation, 161, 161*f*
Operators, 135–38, 136*f*, 148*f*–149*f*, 149–50; bass settings, 192, 192*f*; Freeze Track, 194–95, 195*f*; Grouped, 150, 150*f*; MIDI Clip, 195*f*; treble leads, 198, 198*f*; white noise, 153*f*; wobble bass on, 194, 194*f*
Osc A, 192, 192*f*
Osc B, 193, 193*f*
Oscillators, 135–36, 148–49, 148*f*–149*f*, 162–65, 163*f*–164*f*, 168

Other Menus, 4, 4*f*
outlets, 47, 51
output channel, 83–84
output tracks, 84*f*–85*f*, 90, 90*f*
overdubbing, 32

pack object, 52, 52*f*–54*f*
pack O O, 166
pasting. *See* copying and pasting
patch cords, 45, 47–49, 51
Patcher Inspector, 55, 161, 161*f*
patches, 44
Patching Mode, 49–50, 54, 233, 235
Patching View, 49
patch velocity, 71*f*
pause function, 7
Pedalman Pro, 237–39, 238*f*
pencil tool, 123
performance: computer and, 82; Electro-acoustic music, 111–13, 111*f*–113*f*; monitoring stage setup, 89, 89*f*; Preview/Cue, 82–84, 82*f*, 232; Rock and Pop music, 81–86; Session View recording to Arrangement View, 41–42, 42*f*
phaser, 98
Phrygian Mode, 195
piano, 60–62, 61*f*
Ping Pong Delay, 37, 37*f*
Pitch Bend, 201, 201*f*
Pitch device, 149*f*
pitches, 16*f*, 52, 52*f*, 214–17
pitch mode, 153*f*
Places Browser, 4–6, 4*f*–5*f*
Play at Double Tempo, 13–14
Play at Half Tempo, 13–14
playback control transport, 6–7, 6*f*
Play buttons, 29–30, 29*f*
plug-ins, MIDI, 126–27
Plug-Ins Browser, 4, 4*f*
plugout object, 234
poly, 170
polyphony, 170
p oscillators, 162–65, 163*f*–164*f*, 168
practicing, 94–95, 95*f*
Preferences, 3, 4
Presentation Mode, 54–55, 54*f*–56*f*, 164–65
Preview/Cue, 82–84, 82*f*, 232
Preview headphone button, 10–11, 31
Price, Clifford. *See* Goldie
program interface, 2, 2*f*
programming, 45
projects. *See* My Live Projects
"punch," 178–79, 179*f*, 182, 182*f*

Quantization, 21, 21*f*, 112, 130, 196, 196*f*

Rally-X, 159
Raname, 23
Random Atonal Trash (RAT), 67, 67f–69f
random object, 64–65, 64f, 65f
random-pitch maker, 73, 73f
Range/Enum, 164–66, 165f
RAT. *See* Random Atonal Trash
Raw MIDI Messages, 47
recording: Arm Arrangement Recording
     switch, 18; arming MIDI track for, 18, 18f,
     30; Arm Session Recording button, 30, 30f;
     in Arrangement View, 35; to Arrangement
     View, 41–42, 42f, 131, 140f, 202–3; audio
     in Session View, 31–35, 32f–34f; clips in
     Session View, 30–31, 30f; with effects,
     enhancing, 75–78; with MIDI Keyboard,
     18; Vox track, 82. *See also* channels;
     mastering; overdubbing
rect, 162–63, 163f
Redux, 61–62, 173–74, 174f
Reese bass, 148–51, 148f–151f
release value, 58
remixing: acapella, 209, 209f, 214–17; Arrange-
     ment View, 217, 217f; Beat 1, 206–7, 207f;
     complete, 205; defining, 205; DJ Shadow,
     206; loop sampling, 209–14, 210f–213f;
     mashups, 205, 207–9, 208f–209f; simple,
     205, 206–7, 207f; tempo and, 209, 209f,
     210; Warp From Here, 208–9, 208–9f
Remote button, 41
Remove Stop Button, 216
Renegade, 142
resampling, 192–97
Return tracks, 85, 86–90, 86f, 232, 232f
reverb, 103, 103f; Decay Time, 59, 59f; Dry/Wet
     parameter knob, 38, 40, 61, 80, 80f, 104,
     236; effect added to Vox track, 79, 80f;
     Wooden Room, 59, 59f
Reverse, 109
Reznor, Trent, 79
risers, 199–201, 199f, 201f. *See also* buildup
     patterns
Robinson, Porter, 199
Rock and Pop music, 75; Automation in, 79–81,
     80f; enhancing recording with effects,
     75–78; multichannel concepts, 92–93, 93f;
     multiple sessions in one session, 90–92,
     91f–92f; performance, 81–86; practicing,
     94–95, 95f; Return Tracks as Monitoring
     mixes, 86–90; Reznor, 79
Ross, Rick, 121, 131

Sadness Pad, 58, 58f
Sakaguchi, Yoshihiro, 160
Sample Display/Note Editor, 106, 106f
samplers, MIDI, 19, 177

samples, 1, 4, 4f, 19; Auto-Warp Long Samples,
     28; chip sounds, 173; correctly warping,
     212, 212f; defining, 36; drum, 19–20, 19f,
     145; granular synthesis, 178–81, 179f–181f;
     licensing for, 209; loop creation, 143–48,
     144f; loops, 209–14, 210f–213f; MIDI, 19;
     rate, 36, 62, 174; resampling, 192–97;
     sirens, 151–53; vocal, 179, 180f
Saturator, 150, 193–94
Saunderson, Kevin, 148
Saving sets, 22–23
saw, 164
Saw D, 192, 192f
Scale, 71–72, 72f, 180–81, 181f
scenes, 29–30, 30f
Scratch Sample, 125, 125f
segmented patch cords, 47–48, 49
selecting, region of MIDI track, 15, 15f
selector, 164
send and receive objects, 237, 237f
Sends Only, 90, 90f
send tracks, 85, 221, 232
Send volumes, 85–86, 85f
Session Record Button, 111, 111f
Session View, 6; Breakbeat/Drum and Bass
     music, 157, 157f; Chiptune music, 175f;
     clip slots, 27–30, 27f–28f, 30f; editing clips
     in, 30–31, 30f; granular synthesis, 187f;
     Live Rig, 230–31, 231f; Master Track, 221;
     New, 27; Project, 26; recording audio in,
     31–35, 32f–34f; recording clips in, 30–31,
     30f; recording performance to Arrange-
     ment View, 41–42, 42f; toggle, 6f
"sets." *See* My Live Projects
sfplay object, 234
shouts, 129–31, 130f
Sidechain Compressor, 156, 156f
Sidechain ducking, 138, 138f
signal-flow diagram, 33f, 45, 45f, 84f–85f, 93f
signal path, 84
Simple Delay, 77 78, 86, 103
simple math, 51–54
Simpler, 125–26, 126f, 151–53, 152f–153f,
     181–82, 182f
simple remixing, 205, 206–7, 207f
Simple Transposer, 236–37, 236f
siren samples, 151–53
16-bar accelerating buildup pattern, 155f
16-bar consolidated bass drop, 197, 197f
16-bit, 36
Size, Roni, 142
Skream, 189, 190
Skrillex, 190
Snap to Grid, 11, 110
snare, 122, 135f, 186–87, 187f, 191, 191f, 220
solfege, 215–17

solid state overdrive, 98
soundcards, 32, 32*f*, 76, 84*f*, 92–93, 93*f*. *See also* audio interface
Sounds, 3, 3*f*
space, 103. *See also* reverb
Spacious, 61
Spectrum, 183, 214–15
square wave synth, 163, 163*f*
stabs, 127–28, 128*f*
stage setup, monitoring, 89, 89*f*
Start Marker, 18
"The State," 199
stereo pair, 32, 33
stompboxes, 76
Stop All Clips Button, 29, 29*f*, 42
Stop buttons, 2–309, 30*f*
stopping playback, 6
stretch function, 185
Strings, 85*f*
Sub2 Sine Bass.adv., 123–24, 124*f*
sub bass, 150–51, 202
sub kicks, 123–24, 124*f*
substitute sounds, 9
Sucker Delays, 126, 127*f*
Sync, 37
Synchronisms, 100, 101
synthesis, 19. *See also* granular synthesis
Synth Pad, 57–60

TAP tempo tool, 22, 22*f*, 207, 214
Techno music, 139, 178
tempo: Ambient music, 69–72; BPM, 22, 22*f*, 213, 214; changing, 22, 22*f*; global, 206, 210, 214; House music, 134, 141; M4L patch and, 118–19, 118*f*; MIDI Note Editor and, 13–14; Play at Double, 13–14; Play at Half, 13–14; remixing and, 209, 209*f*, 210; TAP, 22, 22*f*, 207, 214; Warping, 94–95, 95*f*, 105, 108–9, 109*f*
Texture, 215
32-bit, 36
Thorns Live Project, 87, 91–92
Threshold, 201–2, 224
T.I., 120
timbres, MIDI information, 19
time, 103. *See also* delay
toggle object, 66–68
Tomita, Isao, 159
tonal center data, 237, 237*f*
tracks: aux, 221; clips slots on separate tracks, 28, 28*f*; display, 8, 9, 15, 15*f*; Freeze Tracks, 88, 194–95, 195*f*, 197*f*; grouped track folder, 75–76, 76*f*, 84*f*; as groups, 84–85; highlighted region of acoustic, 78*f*; hype, 129; In/Out Section, 33–34, 33*f*–34*f*;

loudness war, 227; naming, 23; non-drum, 155–56, 156*f*; output, 84*f*–85*f*, 90, 90*f*; Return, 85, 86–90, 86*f*, 232, 232*f*; send, 85, 221, 232; two overlapping folder, 91, 91*f*. *See also* Master Track; MIDI tracks
Trance music, 139
transport object, 69–70, 70*f*, 233
Transpose knob, 109, 215–16, 215*f*
Transposer Control, 234–37, 236*f*
transposition, 12, 152
Trap music. *See* Hip-Hop music
Trap Muzik, 120
treble leads, 198, 198*f*
Triangular setting, 228
Triplet grid, 122, 122*f*
tube overdrive, 98–99
24-bit, 36

univibe, 99
unpack object, 50–52, 50*f*, 52*f*–53*f*
un-warp, 214

Velocity Editor, MIDI, 11–12, 11*f*
velocity patch, 71*f*
Velocity value, 163
Vibrato, 166–67, 168*f*
video games, 159–60, 173. *See also* Chiptune music
Vocalist Monitor Mix Out 7, 89
vocals, 79–85, 80*f*–81*f*, 85*f*, 129–31, 130*f*, 220
voice, drums from, 185–87

Waka Flocka Flame, 121, 129
"The Warning," 79*f*
Warp From Here, 208–9, 208–9*f*, 213
Warping, 94–95, 95*f*, 105, 108–9, 109*f*; Breakbeat/Drum and Bass music, 144, 144*f*–145*f*; markers, 208–9, 208*f*–209*f*, 212–13, 213*f*; right-click menu options, 213, 213*f*; samples, correctly, 212, 212*f*; strategies, 213, 213*f*; un-warp, 214
waveforms, 19
wavetable synthesis, granular synthesis with Simpler, 181–82, 182*f*
West, Kanye, 120
white noise, 153–54, 153*f*–154*f*, 200–201, 201*f*
Wise, David, 160
wobble bass, 194, 194*f*
Wooden Room reverb, 59, 59*f*

Yellow Magic Orchestra (YMO), 159, 160

+0 object, 51–52, 52*f*
Zooming Hotspot, 91

CPSIA information can be obtained
at www.ICGtesting.com
Printed in the USA
BVHW020316211222
654703BV00003B/5